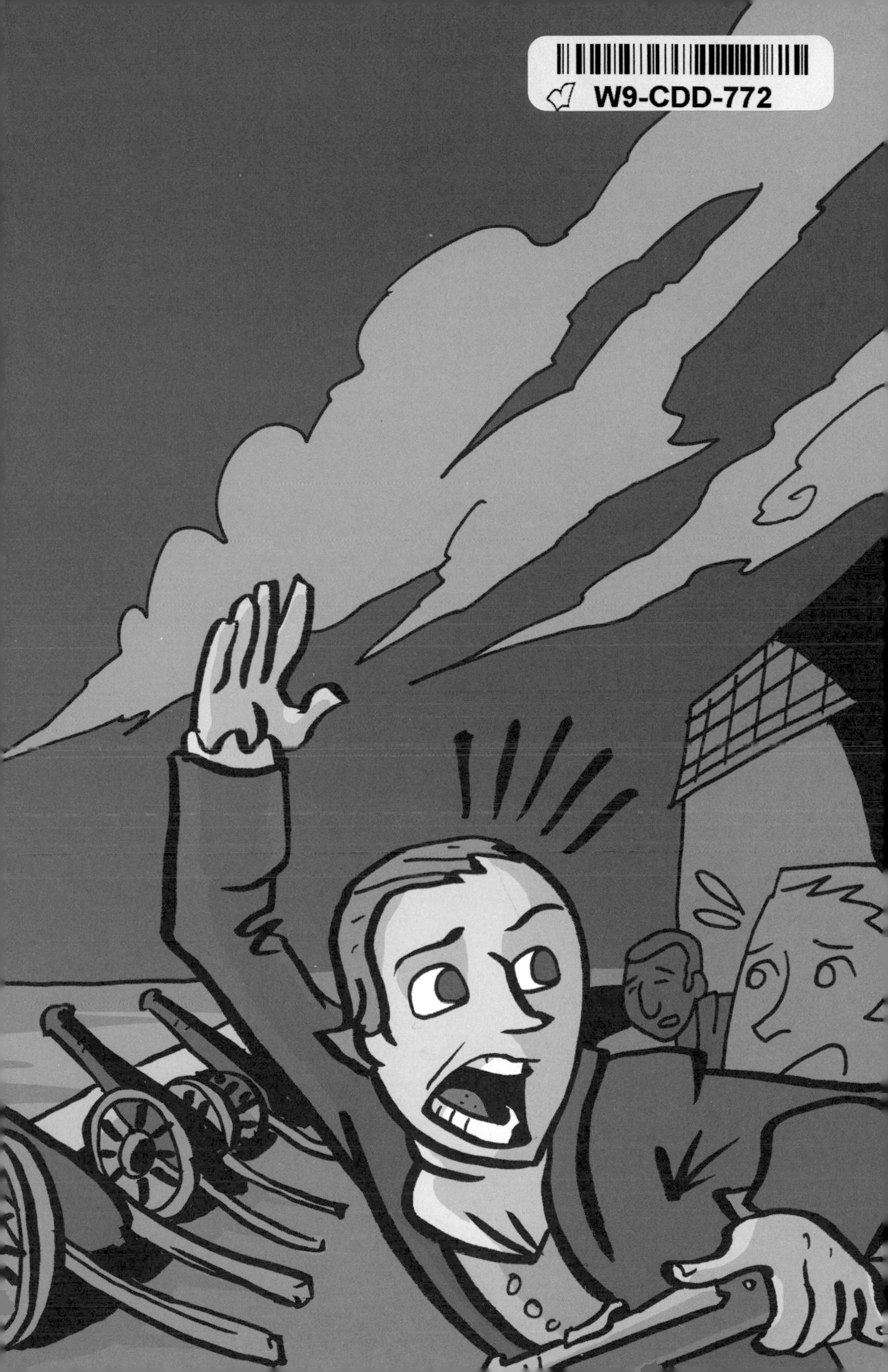

SHOW ME HISTORY!

ALEXANDER HAMILTON
The FIGHTING FOUNDING FATHER!

BY
MARK SHULMAN

ILLUSTRATED BY
KELLY TINDALL

LETTERING & DESIGN BY
COMICRAFT

COVER ART BY
IAN CHURCHILL

PORTABLE
PRESS

SAN DIEGO, CALIFORNIA

Portable Press

An imprint of Printers Row Publishing Group
10350 Barnes Canyon Road, Suite 100, San Diego, CA 92121
www.portablepress.com • e-mail: mail@portablepress.com

Printers Row Publishing Group is a division of Readerlink Distribution Services, LLC. Portable Press is a registered trademark of Readerlink Distribution Services, LLC.

Correspondence regarding the content of this book should be addressed to Portable Press, Editorial Department, at the above address. Author and illustration inquiries should be addressed to Oomf, Inc., www.oomf.com.

Publisher: Peter Norton
Associate Publisher: Ana Parker
Developmental Editor: Vicki Jaeger
Publishing Team: Kathryn C. Dalby, Lauren Taniguchi
Production Team: Jonathan Lopes, Rusty von Dyl

O•MF Created at Oomf, Inc., www.Oomf.com
Director: Mark Shulman
Producer: James Buckley Jr.

Written by Mark Shulman
Illustrated by Kelly Tindall
Lettering & design by Comicraft: John Roshell, Sarah Jacobs,
    Drewes McFarling, Jimmy Betancourt, Forest Dempsey
Cover illustration by Ian Churchill

Library of Congress Cataloging-in-Publication Data

Names: Shulman, Mark, 1962- author.
Title: Alexander Hamilton : the fighting founding father! / Mark Shulman ;
    illustrated by Kelly Tindall ; illustrated by John Roshell.
Description: San Diego : Portable Press, 2019. | Series: Show me history!
Identifiers: LCCN 2018037752 | ISBN 9781684125432 (hardback)
Subjects: LCSH: Hamilton, Alexander, 1757-1804--Juvenile literature. |
    Hamilton, Alexander, 1757-1804--Comic books, strips, etc. |
    Statesmen--United States--Biography--Juvenile literature. |
    Statesmen--United States--Biography--Comic books, strips, etc. | United
    States--Politics and government--1783-1809--Juvenile literature. | United
    States--Politics and government--1783-1809 $v Comic books, strips, etc. |
    Graphic novels. | BISAC: JUVENILE NONFICTION / Biography & Autobiography /
    Historical. | JUVENILE NONFICTION / History / United States / Colonial &
    Revolutionary Periods. | JUVENILE NONFICTION / Biography & Autobiography /
    Political.
Classification: LCC E302.6.H2 S55 2019 | DDC 973.4092 [B] --dc23 LC record
available at https://lccn.loc.gov/2018037752

Printed in China

22 21 20 19 18   1 2 3 4 5

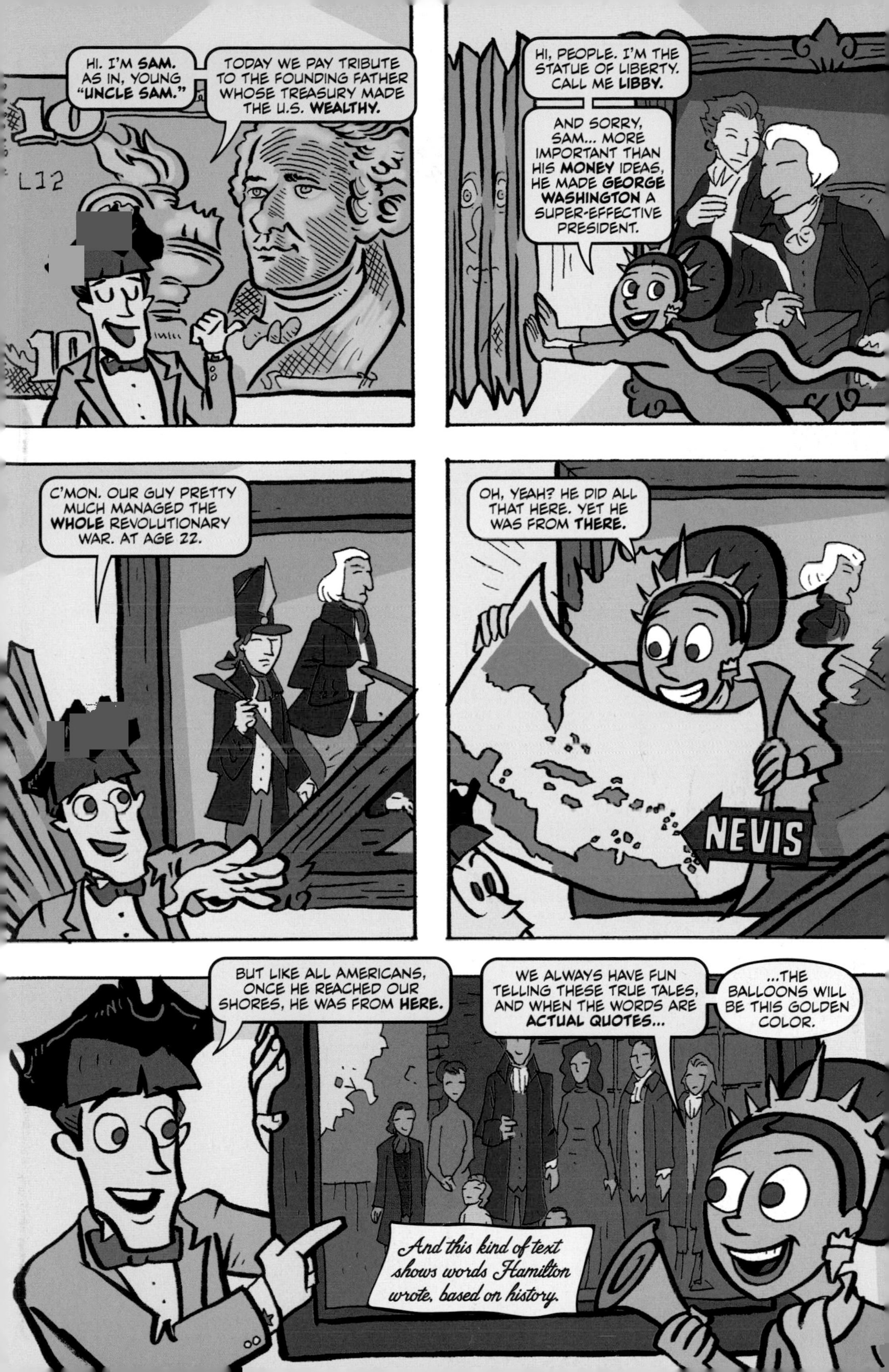

HI. I'M **SAM.** AS IN, YOUNG "**UNCLE SAM.**"
TODAY WE PAY TRIBUTE TO THE FOUNDING FATHER WHOSE TREASURY MADE THE U.S. **WEALTHY.**
HI, PEOPLE. I'M THE STATUE OF LIBERTY. CALL ME **LIBBY.**
AND SORRY, SAM... MORE IMPORTANT THAN HIS **MONEY** IDEAS, HE MADE **GEORGE WASHINGTON** A SUPER-EFFECTIVE PRESIDENT.
C'MON. OUR GUY PRETTY MUCH MANAGED THE **WHOLE** REVOLUTIONARY WAR. AT AGE 22.
OH, YEAH? HE DID ALL THAT HERE. YET HE WAS FROM **THERE.**
NEVIS
BUT LIKE ALL AMERICANS, ONCE HE REACHED OUR SHORES, HE WAS FROM **HERE.**
WE ALWAYS HAVE FUN TELLING THESE TRUE TALES, AND WHEN THE WORDS ARE **ACTUAL QUOTES...**
...THE BALLOONS WILL BE THIS GOLDEN COLOR.
And this kind of text shows words Hamilton wrote, based on history.

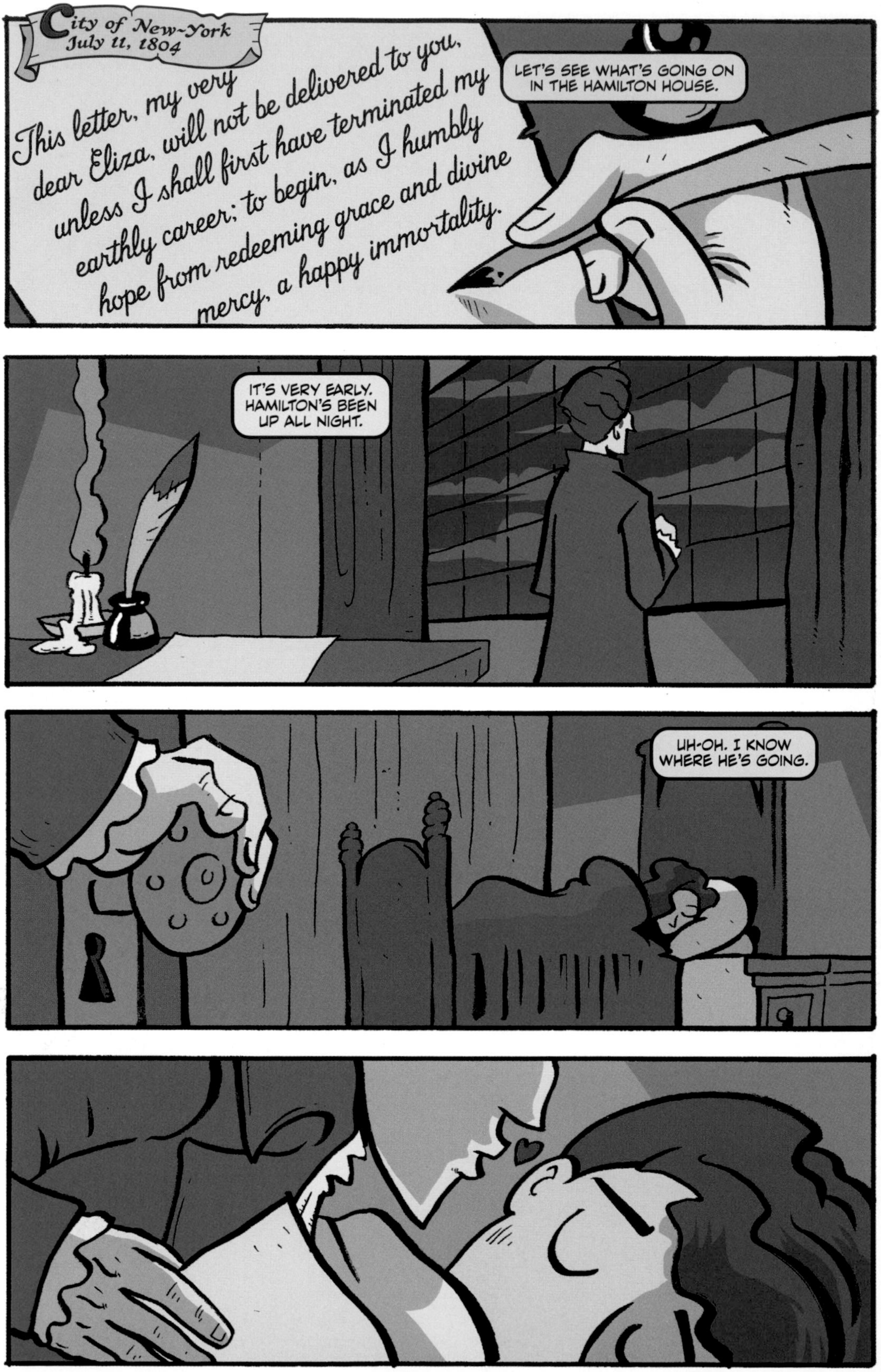
City of New-York
July 11, 1804
This letter, my very dear Eliza, will not be delivered to you, unless I shall first have terminated my earthly career; to begin, as I humbly hope from redeeming grace and divine mercy, a happy immortality.
LET'S SEE WHAT'S GOING ON IN THE HAMILTON HOUSE.
IT'S VERY EARLY. HAMILTON'S BEEN UP ALL NIGHT.
UH-OH. I KNOW WHERE HE'S GOING.

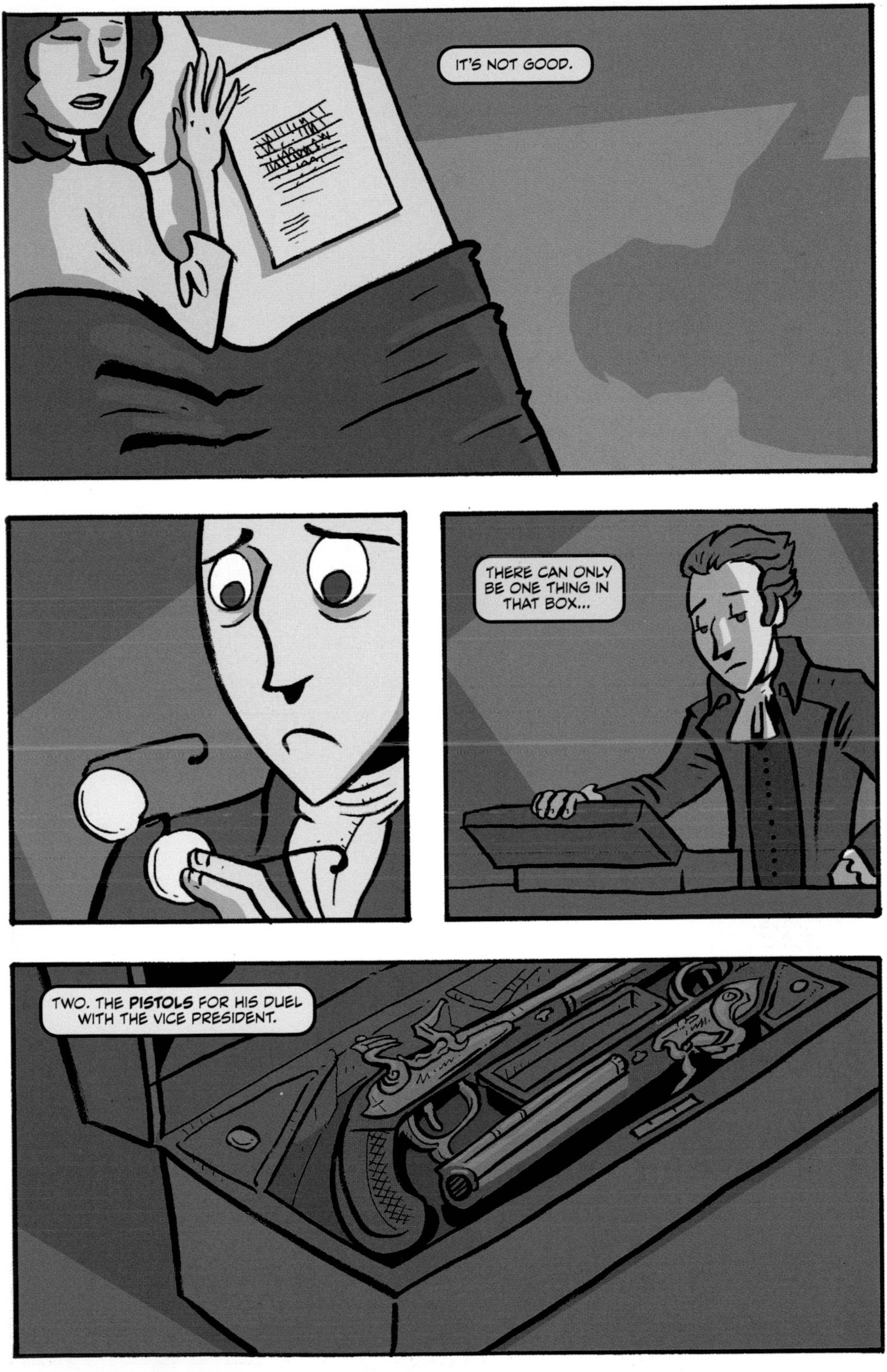
IT'S NOT GOOD.
THERE CAN ONLY BE ONE THING IN THAT BOX...
TWO. THE **PISTOLS** FOR HIS DUEL WITH THE VICE PRESIDENT.

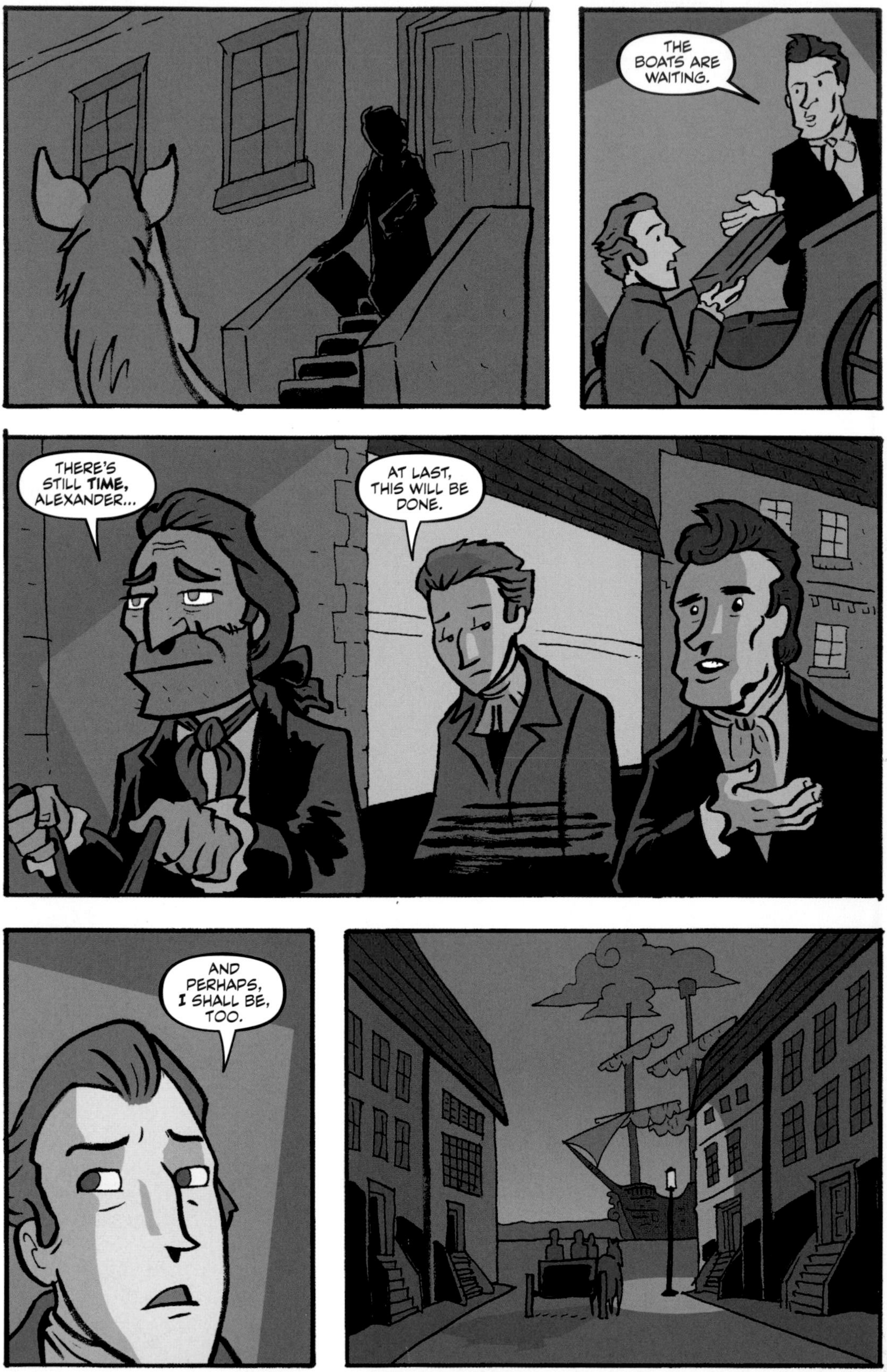
THE BOATS ARE WAITING.
THERE'S STILL **TIME,** ALEXANDER...
AT LAST, THIS WILL BE DONE.
AND PERHAPS, **I** SHALL BE, TOO.

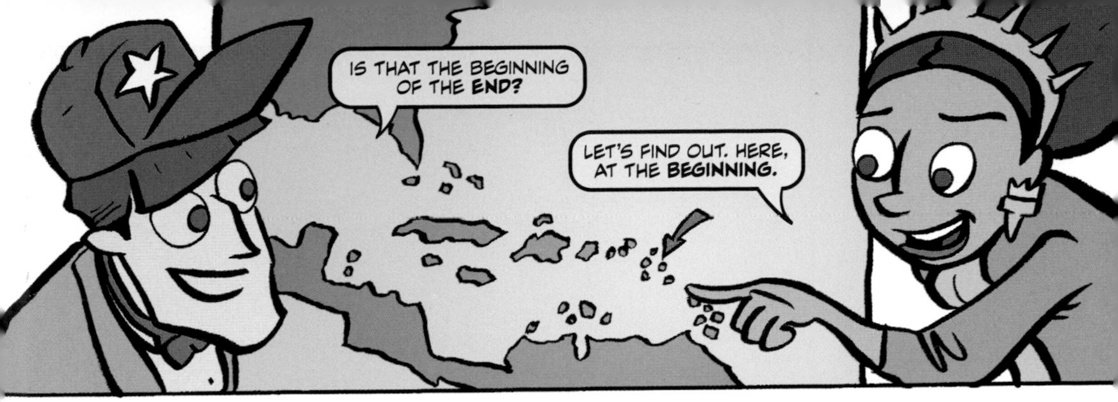
IS THAT THE BEGINNING OF THE END?
LET'S FIND OUT. HERE, AT THE BEGINNING.

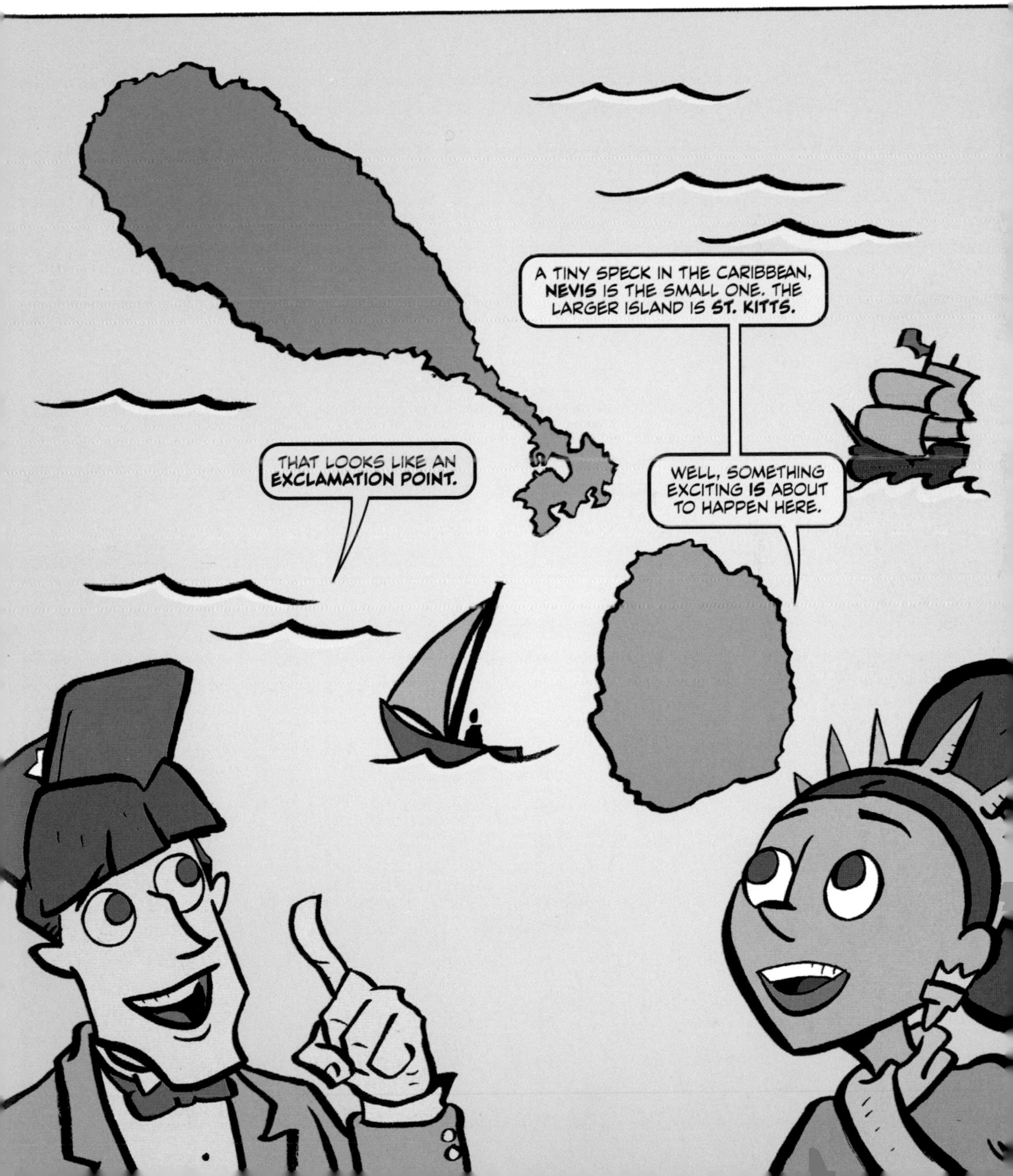
A TINY SPECK IN THE CARIBBEAN, NEVIS IS THE SMALL ONE. THE LARGER ISLAND IS ST. KITTS.
THAT LOOKS LIKE AN EXCLAMATION POINT.
WELL, SOMETHING EXCITING IS ABOUT TO HAPPEN HERE.

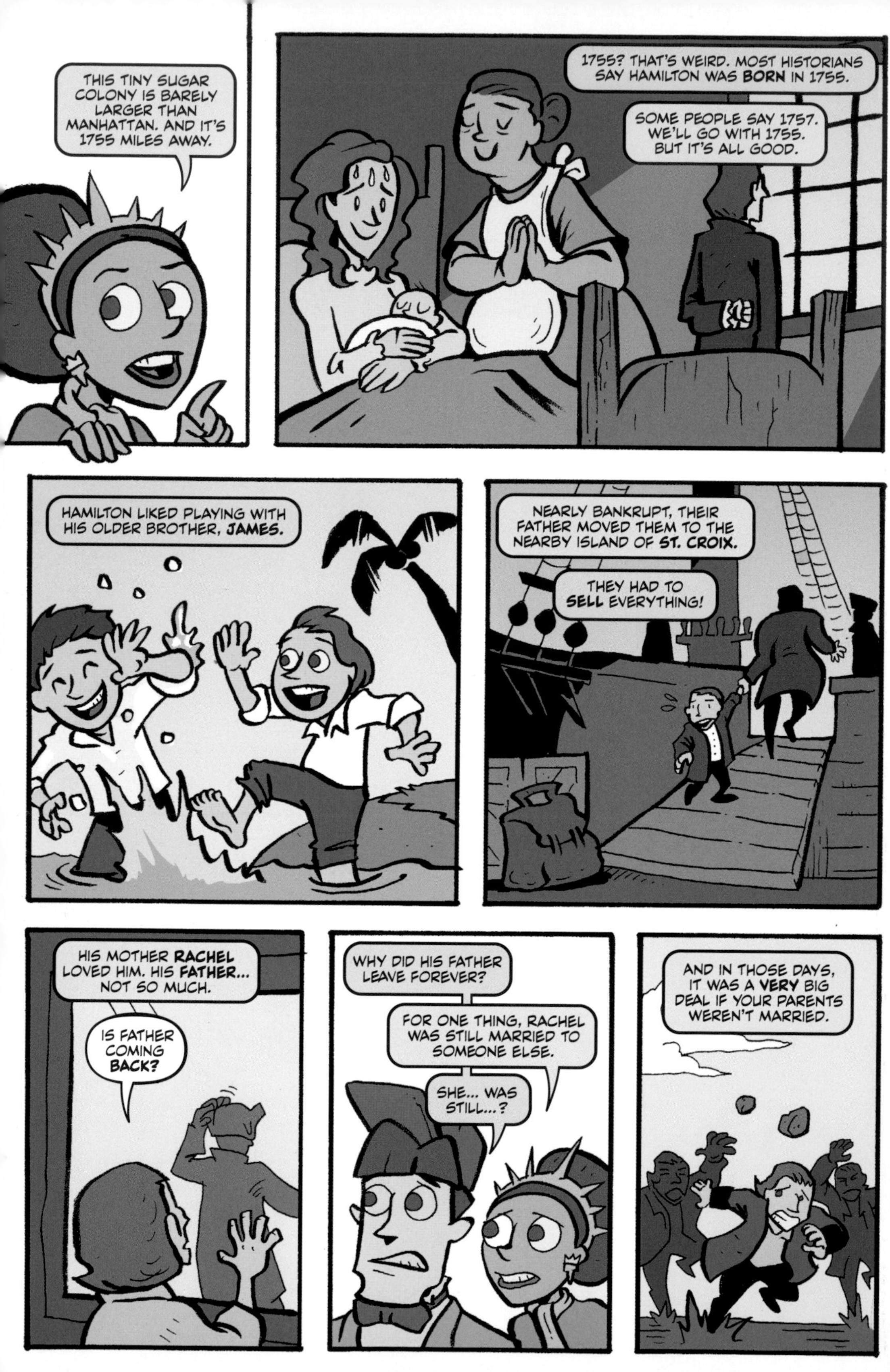
THIS TINY SUGAR COLONY IS BARELY LARGER THAN MANHATTAN. AND IT'S 1755 MILES AWAY.
1755? THAT'S WEIRD. MOST HISTORIANS SAY HAMILTON WAS **BORN** IN 1755.
SOME PEOPLE SAY 1757. WE'LL GO WITH 1755. BUT IT'S ALL GOOD.
HAMILTON LIKED PLAYING WITH HIS OLDER BROTHER, **JAMES.**
NEARLY BANKRUPT, THEIR FATHER MOVED THEM TO THE NEARBY ISLAND OF **ST. CROIX.**
THEY HAD TO **SELL** EVERYTHING!
HIS MOTHER **RACHEL** LOVED HIM. HIS **FATHER...** NOT SO MUCH.
IS FATHER COMING **BACK?**
WHY DID HIS FATHER LEAVE FOREVER?
FOR ONE THING, RACHEL WAS STILL MARRIED TO SOMEONE ELSE.
SHE... WAS STILL...?
AND IN THOSE DAYS, IT WAS A **VERY** BIG DEAL IF YOUR PARENTS WEREN'T MARRIED.

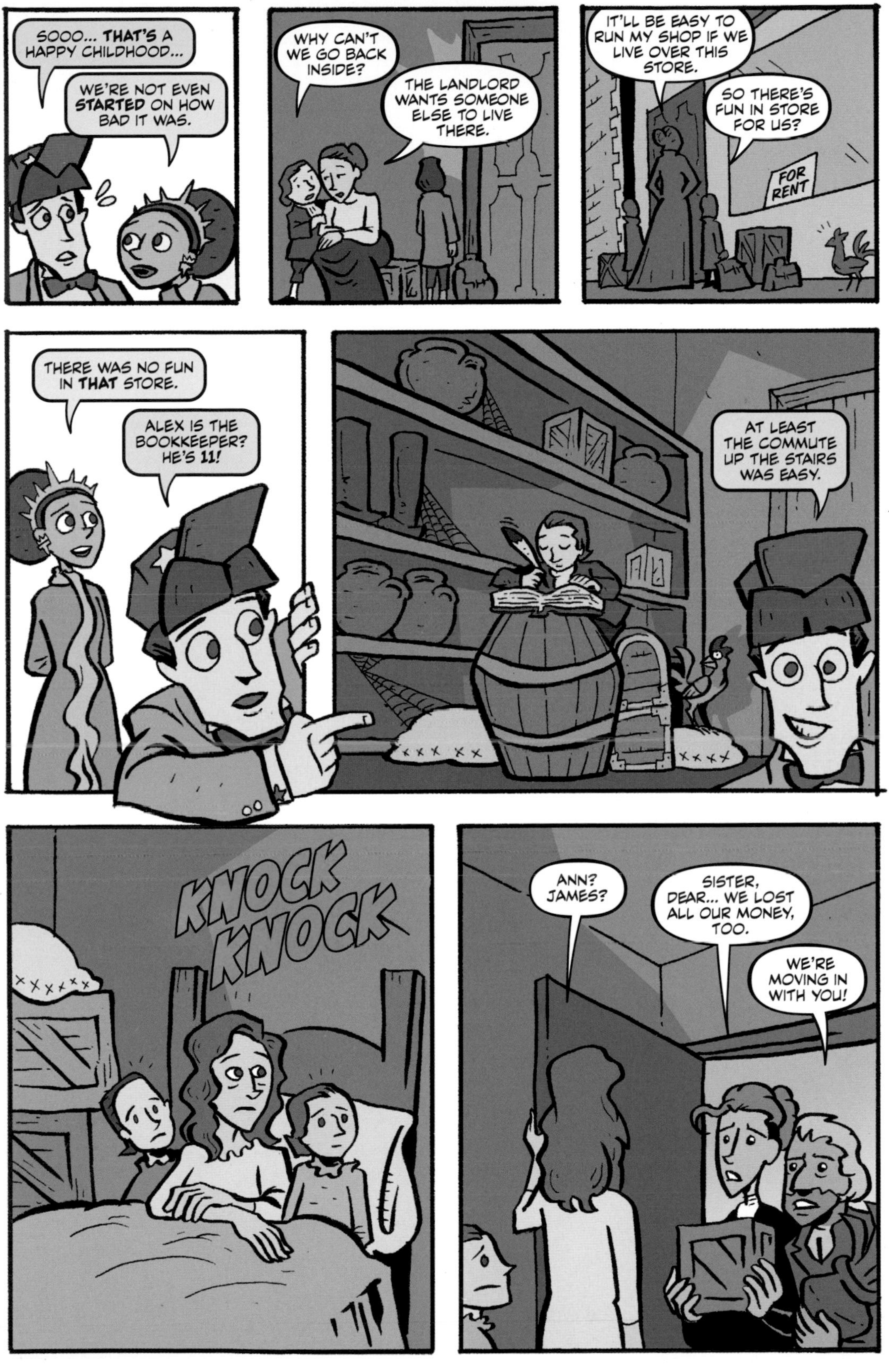
SOOO... THAT'S A HAPPY CHILDHOOD...
WE'RE NOT EVEN STARTED ON HOW BAD IT WAS.
WHY CAN'T WE GO BACK INSIDE?
THE LANDLORD WANTS SOMEONE ELSE TO LIVE THERE.
IT'LL BE EASY TO RUN MY SHOP IF WE LIVE OVER THIS STORE.
SO THERE'S FUN IN STORE FOR US?
FOR RENT
THERE WAS NO FUN IN THAT STORE.
ALEX IS THE BOOKKEEPER? HE'S 11!
AT LEAST THE COMMUTE UP THE STAIRS WAS EASY.
KNOCK KNOCK
ANN? JAMES?
SISTER, DEAR... WE LOST ALL OUR MONEY, TOO.
WE'RE MOVING IN WITH YOU!

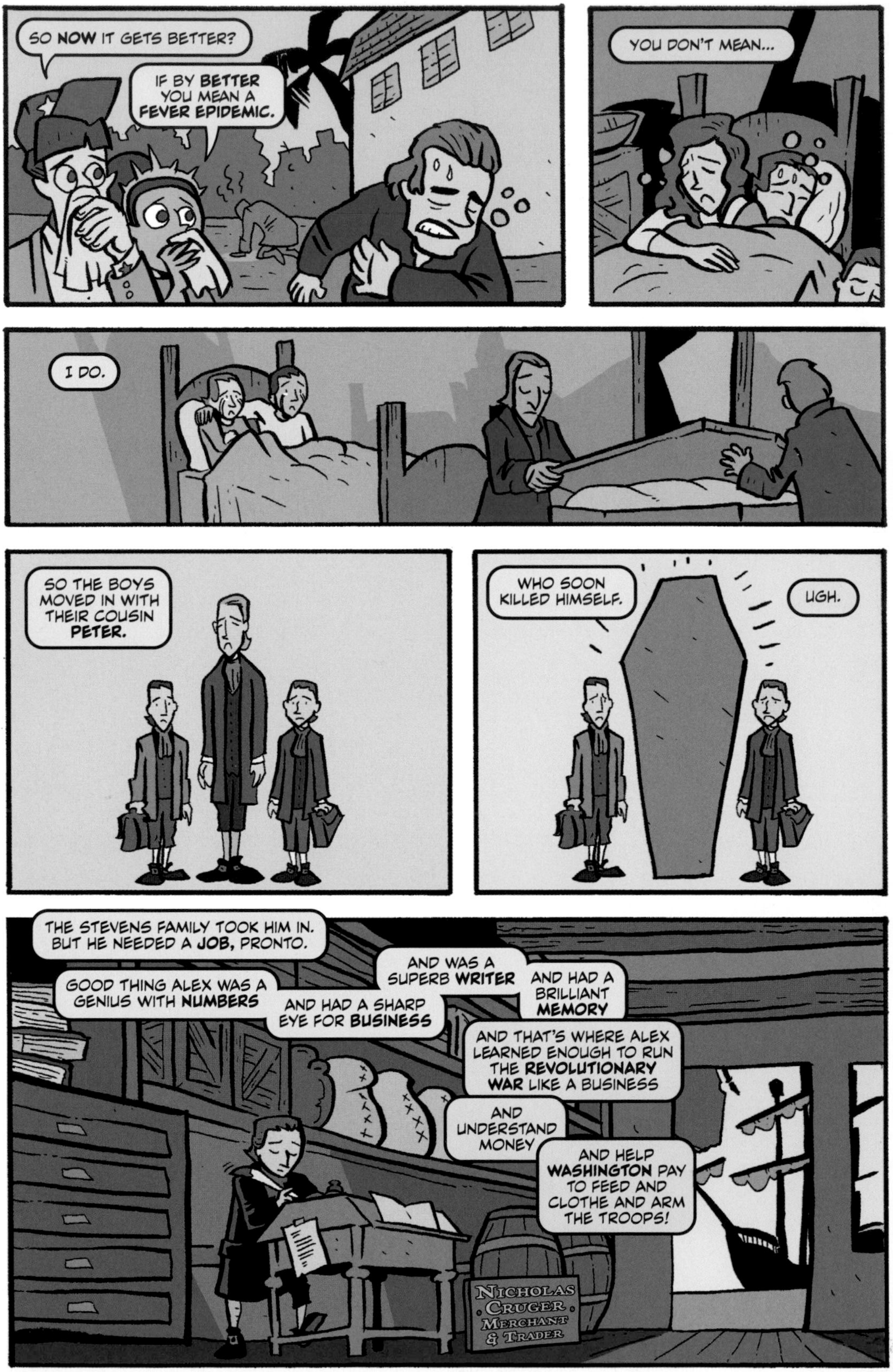
SO NOW IT GETS BETTER?
IF BY BETTER YOU MEAN A FEVER EPIDEMIC.
YOU DON'T MEAN...
I DO.
SO THE BOYS MOVED IN WITH THEIR COUSIN PETER.
WHO SOON KILLED HIMSELF.
UGH.
THE STEVENS FAMILY TOOK HIM IN. BUT HE NEEDED A JOB, PRONTO.
GOOD THING ALEX WAS A GENIUS WITH NUMBERS
AND HAD A SHARP EYE FOR BUSINESS
AND WAS A SUPERB WRITER
AND HAD A BRILLIANT MEMORY
AND THAT'S WHERE ALEX LEARNED ENOUGH TO RUN THE REVOLUTIONARY WAR LIKE A BUSINESS
AND UNDERSTAND MONEY
AND HELP WASHINGTON PAY TO FEED AND CLOTHE AND ARM THE TROOPS!
NICHOLAS CRUGER MERCHANT & TRADER

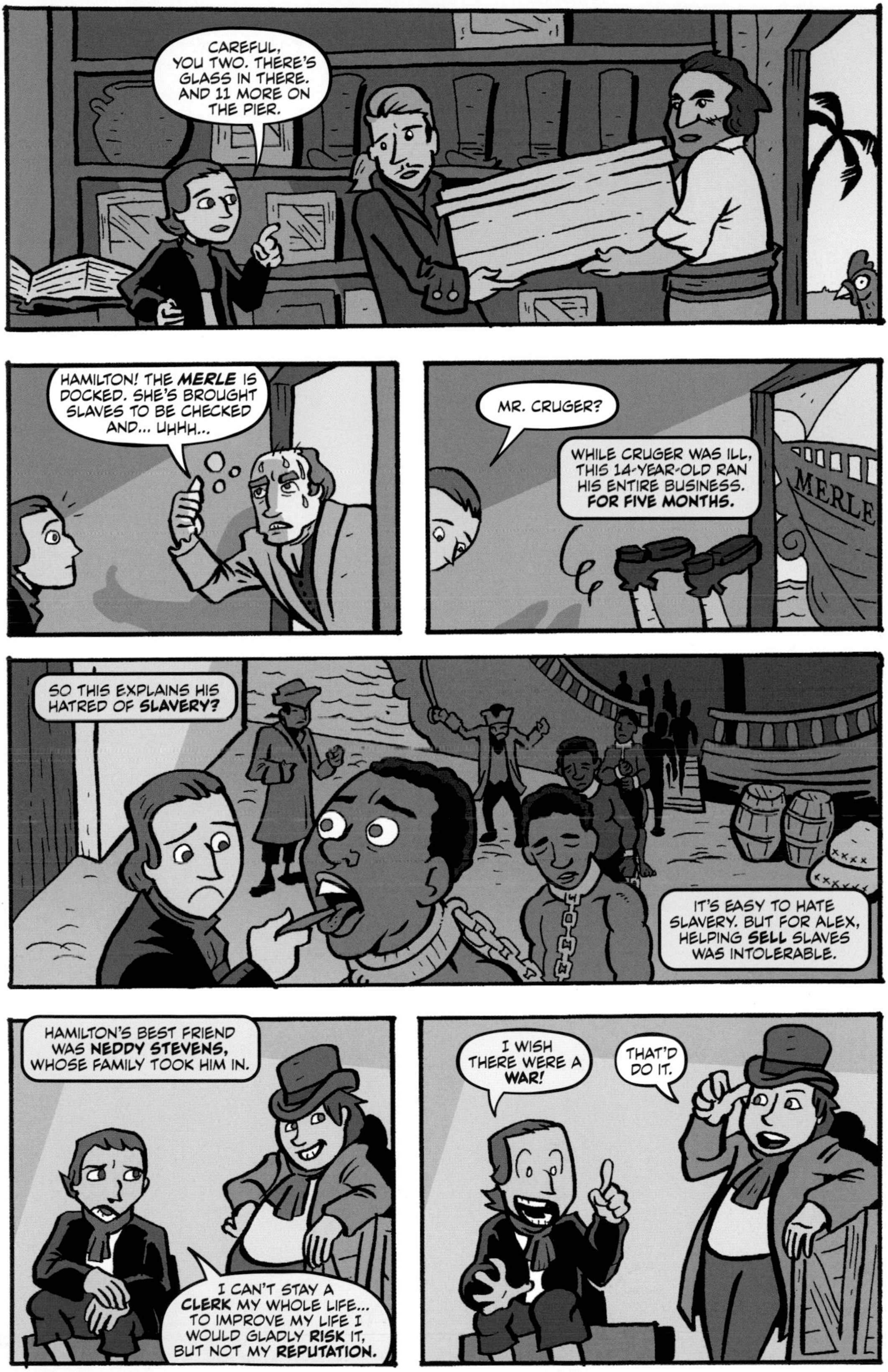
CAREFUL, YOU TWO. THERE'S GLASS IN THERE. AND 11 MORE ON THE PIER.
HAMILTON! THE MERLE IS DOCKED. SHE'S BROUGHT SLAVES TO BE CHECKED AND... UHHH...
MR. CRUGER?
WHILE CRUGER WAS ILL, THIS 14-YEAR-OLD RAN HIS ENTIRE BUSINESS. FOR FIVE MONTHS.
MERLE
SO THIS EXPLAINS HIS HATRED OF SLAVERY?
IT'S EASY TO HATE SLAVERY. BUT FOR ALEX, HELPING SELL SLAVES WAS INTOLERABLE.
HAMILTON'S BEST FRIEND WAS NEDDY STEVENS, WHOSE FAMILY TOOK HIM IN.
I CAN'T STAY A CLERK MY WHOLE LIFE... TO IMPROVE MY LIFE I WOULD GLADLY RISK IT, BUT NOT MY REPUTATION.
I WISH THERE WERE A WAR!
THAT'D DO IT.

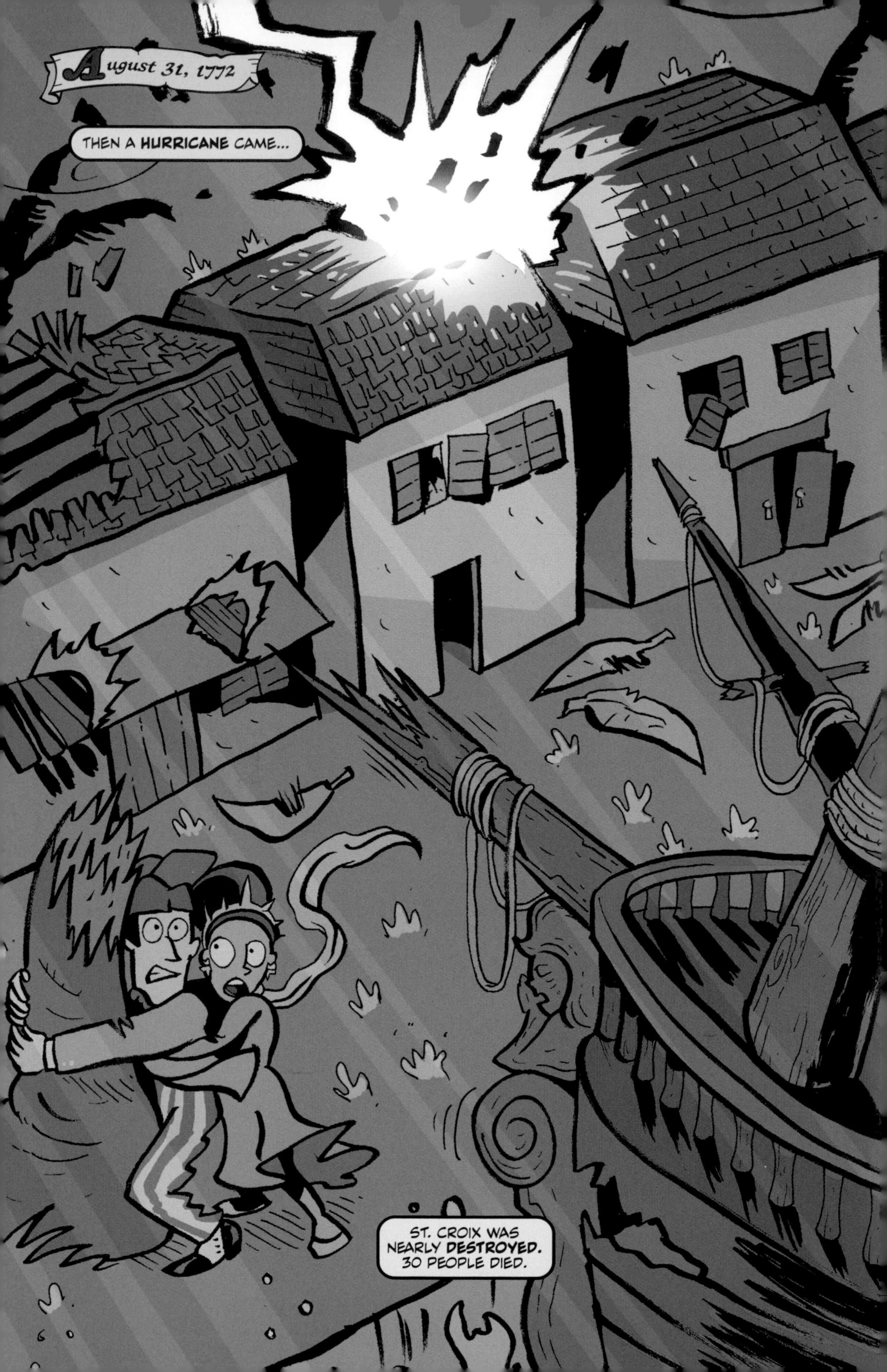
August 31, 1772
THEN A HURRICANE CAME...
ST. CROIX WAS NEARLY DESTROYED. 30 PEOPLE DIED.

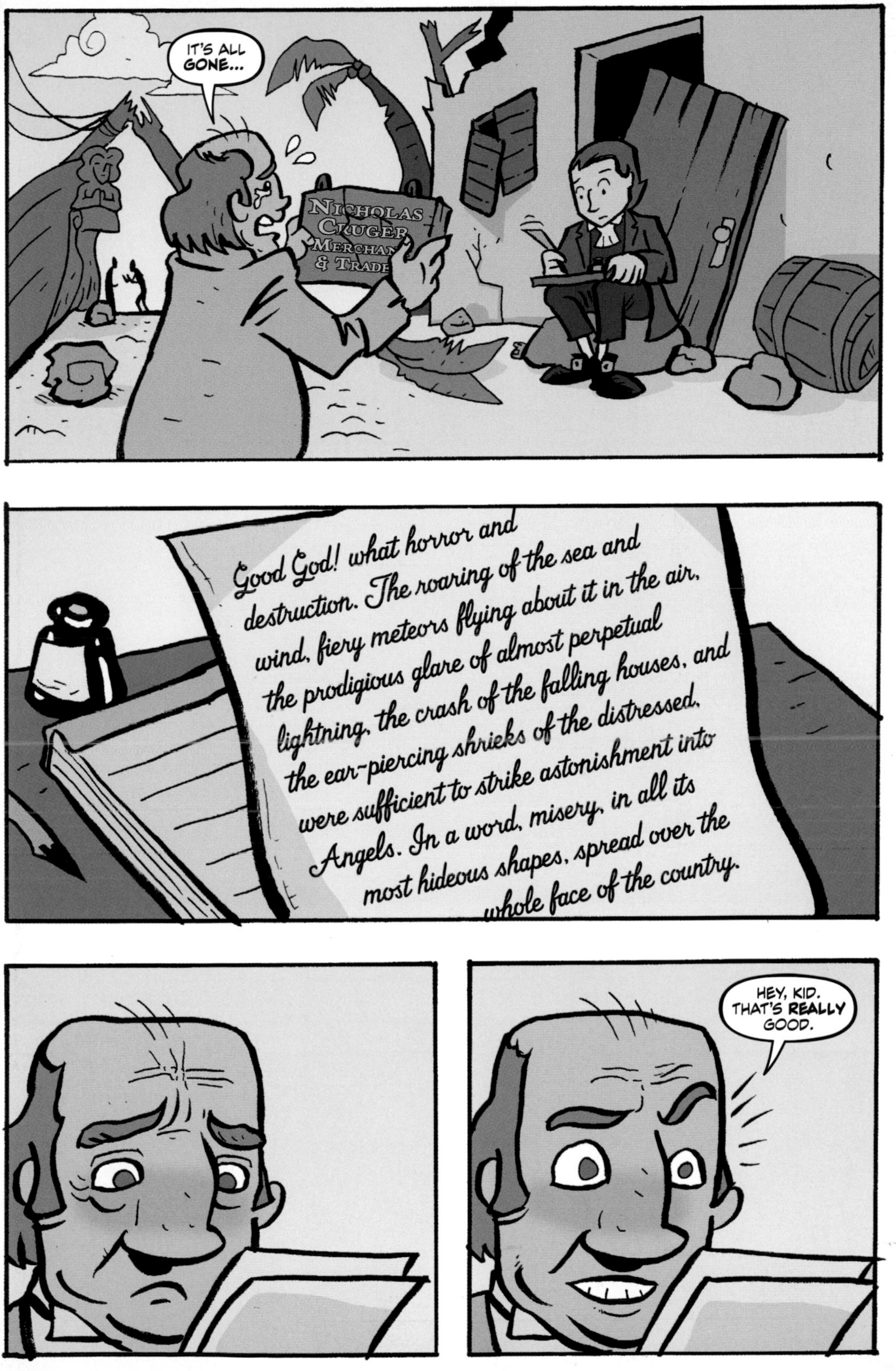
IT'S ALL GONE...
NICHOLAS CRUGER MERCHAN[T] & TRADE[R]
Good God! what horror and destruction. The roaring of the sea and wind, fiery meteors flying about it in the air, the prodigious glare of almost perpetual lightning, the crash of the falling houses, and the ear-piercing shrieks of the distressed, were sufficient to strike astonishment into Angels. In a word, misery, in all its most hideous shapes, spread over the whole face of the country.
HEY, KID. THAT'S REALLY GOOD.

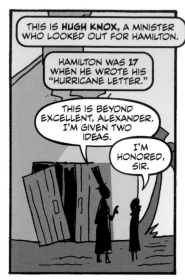

THIS IS **HUGH KNOX,** A MINISTER WHO LOOKED OUT FOR HAMILTON.

HAMILTON WAS **17** WHEN HE WROTE HIS "HURRICANE LETTER."

THIS IS BEYOND EXCELLENT, ALEXANDER. I'M GIVEN TWO IDEAS.

I'M HONORED, SIR.

I'LL SEND IT TO THE *ROYAL DANISH AMERICAN GAZETTE.*

THE LEADING NEWSPAPER. WHOA!

THEY WILL PUBLISH THIS IF I ASK.

AND THE **OTHER** IDEA, SIR?

AH, YES. ONCE YOU PUBLISH, I'LL TALK TO THE LOCAL BUSINESSMEN...

HE'S **HOW** OLD?

SEVENTEEN.

I'M 57. I CAN'T WRITE LIKE THIS.

AND **YOU** HAVE AN EDUCATION.

SPEAKING OF EDUCATION...

PUT OUT YOUR HAND, ALEXANDER.

THE COMMUNITY LEADERS WANT YOU TO GET A **GREAT EDUCATION,** SON.

AND IT WON'T HAPPEN ON **THIS** PILE OF BUSTED LUMBER. THAT'S FOR SURE.

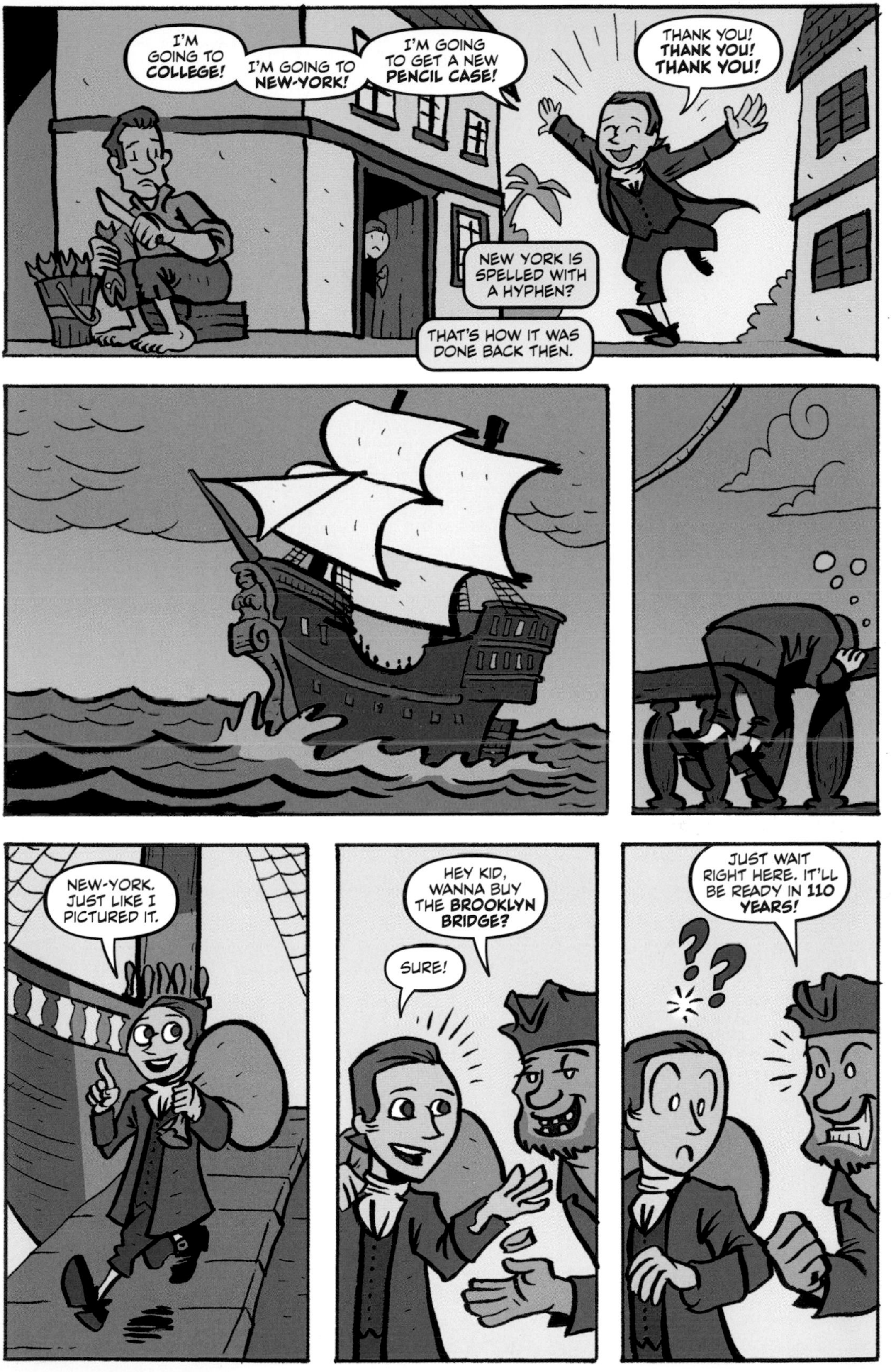
I'M GOING TO COLLEGE!
I'M GOING TO NEW-YORK!
I'M GOING TO GET A NEW PENCIL CASE!
THANK YOU! THANK YOU! THANK YOU!
NEW YORK IS SPELLED WITH A HYPHEN?
THAT'S HOW IT WAS DONE BACK THEN.
NEW-YORK. JUST LIKE I PICTURED IT.
HEY KID, WANNA BUY THE BROOKLYN BRIDGE?
SURE!
JUST WAIT RIGHT HERE. IT'LL BE READY IN 110 YEARS!

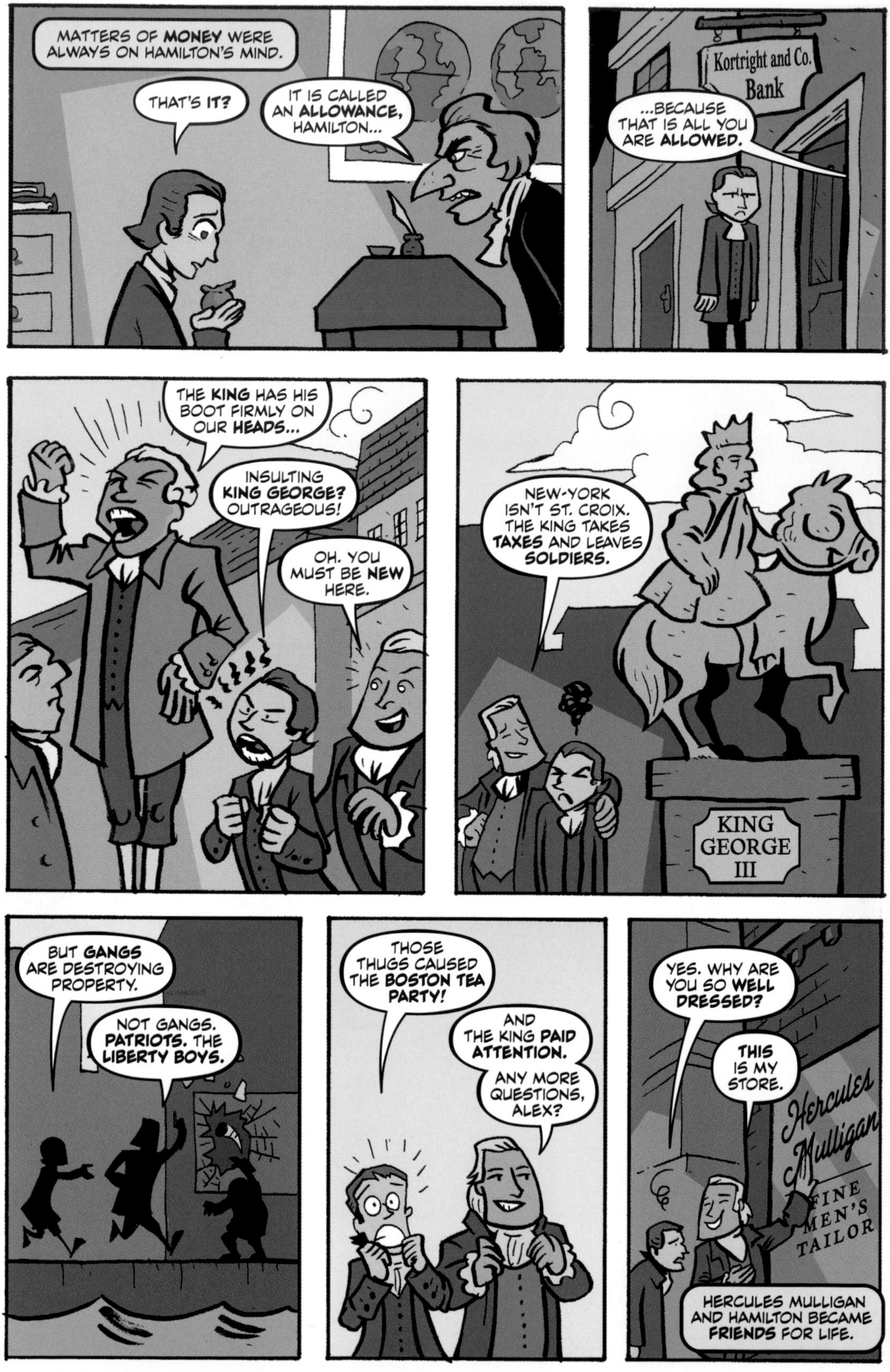
MATTERS OF MONEY WERE ALWAYS ON HAMILTON'S MIND.
THAT'S IT?
IT IS CALLED AN ALLOWANCE, HAMILTON...
Kortright and Co. Bank
...BECAUSE THAT IS ALL YOU ARE ALLOWED.
THE KING HAS HIS BOOT FIRMLY ON OUR HEADS...
INSULTING KING GEORGE? OUTRAGEOUS!
OH. YOU MUST BE NEW HERE.
NEW-YORK ISN'T ST. CROIX. THE KING TAKES TAXES AND LEAVES SOLDIERS.
KING GEORGE III
BUT GANGS ARE DESTROYING PROPERTY.
NOT GANGS. PATRIOTS. THE LIBERTY BOYS.
THOSE THUGS CAUSED THE BOSTON TEA PARTY!
AND THE KING PAID ATTENTION.
ANY MORE QUESTIONS, ALEX?
YES. WHY ARE YOU SO WELL DRESSED?
THIS IS MY STORE.
Hercules Mulligan
FINE MEN'S TAILOR
HERCULES MULLIGAN AND HAMILTON BECAME FRIENDS FOR LIFE.

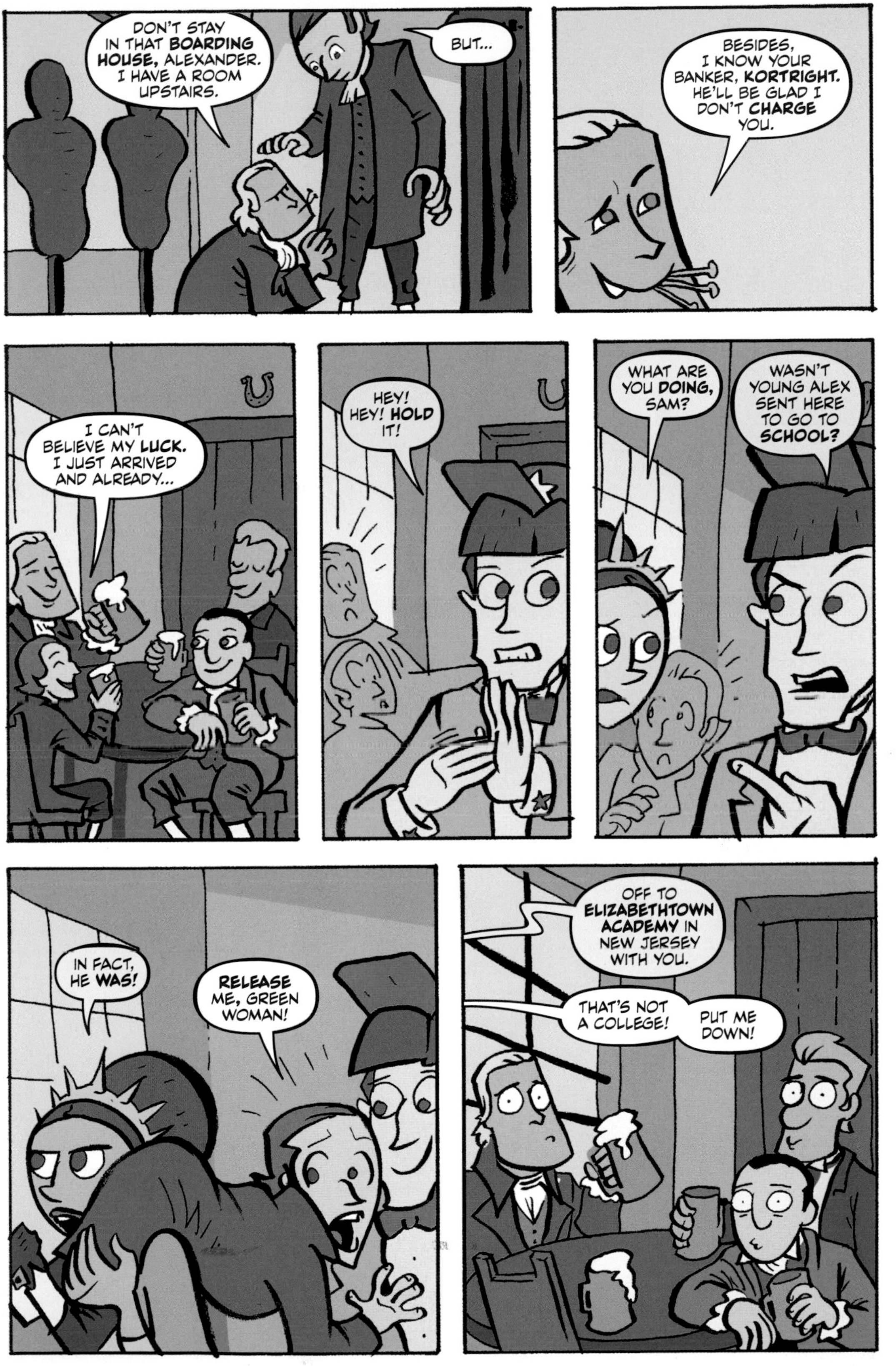
DON'T STAY IN THAT **BOARDING HOUSE,** ALEXANDER. I HAVE A ROOM UPSTAIRS.
BUT...
BESIDES, I KNOW YOUR BANKER, **KORTRIGHT.** HE'LL BE GLAD I DON'T **CHARGE** YOU.
I CAN'T BELIEVE MY **LUCK.** I JUST ARRIVED AND ALREADY...
HEY! HEY! **HOLD** IT!
WHAT ARE YOU **DOING,** SAM?
WASN'T YOUNG ALEX SENT HERE TO GO TO **SCHOOL?**
IN FACT, HE **WAS!**
RELEASE ME, GREEN WOMAN!
OFF TO **ELIZABETHTOWN ACADEMY** IN NEW JERSEY WITH YOU.
THAT'S NOT A COLLEGE!
PUT ME DOWN!

EVEN A **GREAT READER** LIKE ALEX NEEDED **MORE SCHOOLING** BEFORE GOING TO COLLEGE...

ENGLISH LITERATURE...
MY NAME IS ALEXANDER.

LATIN...
ALEXANDER NOMEN MEUM.

ANCIENT GREEK...
TO ÓNOMÁ MOU EÍNAI O ALÉXANDROS.

FRENCH...
MON NOM EST ALEXANDER.

PHILOSOPHY...
I **THINK** MY NAME IS ALEXANDER.

AND PROPER MANNERS...
PARDON THE INTRUSION, I AM REFERRED TO AS ALEXANDER.

NOW GO TO COLLEGE!

UNHAND ME, VERDANT FEMALE!

AND DO YOUR HOMEWORK!

WELCOME TO PRINCETON COLLEGE. I'M **AARON BURR.**

MY GRANDFATHER RUNS THIS PLACE.

PRINCE COLL NEW-JER

...HAMILTON WAS **SUPPOSED** TO GO TO PRINCETON...

THEY WON'T GIVE ME A FOUR-YEAR EDUCATION IN TWO YEARS.

PRINC N COLL NEW-JE

BUT **KING'S COLLEGE** WOULD DO IT IN TWO.

WHO NEEDS THE **PRINCE** WHEN YOU CAN GO WITH THE **KING?**

IT'S CALLED **COLUMBIA UNIVERSITY** NOW.

KING'S COLLEGE NEW-YORK

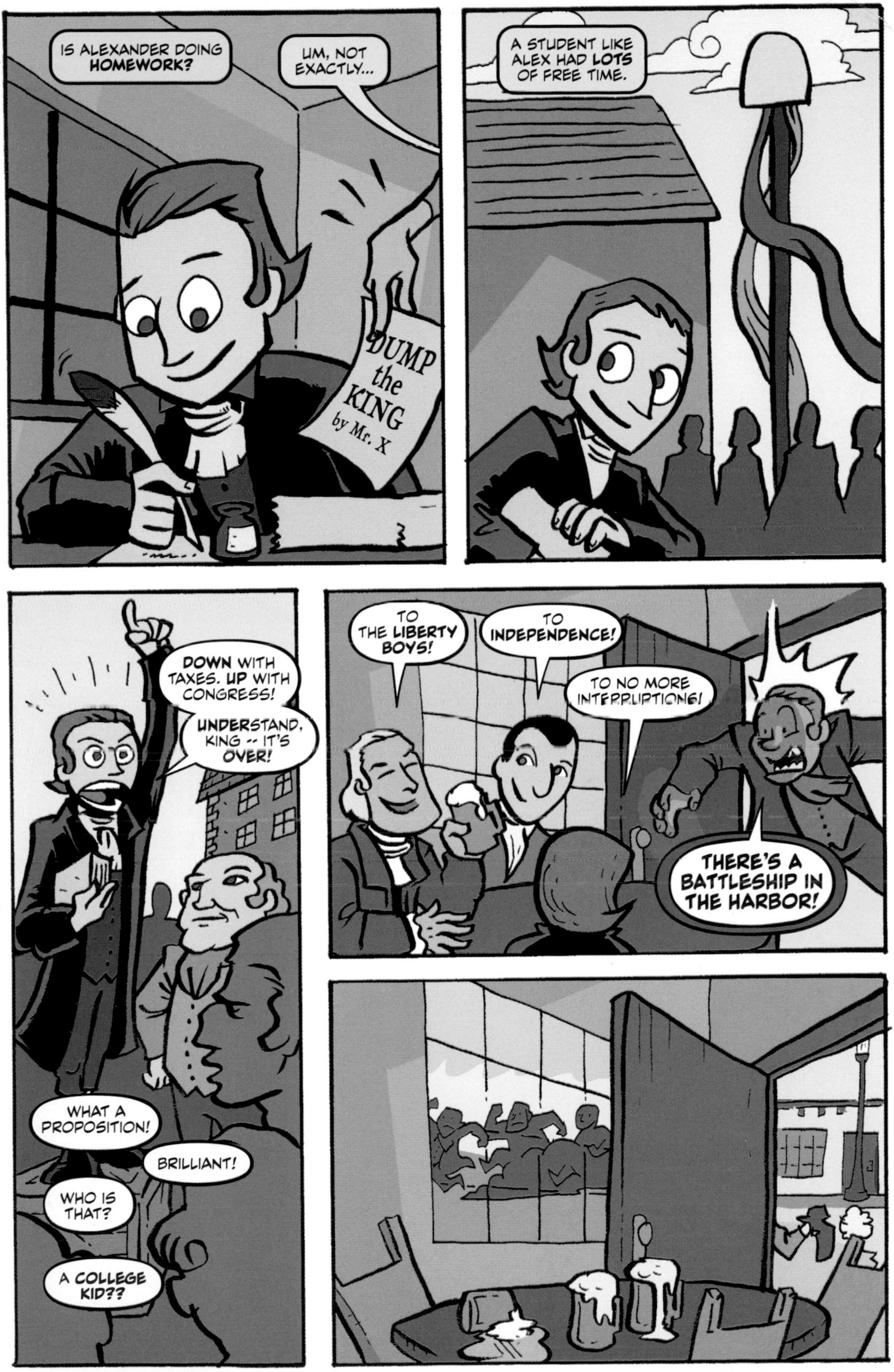
IS ALEXANDER DOING HOMEWORK?
UM, NOT EXACTLY...
DUMP the KING by Mr. X
A STUDENT LIKE ALEX HAD LOTS OF FREE TIME.
DOWN WITH TAXES. UP WITH CONGRESS!
UNDERSTAND, KING -- IT'S OVER!
WHAT A PROPOSITION!
BRILLIANT!
WHO IS THAT?
A COLLEGE KID??
TO THE LIBERTY BOYS!
TO INDEPENDENCE!
TO NO MORE INTERRUPTIONS!
THERE'S A BATTLESHIP IN THE HARBOR!

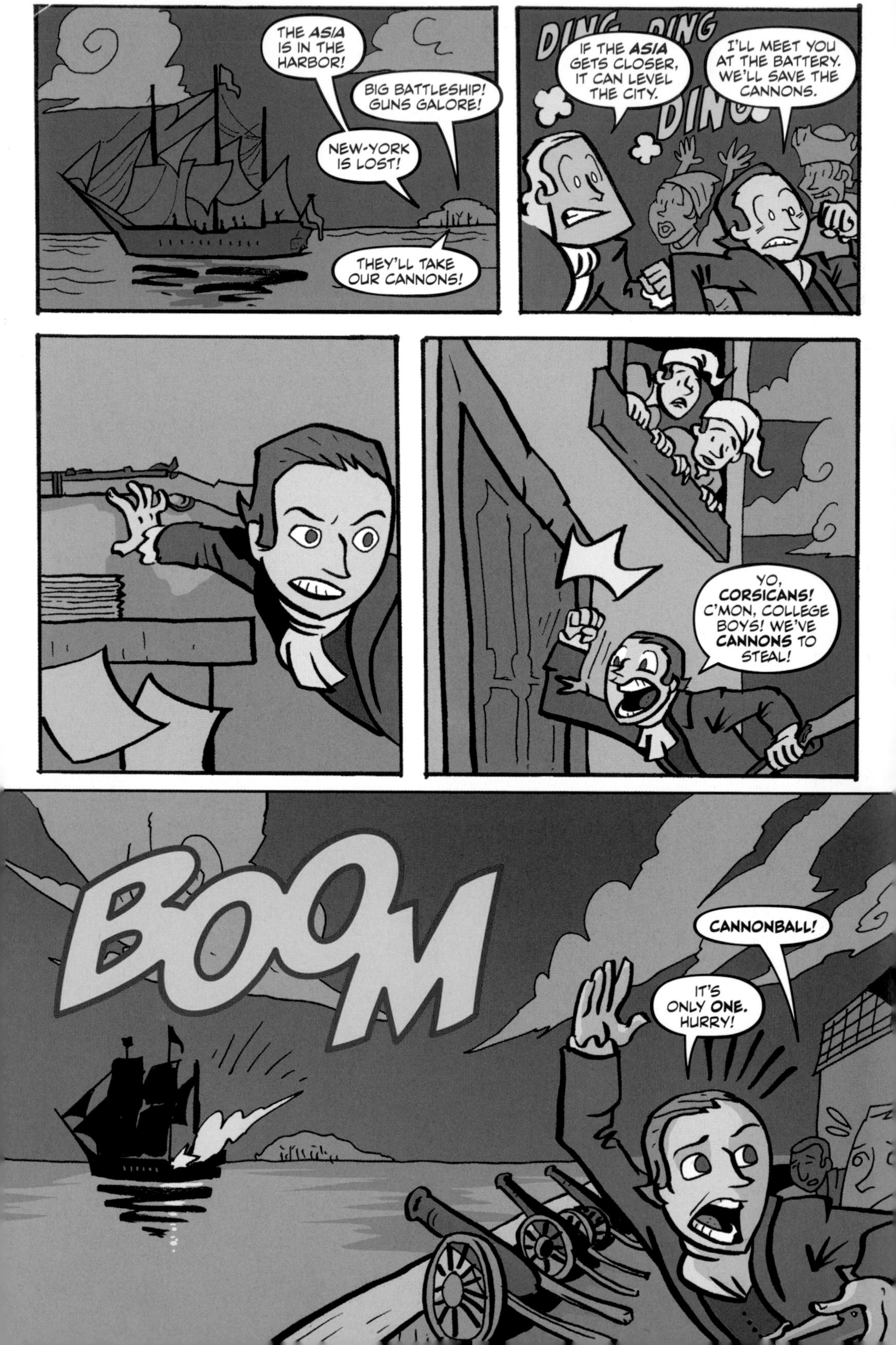
THE ASIA IS IN THE HARBOR!
BIG BATTLESHIP! GUNS GALORE!
NEW-YORK IS LOST!
THEY'LL TAKE OUR CANNONS!
DING DING
IF THE ASIA GETS CLOSER, IT CAN LEVEL THE CITY.
I'LL MEET YOU AT THE BATTERY. WE'LL SAVE THE CANNONS.
YO, CORSICANS! C'MON, COLLEGE BOYS! WE'VE CANNONS TO STEAL!
BOOM
CANNONBALL!
IT'S ONLY ONE. HURRY!

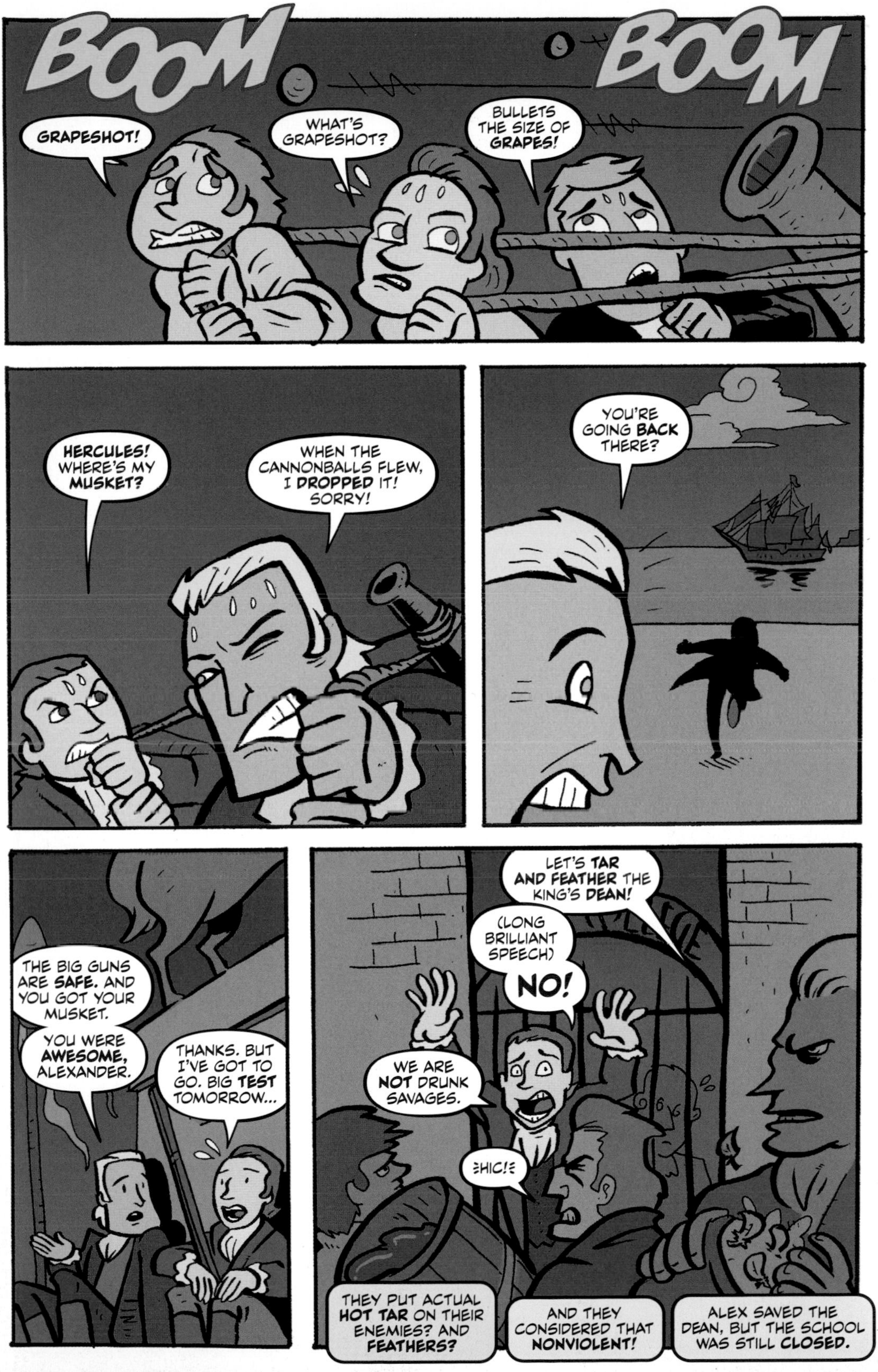

BOOM
BOOM
GRAPESHOT!
WHAT'S GRAPESHOT?
BULLETS THE SIZE OF GRAPES!
HERCULES! WHERE'S MY MUSKET?
WHEN THE CANNONBALLS FLEW, I DROPPED IT! SORRY!
YOU'RE GOING BACK THERE?
THE BIG GUNS ARE SAFE. AND YOU GOT YOUR MUSKET.
YOU WERE AWESOME, ALEXANDER.
THANKS. BUT I'VE GOT TO GO. BIG TEST TOMORROW...
LET'S TAR AND FEATHER THE KING'S DEAN!
(LONG BRILLIANT SPEECH)
NO!
WE ARE NOT DRUNK SAVAGES.
HIC!
THEY PUT ACTUAL HOT TAR ON THEIR ENEMIES? AND FEATHERS?
AND THEY CONSIDERED THAT NONVIOLENT!
ALEX SAVED THE DEAN, BUT THE SCHOOL WAS STILL CLOSED.

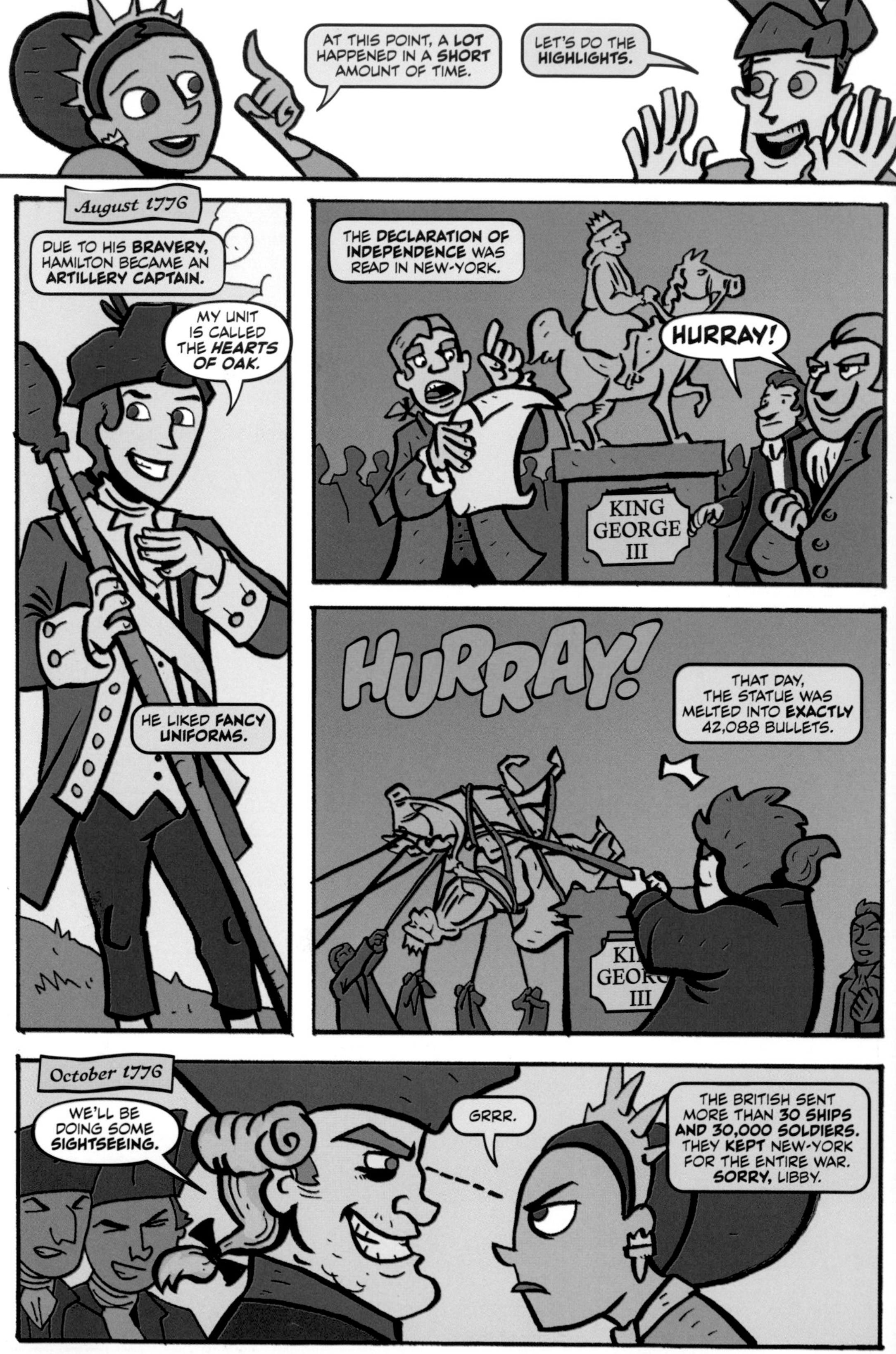

AT THIS POINT, A LOT HAPPENED IN A SHORT AMOUNT OF TIME.
LET'S DO THE HIGHLIGHTS.
August 1776
DUE TO HIS BRAVERY, HAMILTON BECAME AN ARTILLERY CAPTAIN.
MY UNIT IS CALLED THE HEARTS OF OAK.
HE LIKED FANCY UNIFORMS.
THE DECLARATION OF INDEPENDENCE WAS READ IN NEW-YORK.
HURRAY!
KING GEORGE III
HURRAY!
THAT DAY, THE STATUE WAS MELTED INTO EXACTLY 42,088 BULLETS.
October 1776
WE'LL BE DOING SOME SIGHTSEEING.
GRRR.
THE BRITISH SENT MORE THAN 30 SHIPS AND 30,000 SOLDIERS. THEY KEPT NEW-YORK FOR THE ENTIRE WAR. SORRY, LIBBY.

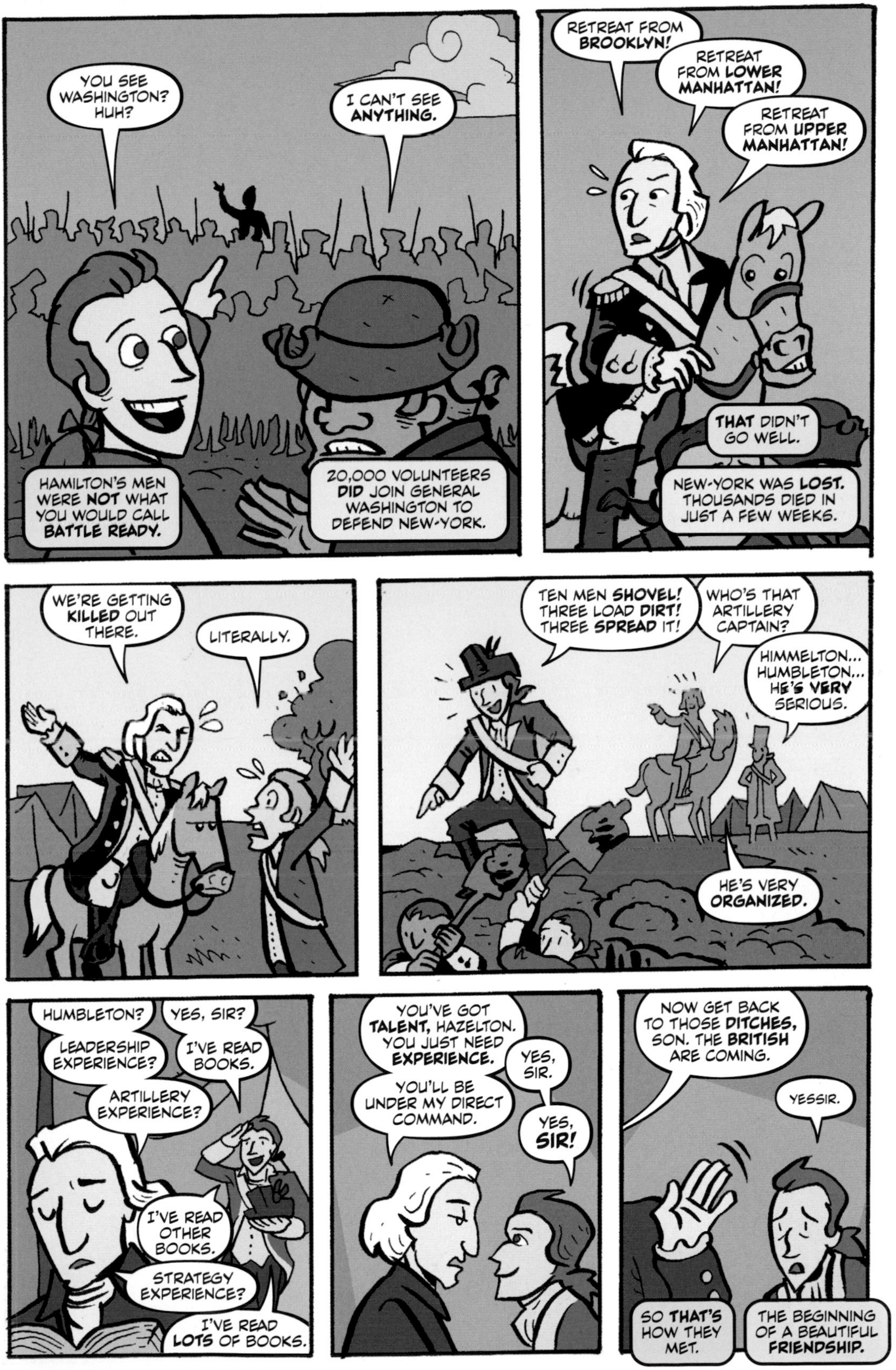

YOU SEE WASHINGTON? HUH?
I CAN'T SEE **ANYTHING.**
HAMILTON'S MEN WERE **NOT** WHAT YOU WOULD CALL **BATTLE READY.**
20,000 VOLUNTEERS **DID** JOIN GENERAL WASHINGTON TO DEFEND NEW-YORK.
RETREAT FROM **BROOKLYN!**
RETREAT FROM **LOWER MANHATTAN!**
RETREAT FROM **UPPER MANHATTAN!**
THAT DIDN'T GO WELL.
NEW-YORK WAS **LOST.** THOUSANDS DIED IN JUST A FEW WEEKS.
WE'RE GETTING **KILLED** OUT THERE.
LITERALLY.
TEN MEN **SHOVEL!** THREE LOAD **DIRT!** THREE **SPREAD** IT!
WHO'S THAT ARTILLERY CAPTAIN?
HIMMELTON... HUMBLETON... **HE'S VERY** SERIOUS.
HE'S VERY **ORGANIZED.**
HUMBLETON?
YES, SIR?
LEADERSHIP EXPERIENCE?
I'VE READ BOOKS.
ARTILLERY EXPERIENCE?
I'VE READ OTHER BOOKS.
STRATEGY EXPERIENCE?
I'VE READ **LOTS** OF BOOKS.
YOU'VE GOT **TALENT,** HAZELTON. YOU JUST NEED **EXPERIENCE.**
YES, SIR.
YOU'LL BE UNDER MY DIRECT COMMAND.
YES, **SIR!**
NOW GET BACK TO THOSE **DITCHES,** SON. THE **BRITISH** ARE COMING.
YESSIR.
SO **THAT'S** HOW THEY MET.
THE BEGINNING OF A BEAUTIFUL **FRIENDSHIP.**

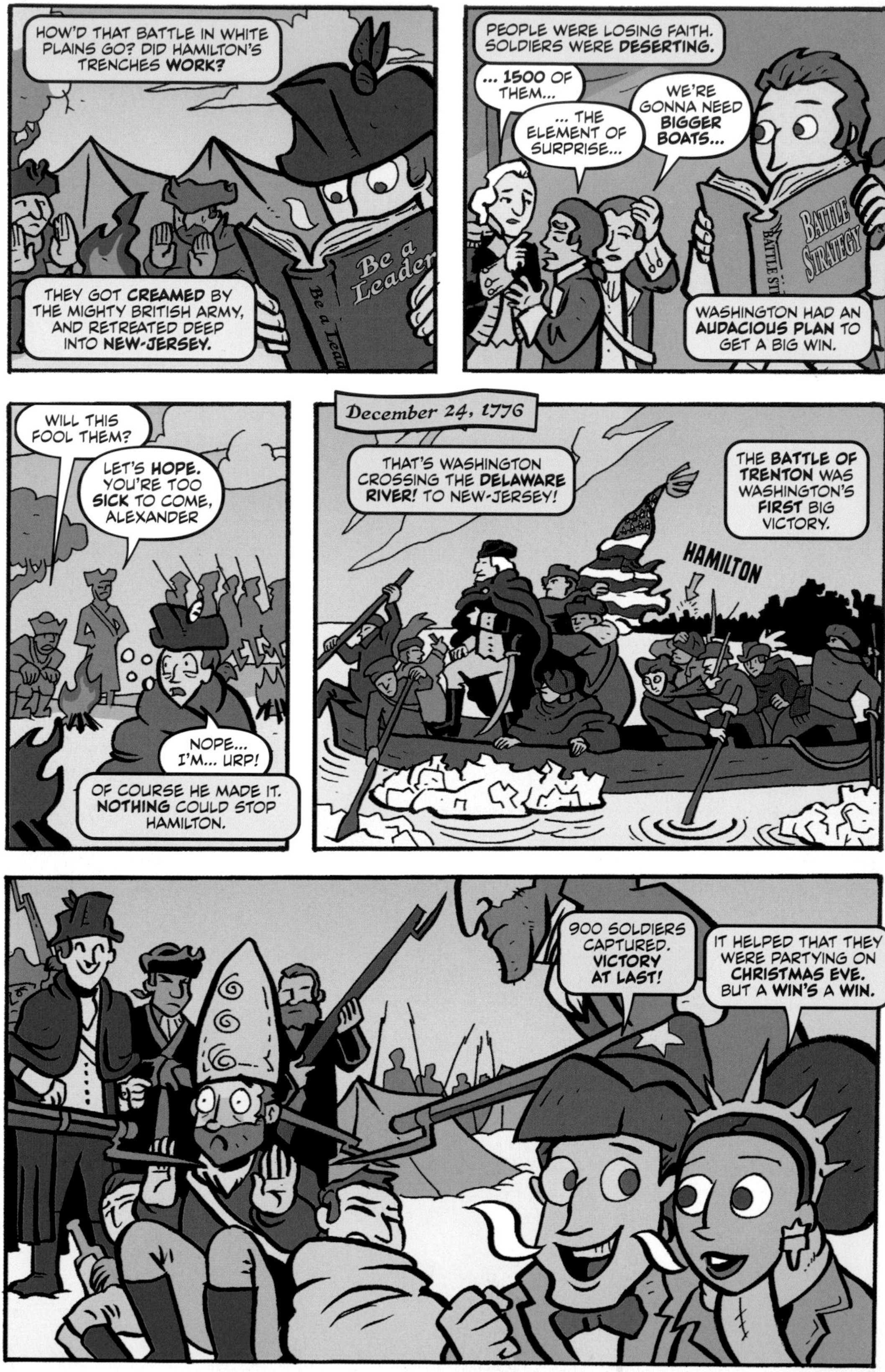
HOW'D THAT BATTLE IN WHITE PLAINS GO? DID HAMILTON'S TRENCHES WORK?
Be a Leader
THEY GOT CREAMED BY THE MIGHTY BRITISH ARMY, AND RETREATED DEEP INTO NEW-JERSEY.
PEOPLE WERE LOSING FAITH. SOLDIERS WERE DESERTING.
... 1500 OF THEM...
... THE ELEMENT OF SURPRISE...
WE'RE GONNA NEED BIGGER BOATS...
BATTLE STRATEGY
WASHINGTON HAD AN AUDACIOUS PLAN TO GET A BIG WIN.
WILL THIS FOOL THEM?
LET'S HOPE. YOU'RE TOO SICK TO COME, ALEXANDER
NOPE... I'M... URP!
OF COURSE HE MADE IT. NOTHING COULD STOP HAMILTON.
December 24, 1776
THAT'S WASHINGTON CROSSING THE DELAWARE RIVER! TO NEW-JERSEY!
THE BATTLE OF TRENTON WAS WASHINGTON'S FIRST BIG VICTORY.
HAMILTON
900 SOLDIERS CAPTURED. VICTORY AT LAST!
IT HELPED THAT THEY WERE PARTYING ON CHRISTMAS EVE. BUT A WIN'S A WIN.

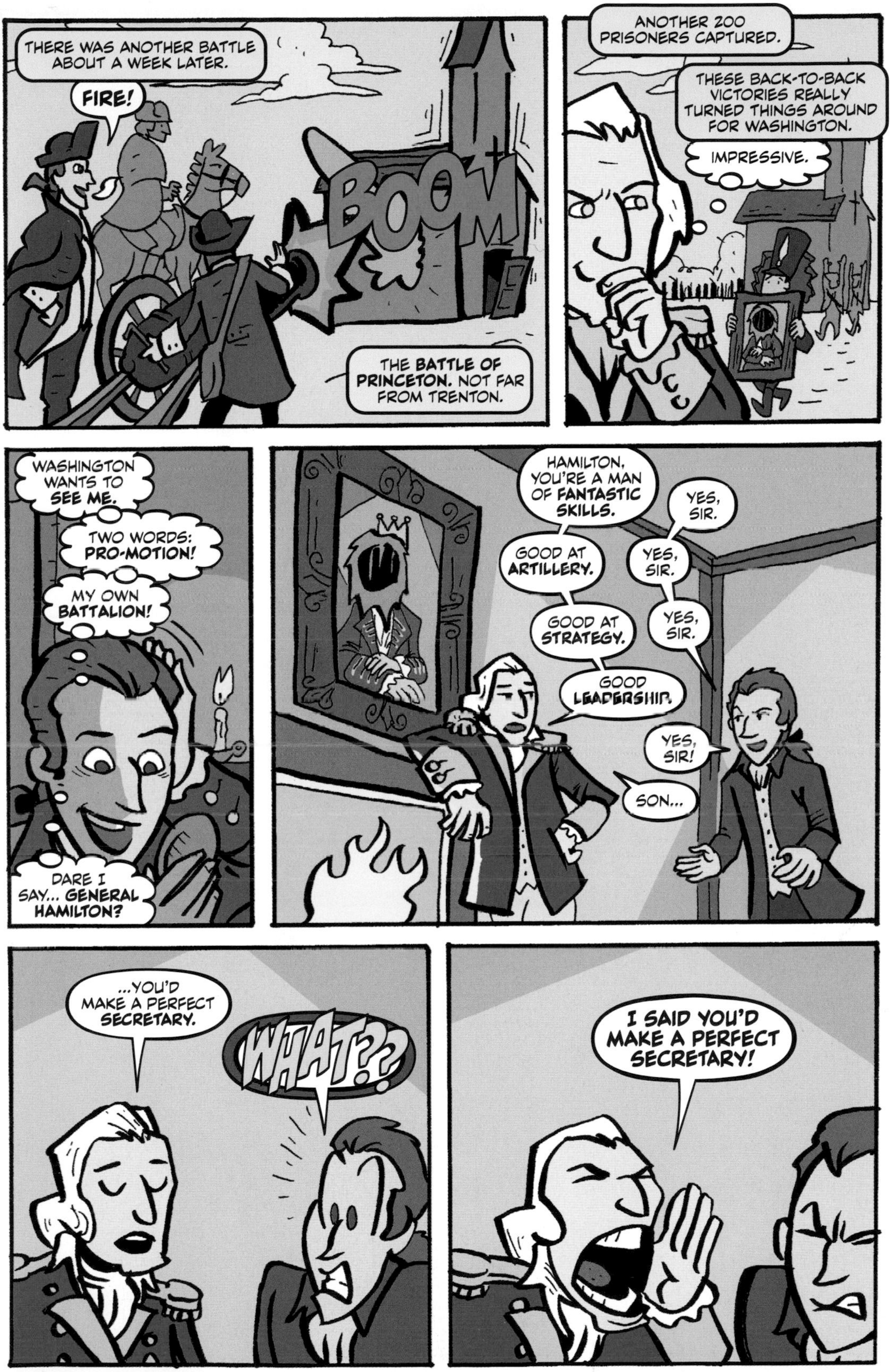
THERE WAS ANOTHER BATTLE ABOUT A WEEK LATER.
FIRE!
BOOM
THE BATTLE OF PRINCETON. NOT FAR FROM TRENTON.
ANOTHER 200 PRISONERS CAPTURED.
THESE BACK-TO-BACK VICTORIES REALLY TURNED THINGS AROUND FOR WASHINGTON.
IMPRESSIVE.
WASHINGTON WANTS TO SEE ME.
TWO WORDS: PRO-MOTION!
MY OWN BATTALION!
DARE I SAY... GENERAL HAMILTON?
HAMILTON, YOU'RE A MAN OF FANTASTIC SKILLS.
YES, SIR.
GOOD AT ARTILLERY.
YES, SIR.
GOOD AT STRATEGY.
YES, SIR.
GOOD LEADERSHIP.
YES, SIR!
SON...
...YOU'D MAKE A PERFECT SECRETARY.
WHAT??
I SAID YOU'D MAKE A PERFECT SECRETARY!

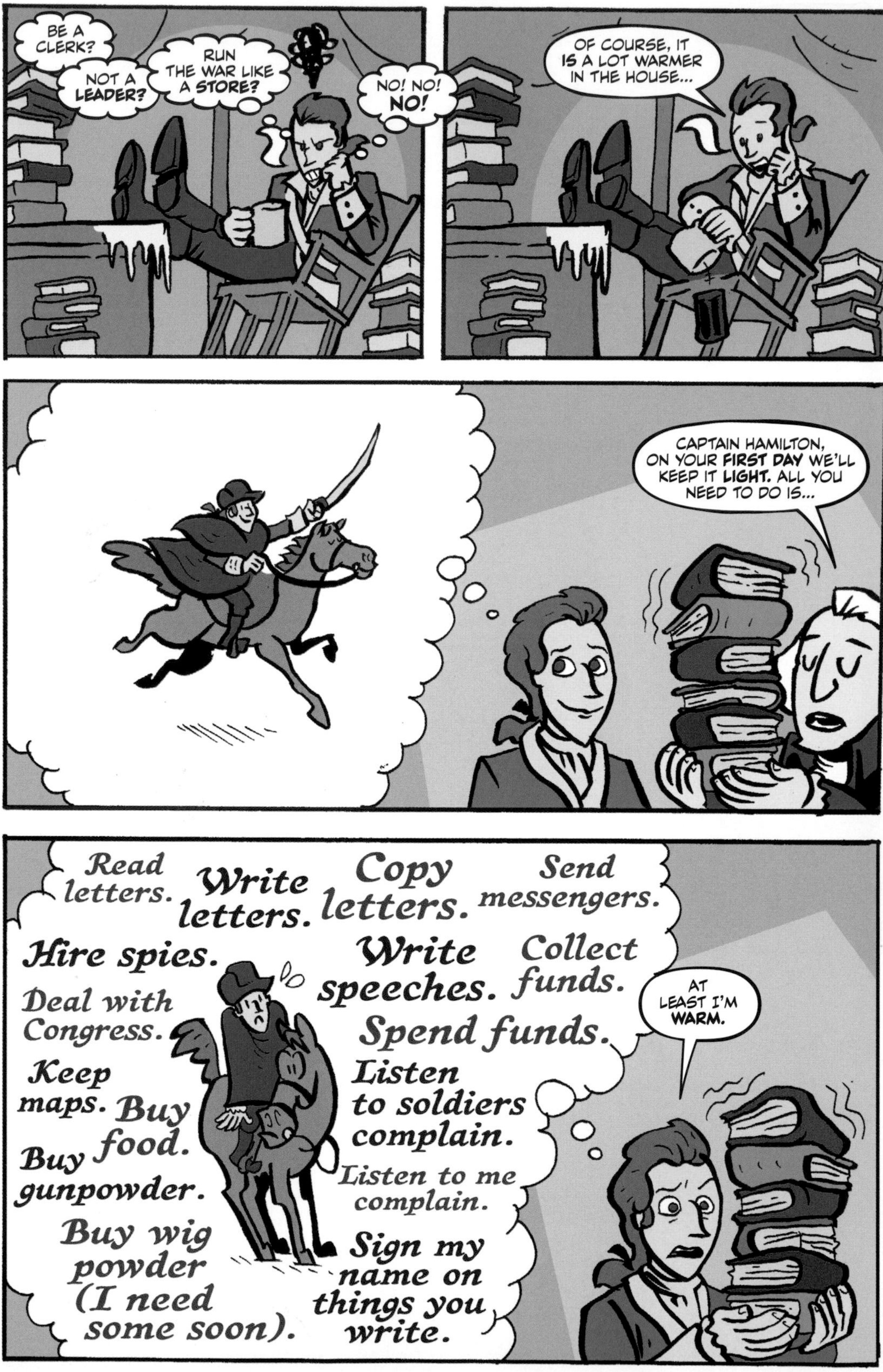
BE A CLERK?
NOT A LEADER?
RUN THE WAR LIKE A STORE?
NO! NO! NO!
OF COURSE, IT IS A LOT WARMER IN THE HOUSE...
CAPTAIN HAMILTON, ON YOUR FIRST DAY WE'LL KEEP IT LIGHT. ALL YOU NEED TO DO IS...
Read letters.
Write letters.
Copy letters.
Send messengers.
Hire spies.
Write speeches.
Collect funds.
Deal with Congress.
Spend funds.
Keep maps.
Buy food.
Listen to soldiers complain.
Buy gunpowder.
Listen to me complain.
Buy wig powder (I need some soon).
Sign my name on things you write.
AT LEAST I'M WARM.

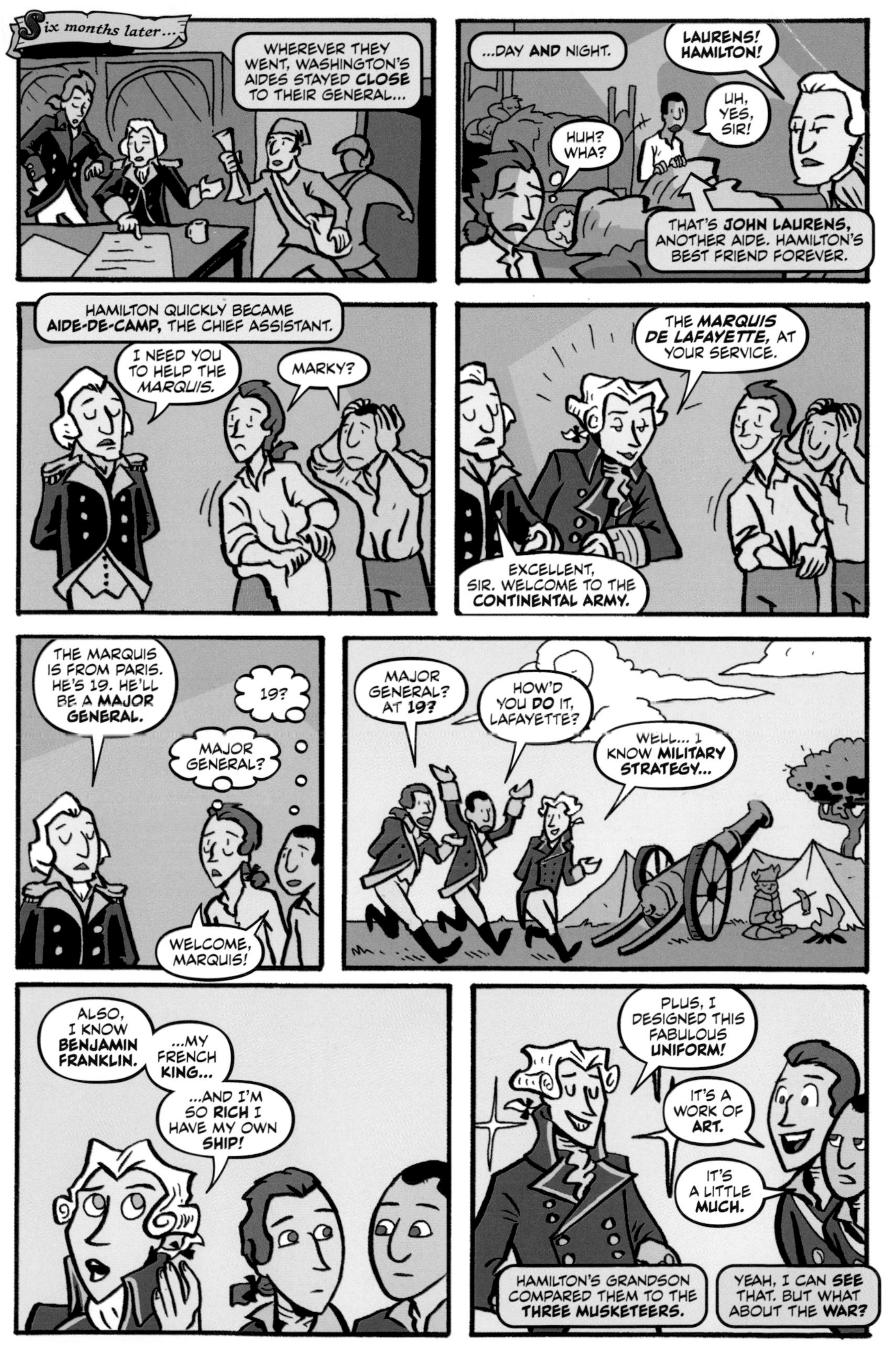

Six months later...
WHEREVER THEY WENT, WASHINGTON'S AIDES STAYED CLOSE TO THEIR GENERAL...
...DAY AND NIGHT.
LAURENS! HAMILTON!
UH, YES, SIR!
HUH? WHA?
THAT'S JOHN LAURENS, ANOTHER AIDE. HAMILTON'S BEST FRIEND FOREVER.
HAMILTON QUICKLY BECAME AIDE-DE-CAMP, THE CHIEF ASSISTANT.
I NEED YOU TO HELP THE MARQUIS.
MARKY?
THE MARQUIS DE LAFAYETTE, AT YOUR SERVICE.
EXCELLENT, SIR. WELCOME TO THE CONTINENTAL ARMY.
THE MARQUIS IS FROM PARIS. HE'S 19. HE'LL BE A MAJOR GENERAL.
19?
MAJOR GENERAL?
WELCOME, MARQUIS!
MAJOR GENERAL? AT 19?
HOW'D YOU DO IT, LAFAYETTE?
WELL... I KNOW MILITARY STRATEGY...
ALSO, I KNOW BENJAMIN FRANKLIN.
...MY FRENCH KING...
...AND I'M SO RICH I HAVE MY OWN SHIP!
PLUS, I DESIGNED THIS FABULOUS UNIFORM!
IT'S A WORK OF ART.
IT'S A LITTLE MUCH.
HAMILTON'S GRANDSON COMPARED THEM TO THE THREE MUSKETEERS.
YEAH, I CAN SEE THAT. BUT WHAT ABOUT THE WAR?

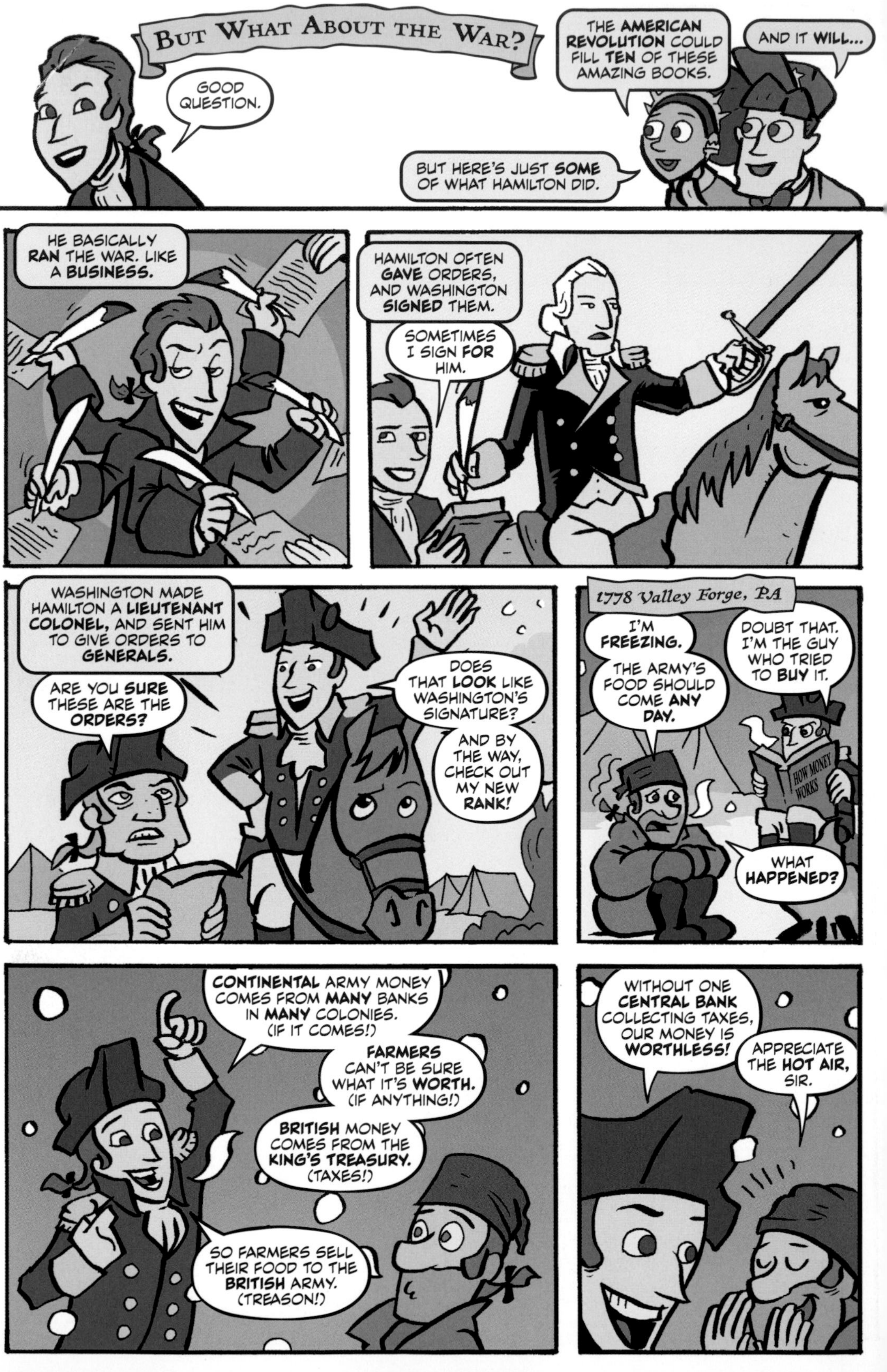
BUT WHAT ABOUT THE WAR?
GOOD QUESTION.
THE AMERICAN REVOLUTION COULD FILL TEN OF THESE AMAZING BOOKS.
AND IT WILL...
BUT HERE'S JUST SOME OF WHAT HAMILTON DID.
HE BASICALLY RAN THE WAR. LIKE A BUSINESS.
HAMILTON OFTEN GAVE ORDERS, AND WASHINGTON SIGNED THEM.
SOMETIMES I SIGN FOR HIM.
WASHINGTON MADE HAMILTON A LIEUTENANT COLONEL, AND SENT HIM TO GIVE ORDERS TO GENERALS.
ARE YOU SURE THESE ARE THE ORDERS?
DOES THAT LOOK LIKE WASHINGTON'S SIGNATURE?
AND BY THE WAY, CHECK OUT MY NEW RANK!
1778 Valley Forge, PA
I'M FREEZING.
THE ARMY'S FOOD SHOULD COME ANY DAY.
DOUBT THAT. I'M THE GUY WHO TRIED TO BUY IT.
HOW MONEY WORKS
WHAT HAPPENED?
CONTINENTAL ARMY MONEY COMES FROM MANY BANKS IN MANY COLONIES. (IF IT COMES!)
FARMERS CAN'T BE SURE WHAT IT'S WORTH. (IF ANYTHING!)
BRITISH MONEY COMES FROM THE KING'S TREASURY. (TAXES!)
SO FARMERS SELL THEIR FOOD TO THE BRITISH ARMY. (TREASON!)
WITHOUT ONE CENTRAL BANK COLLECTING TAXES, OUR MONEY IS WORTHLESS!
APPRECIATE THE HOT AIR, SIR.

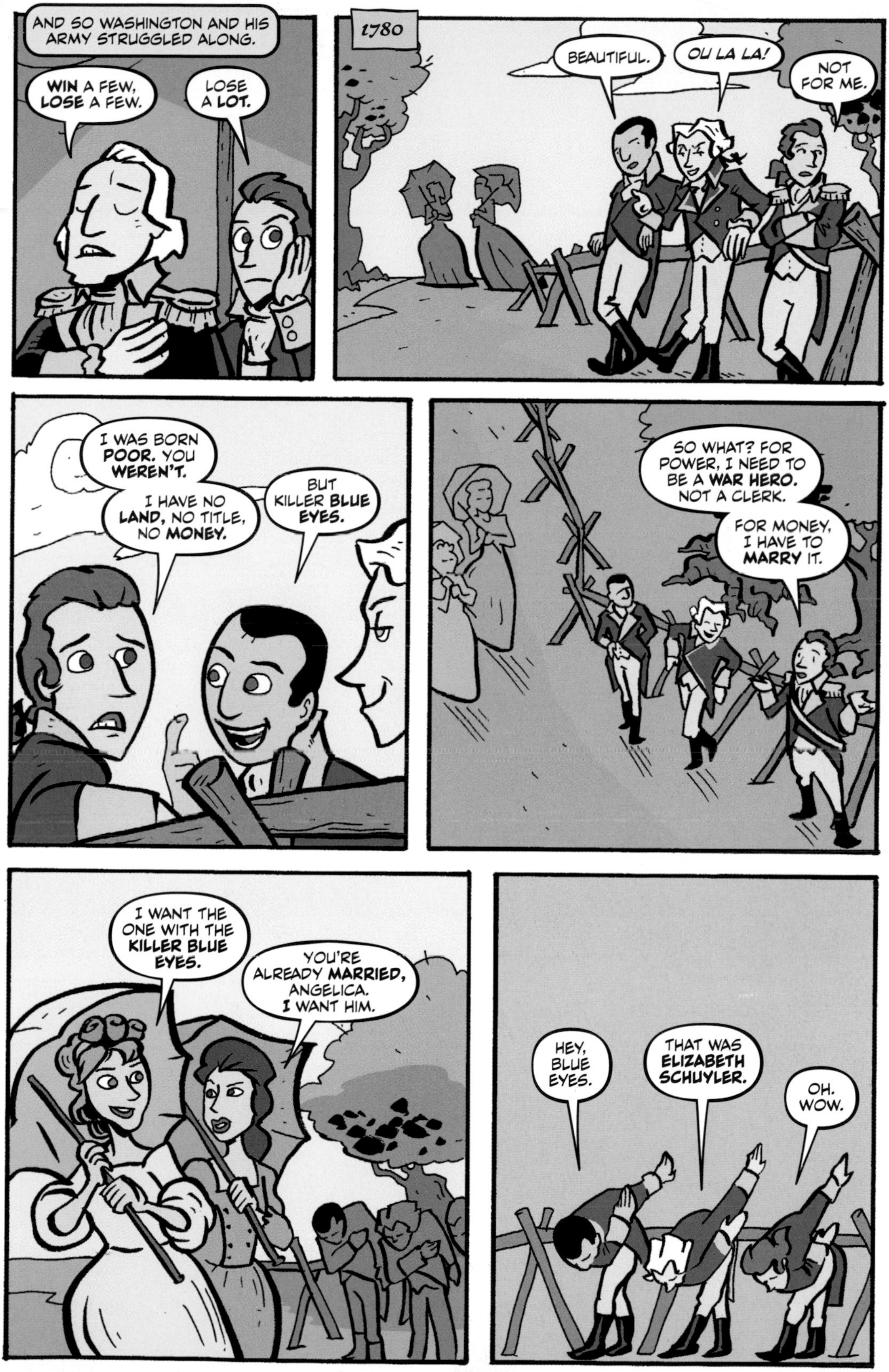
AND SO WASHINGTON AND HIS ARMY STRUGGLED ALONG.
WIN A FEW, LOSE A FEW.
LOSE A LOT.
1780
BEAUTIFUL.
OU LA LA!
NOT FOR ME.
I WAS BORN POOR. YOU WEREN'T.
I HAVE NO LAND, NO TITLE, NO MONEY.
BUT KILLER BLUE EYES.
SO WHAT? FOR POWER, I NEED TO BE A WAR HERO. NOT A CLERK.
FOR MONEY, I HAVE TO MARRY IT.
I WANT THE ONE WITH THE KILLER BLUE EYES.
YOU'RE ALREADY MARRIED, ANGELICA. I WANT HIM.
HEY, BLUE EYES.
THAT WAS ELIZABETH SCHUYLER.
OH. WOW.

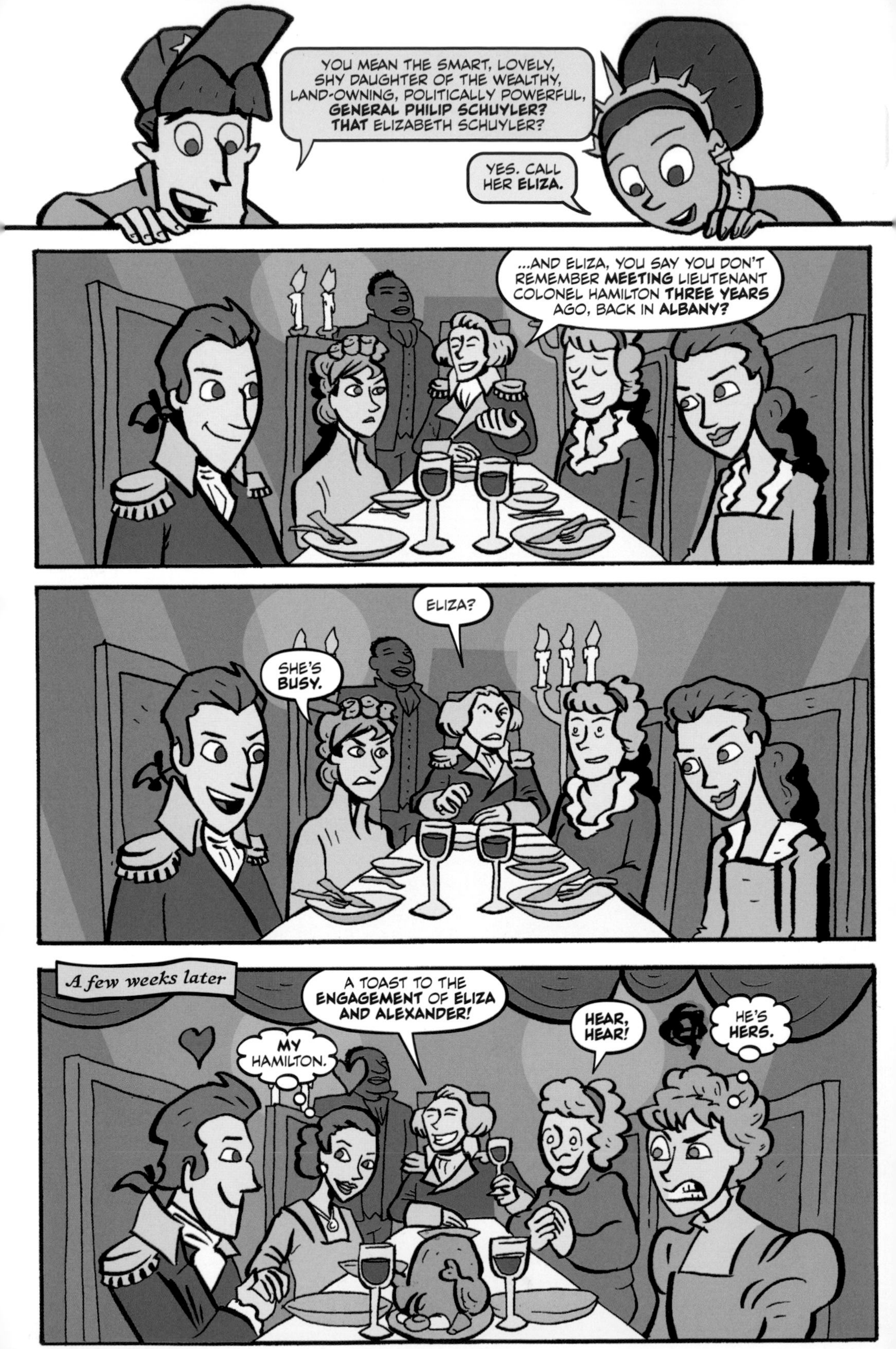
YOU MEAN THE SMART, LOVELY, SHY DAUGHTER OF THE WEALTHY, LAND-OWNING, POLITICALLY POWERFUL, GENERAL PHILIP SCHUYLER? THAT ELIZABETH SCHUYLER?
YES. CALL HER ELIZA.
...AND ELIZA, YOU SAY YOU DON'T REMEMBER MEETING LIEUTENANT COLONEL HAMILTON THREE YEARS AGO, BACK IN ALBANY?
ELIZA?
SHE'S BUSY.
A few weeks later
A TOAST TO THE ENGAGEMENT OF ELIZA AND ALEXANDER!
MY HAMILTON.
HEAR, HEAR!
HE'S HERS.

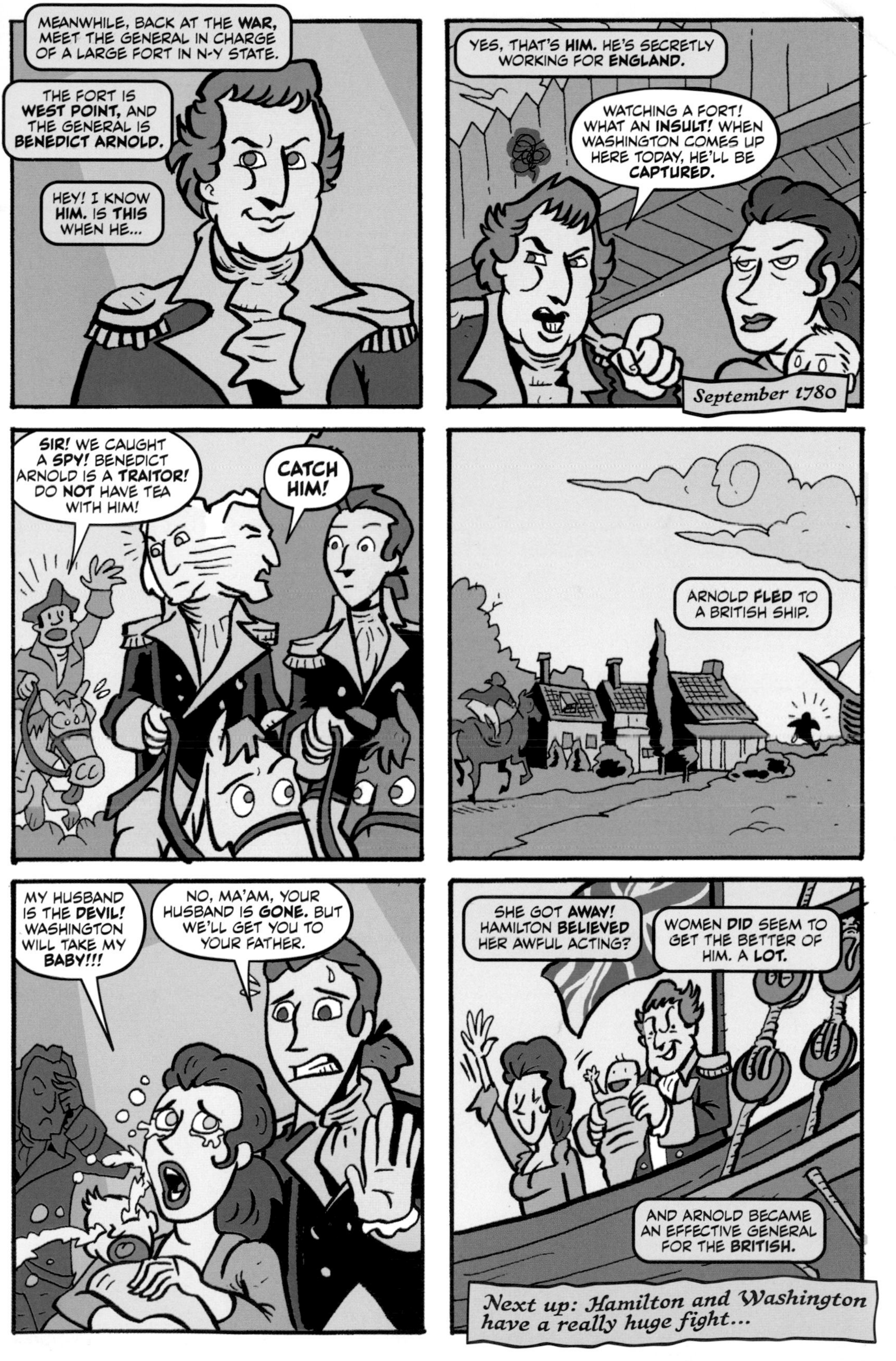
MEANWHILE, BACK AT THE WAR, MEET THE GENERAL IN CHARGE OF A LARGE FORT IN N-Y STATE.
THE FORT IS WEST POINT, AND THE GENERAL IS BENEDICT ARNOLD.
HEY! I KNOW HIM. IS THIS WHEN HE...
YES, THAT'S HIM. HE'S SECRETLY WORKING FOR ENGLAND.
WATCHING A FORT! WHAT AN INSULT! WHEN WASHINGTON COMES UP HERE TODAY, HE'LL BE CAPTURED.
September 1780
SIR! WE CAUGHT A SPY! BENEDICT ARNOLD IS A TRAITOR! DO NOT HAVE TEA WITH HIM!
CATCH HIM!
ARNOLD FLED TO A BRITISH SHIP.
MY HUSBAND IS THE DEVIL! WASHINGTON WILL TAKE MY BABY!!!
NO, MA'AM, YOUR HUSBAND IS GONE. BUT WE'LL GET YOU TO YOUR FATHER.
SHE GOT AWAY! HAMILTON BELIEVED HER AWFUL ACTING?
WOMEN DID SEEM TO GET THE BETTER OF HIM. A LOT.
AND ARNOLD BECAME AN EFFECTIVE GENERAL FOR THE BRITISH.
Next up: Hamilton and Washington have a really huge fight...

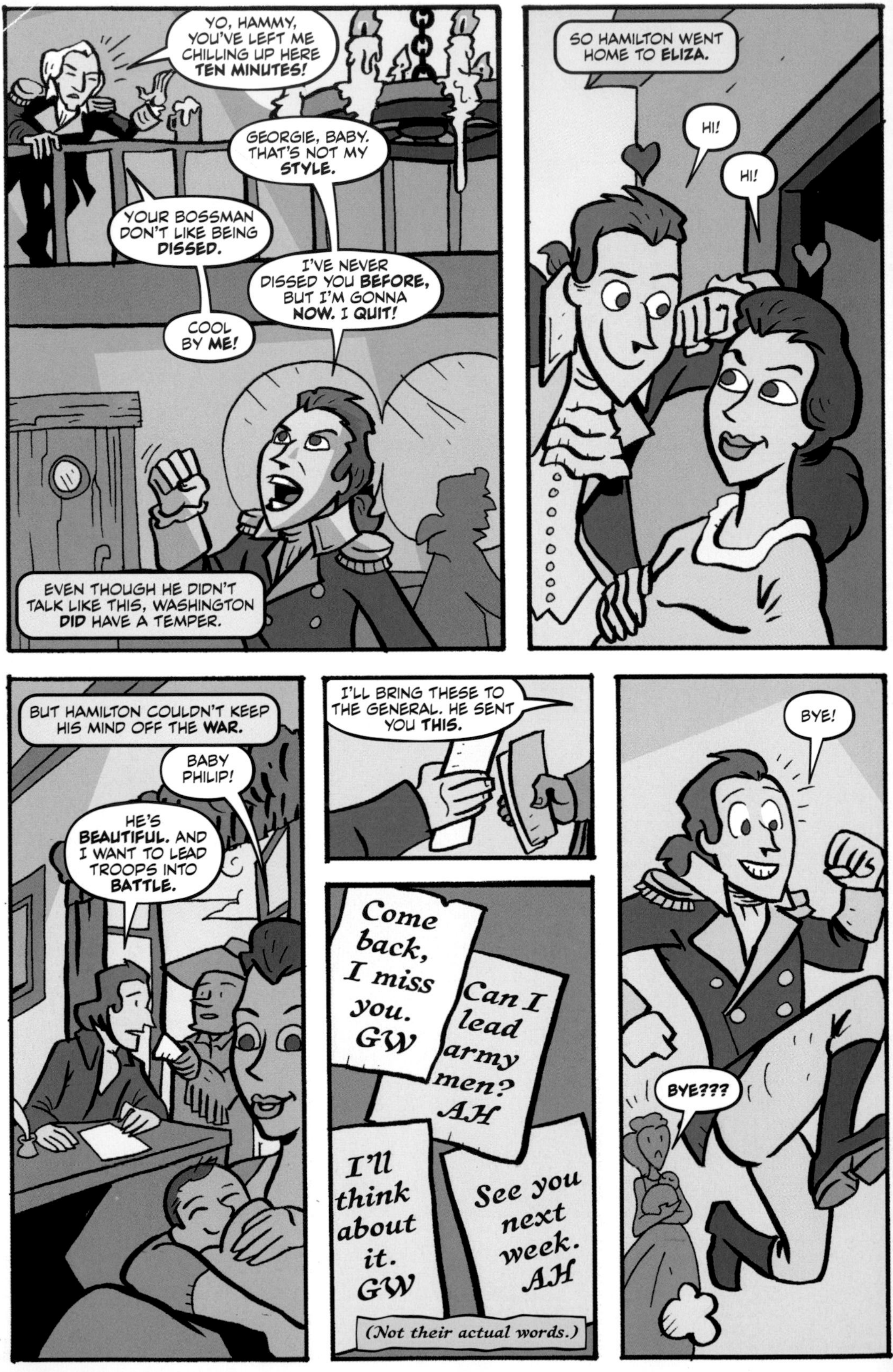
YO, HAMMY, YOU'VE LEFT ME CHILLING UP HERE TEN MINUTES!
GEORGIE, BABY. THAT'S NOT MY STYLE.
YOUR BOSSMAN DON'T LIKE BEING DISSED.
I'VE NEVER DISSED YOU BEFORE, BUT I'M GONNA NOW. I QUIT!
COOL BY ME!
EVEN THOUGH HE DIDN'T TALK LIKE THIS, WASHINGTON DID HAVE A TEMPER.
SO HAMILTON WENT HOME TO ELIZA.
HI!
HI!
BUT HAMILTON COULDN'T KEEP HIS MIND OFF THE WAR.
BABY PHILIP!
HE'S BEAUTIFUL. AND I WANT TO LEAD TROOPS INTO BATTLE.
I'LL BRING THESE TO THE GENERAL. HE SENT YOU THIS.
Come back, I miss you. GW
Can I lead army men? AH
I'll think about it. GW
See you next week. AH
(Not their actual words.)
BYE!
BYE???

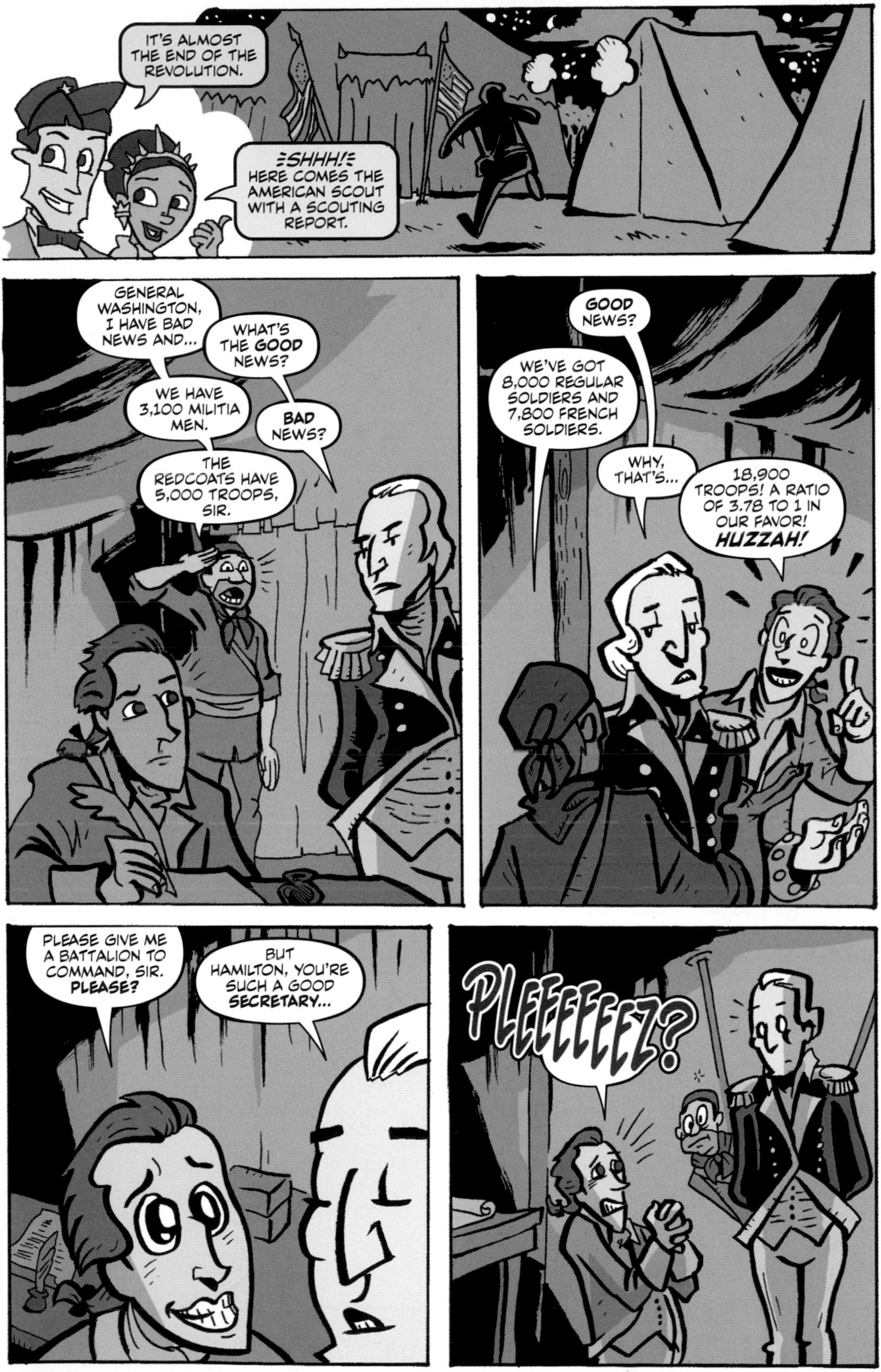
IT'S ALMOST THE END OF THE REVOLUTION.
SHHH! HERE COMES THE AMERICAN SCOUT WITH A SCOUTING REPORT.
GENERAL WASHINGTON, I HAVE BAD NEWS AND...
WHAT'S THE GOOD NEWS?
WE HAVE 3,100 MILITIA MEN.
BAD NEWS?
THE REDCOATS HAVE 5,000 TROOPS, SIR.
GOOD NEWS?
WE'VE GOT 8,000 REGULAR SOLDIERS AND 7,800 FRENCH SOLDIERS.
WHY, THAT'S...
18,900 TROOPS! A RATIO OF 3.78 TO 1 IN OUR FAVOR! HUZZAH!
PLEASE GIVE ME A BATTALION TO COMMAND, SIR. PLEASE?
BUT HAMILTON, YOU'RE SUCH A GOOD SECRETARY...
PLEEEEEEEZ?

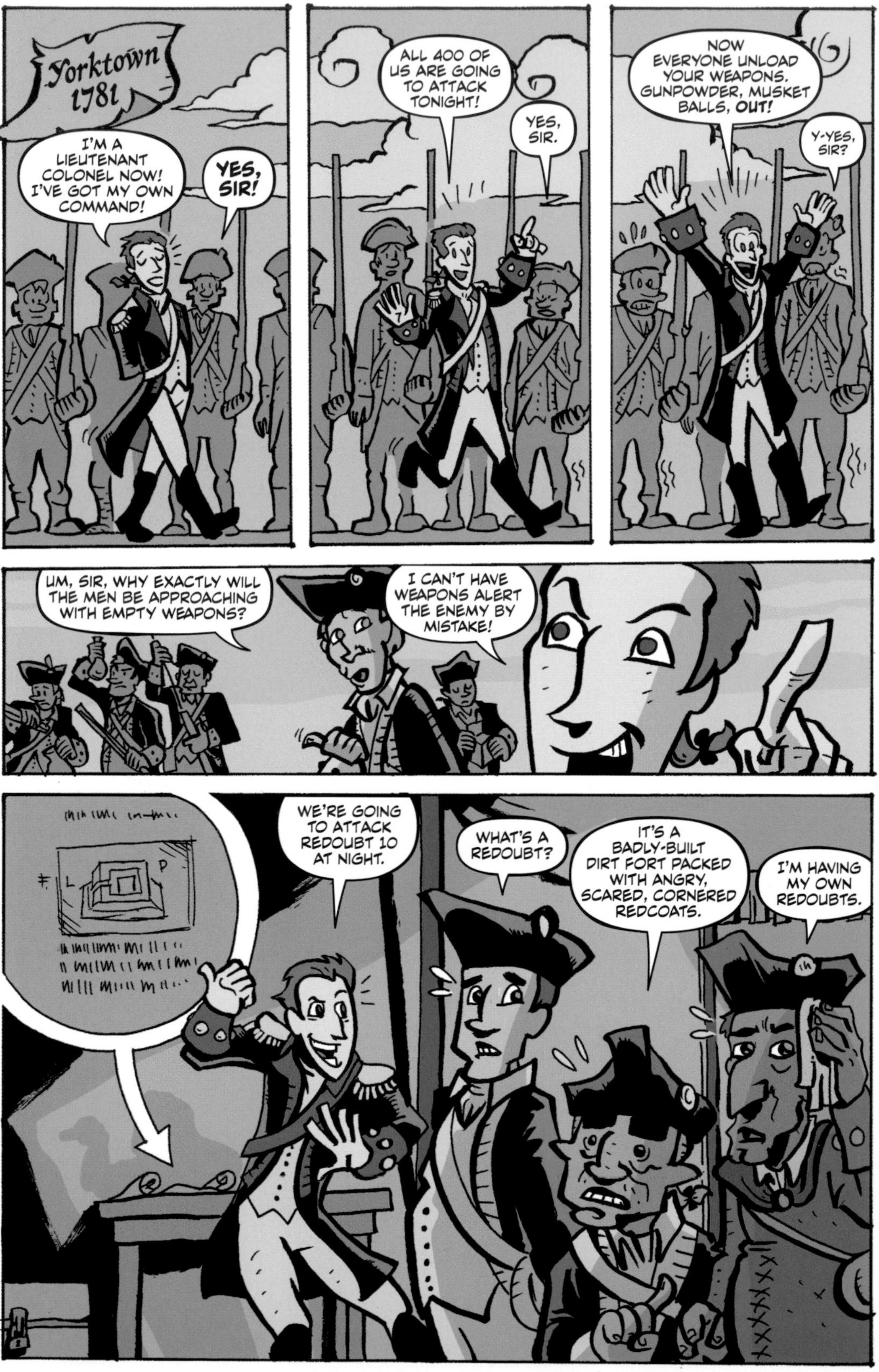
Yorktown 1781
I'M A LIEUTENANT COLONEL NOW! I'VE GOT MY OWN COMMAND!
YES, SIR!
ALL 400 OF US ARE GOING TO ATTACK TONIGHT!
YES, SIR.
NOW EVERYONE UNLOAD YOUR WEAPONS. GUNPOWDER, MUSKET BALLS, OUT!
Y-YES, SIR?
UM, SIR, WHY EXACTLY WILL THE MEN BE APPROACHING WITH EMPTY WEAPONS?
I CAN'T HAVE WEAPONS ALERT THE ENEMY BY MISTAKE!
WE'RE GOING TO ATTACK REDOUBT 10 AT NIGHT.
WHAT'S A REDOUBT?
IT'S A BADLY-BUILT DIRT FORT PACKED WITH ANGRY, SCARED, CORNERED REDCOATS.
I'M HAVING MY OWN REDOUBTS.

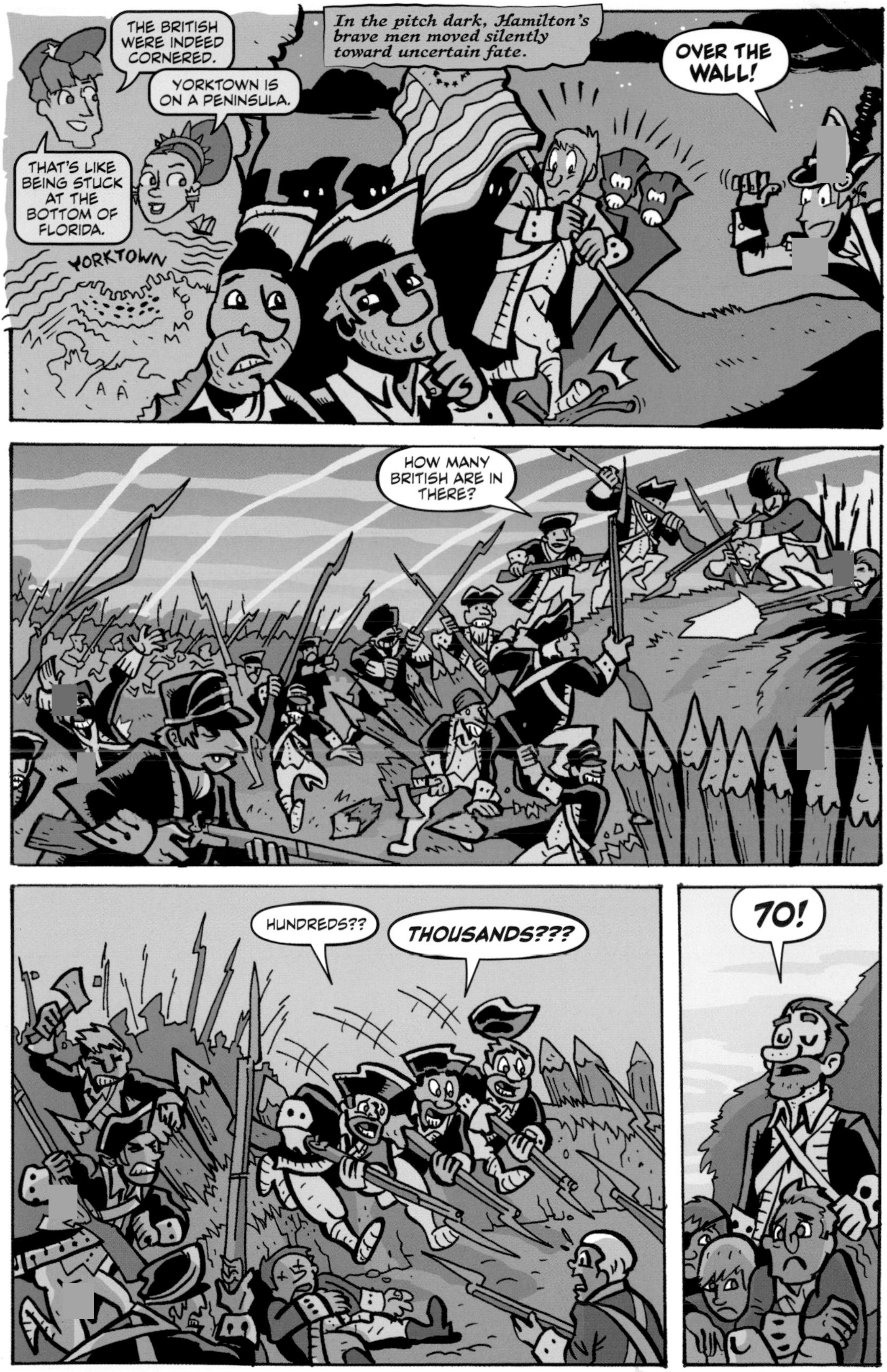
THE BRITISH WERE INDEED CORNERED.
YORKTOWN IS ON A PENINSULA.
THAT'S LIKE BEING STUCK AT THE BOTTOM OF FLORIDA.
YORKTOWN
In the pitch dark, Hamilton's brave men moved silently toward uncertain fate.
OVER THE WALL!
HOW MANY BRITISH ARE IN THERE?
HUNDREDS??
THOUSANDS???
70!

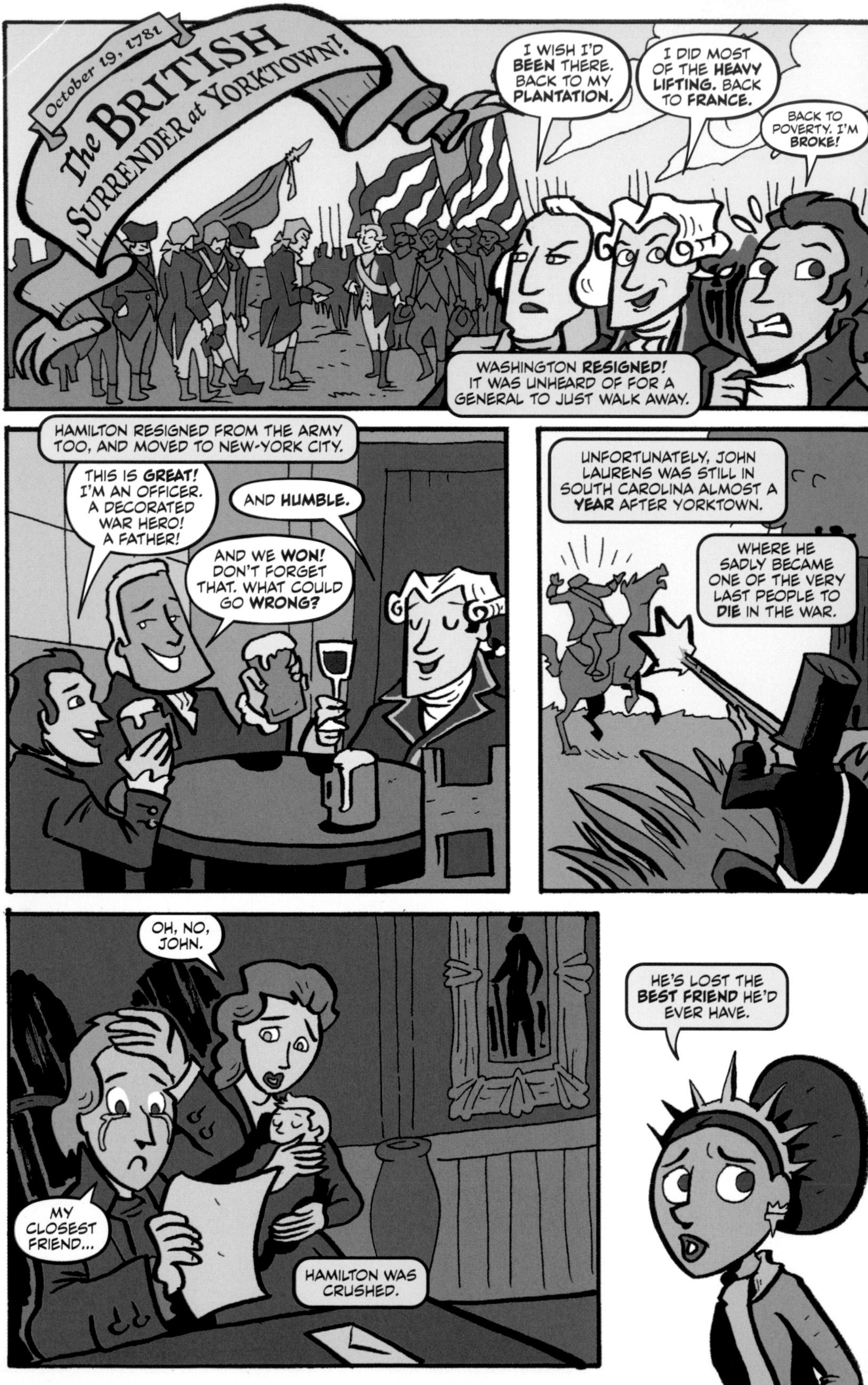
October 19, 1781
The BRITISH SURRENDER at YORKTOWN!
I WISH I'D BEEN THERE. BACK TO MY PLANTATION.
I DID MOST OF THE HEAVY LIFTING. BACK TO FRANCE.
BACK TO POVERTY. I'M BROKE!
WASHINGTON RESIGNED! IT WAS UNHEARD OF FOR A GENERAL TO JUST WALK AWAY.
HAMILTON RESIGNED FROM THE ARMY TOO, AND MOVED TO NEW-YORK CITY.
THIS IS GREAT! I'M AN OFFICER. A DECORATED WAR HERO! A FATHER!
AND HUMBLE.
AND WE WON! DON'T FORGET THAT. WHAT COULD GO WRONG?
UNFORTUNATELY, JOHN LAURENS WAS STILL IN SOUTH CAROLINA ALMOST A YEAR AFTER YORKTOWN.
WHERE HE SADLY BECAME ONE OF THE VERY LAST PEOPLE TO DIE IN THE WAR.
OH, NO, JOHN.
MY CLOSEST FRIEND...
HAMILTON WAS CRUSHED.
HE'S LOST THE BEST FRIEND HE'D EVER HAVE.

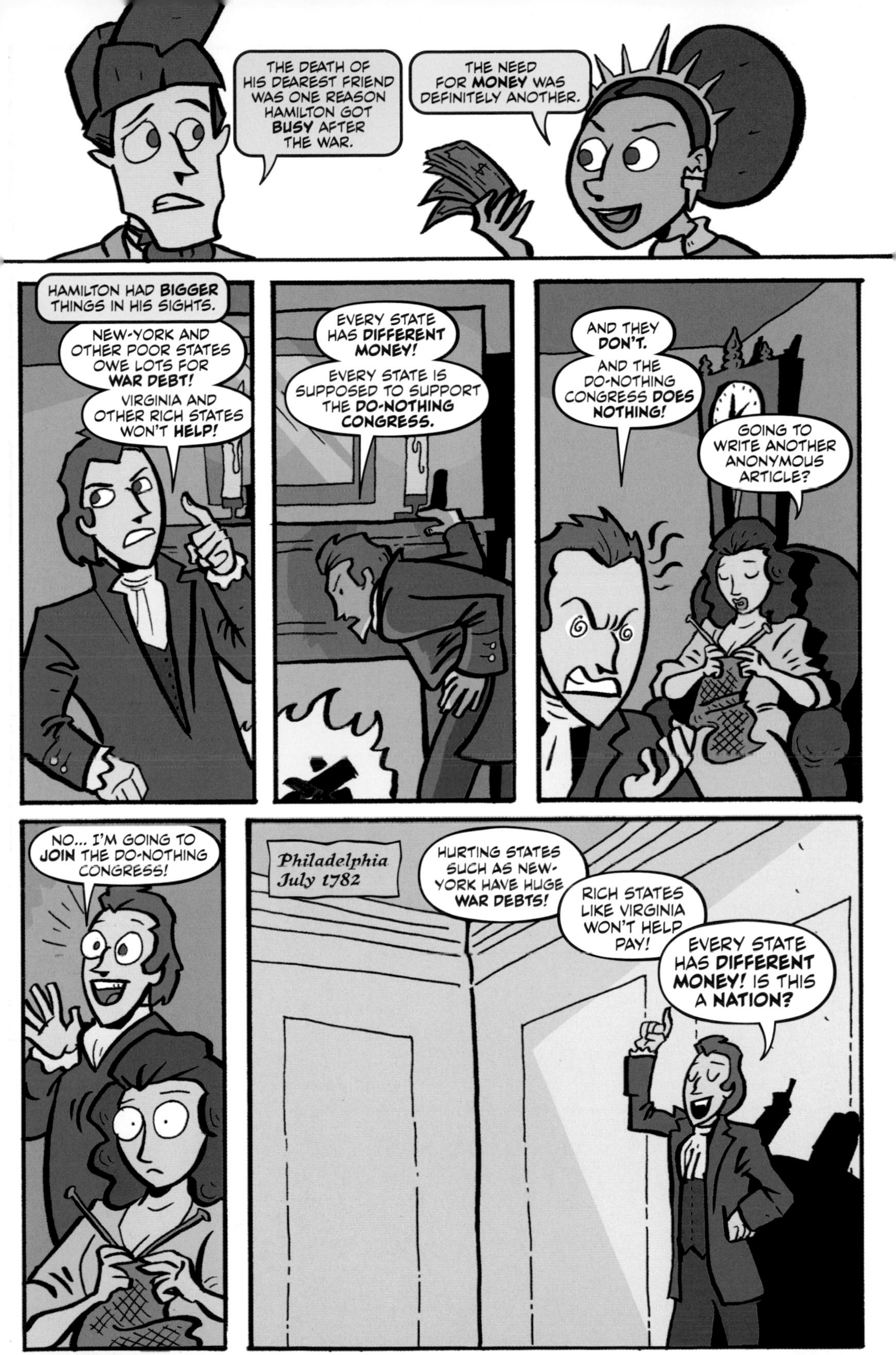
THE DEATH OF HIS DEAREST FRIEND WAS ONE REASON HAMILTON GOT BUSY AFTER THE WAR.
THE NEED FOR MONEY WAS DEFINITELY ANOTHER.
HAMILTON HAD BIGGER THINGS IN HIS SIGHTS.
NEW-YORK AND OTHER POOR STATES OWE LOTS FOR WAR DEBT!
VIRGINIA AND OTHER RICH STATES WON'T HELP!
EVERY STATE HAS DIFFERENT MONEY!
EVERY STATE IS SUPPOSED TO SUPPORT THE DO-NOTHING CONGRESS.
AND THEY DON'T.
AND THE DO-NOTHING CONGRESS DOES NOTHING!
GOING TO WRITE ANOTHER ANONYMOUS ARTICLE?
NO... I'M GOING TO JOIN THE DO-NOTHING CONGRESS!
Philadelphia July 1782
HURTING STATES SUCH AS NEW-YORK HAVE HUGE WAR DEBTS!
RICH STATES LIKE VIRGINIA WON'T HELP PAY!
EVERY STATE HAS DIFFERENT MONEY! IS THIS A NATION?

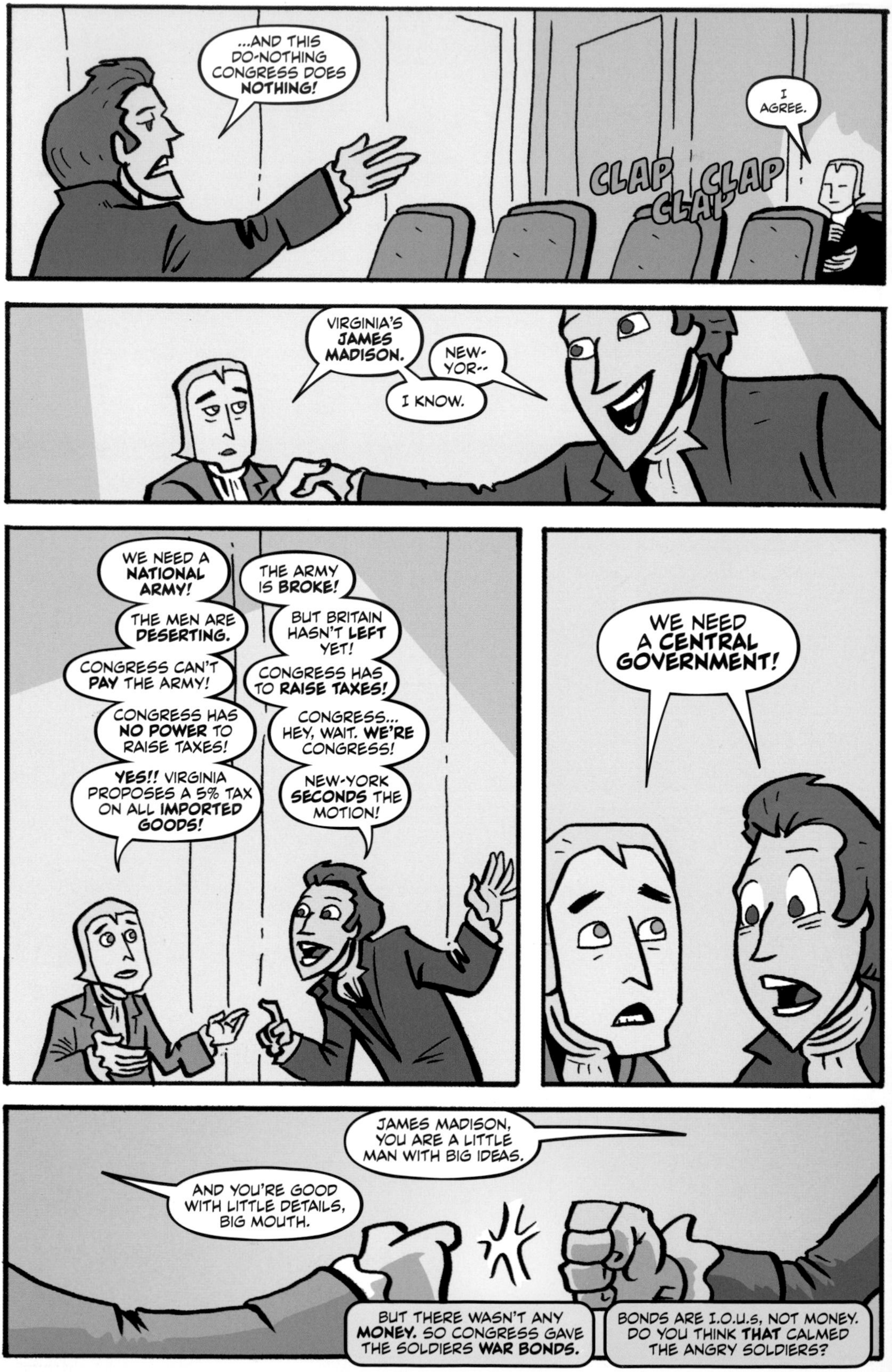
...AND THIS DO-NOTHING CONGRESS DOES **NOTHING!**
I AGREE.
CLAP CLAP CLAP
VIRGINIA'S **JAMES MADISON.**
NEW-YOR--
I KNOW.
WE NEED A **NATIONAL ARMY!**
THE ARMY IS **BROKE!**
THE MEN ARE **DESERTING.**
BUT BRITAIN HASN'T **LEFT** YET!
CONGRESS CAN'T **PAY** THE ARMY!
CONGRESS HAS TO **RAISE TAXES!**
CONGRESS HAS **NO POWER** TO RAISE TAXES!
CONGRESS... HEY, WAIT. **WE'RE** CONGRESS!
YES!! VIRGINIA PROPOSES A 5% TAX ON ALL **IMPORTED GOODS!**
NEW-YORK **SECONDS** THE MOTION!
WE NEED A **CENTRAL GOVERNMENT!**
JAMES MADISON, YOU ARE A LITTLE MAN WITH BIG IDEAS.
AND YOU'RE GOOD WITH LITTLE DETAILS, BIG MOUTH.
BUT THERE WASN'T ANY **MONEY.** SO CONGRESS GAVE THE SOLDIERS **WAR BONDS.**
BONDS ARE I.O.U.s, NOT MONEY. DO YOU THINK **THAT** CALMED THE ANGRY SOLDIERS?

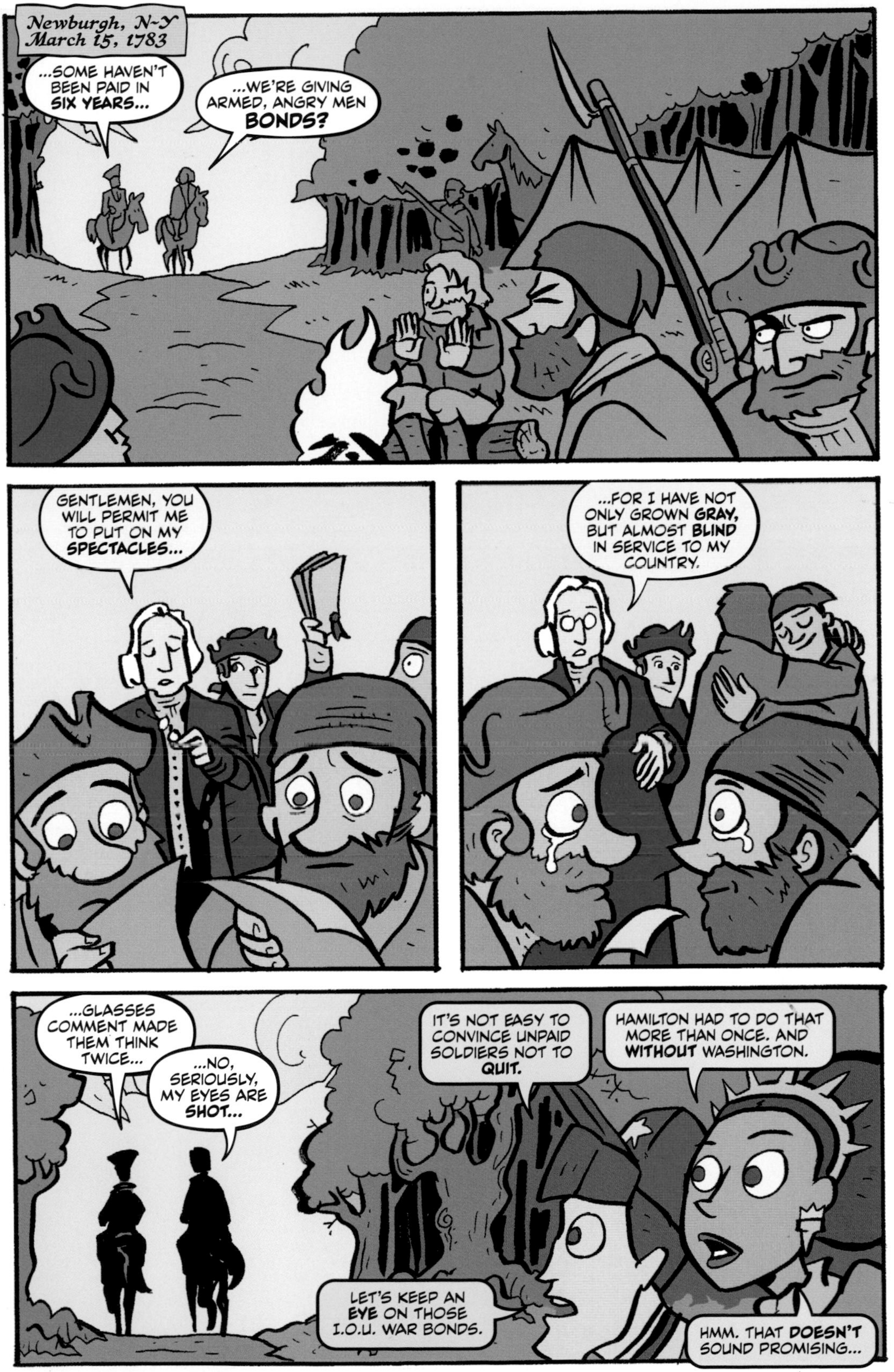
Newburgh, N-Y March 15, 1783
...SOME HAVEN'T BEEN PAID IN SIX YEARS...
...WE'RE GIVING ARMED, ANGRY MEN BONDS?
GENTLEMEN, YOU WILL PERMIT ME TO PUT ON MY SPECTACLES...
...FOR I HAVE NOT ONLY GROWN GRAY, BUT ALMOST BLIND IN SERVICE TO MY COUNTRY.
...GLASSES COMMENT MADE THEM THINK TWICE...
...NO, SERIOUSLY, MY EYES ARE SHOT...
IT'S NOT EASY TO CONVINCE UNPAID SOLDIERS NOT TO QUIT.
HAMILTON HAD TO DO THAT MORE THAN ONCE. AND WITHOUT WASHINGTON.
LET'S KEEP AN EYE ON THOSE I.O.U. WAR BONDS.
HMM. THAT DOESN'T SOUND PROMISING...

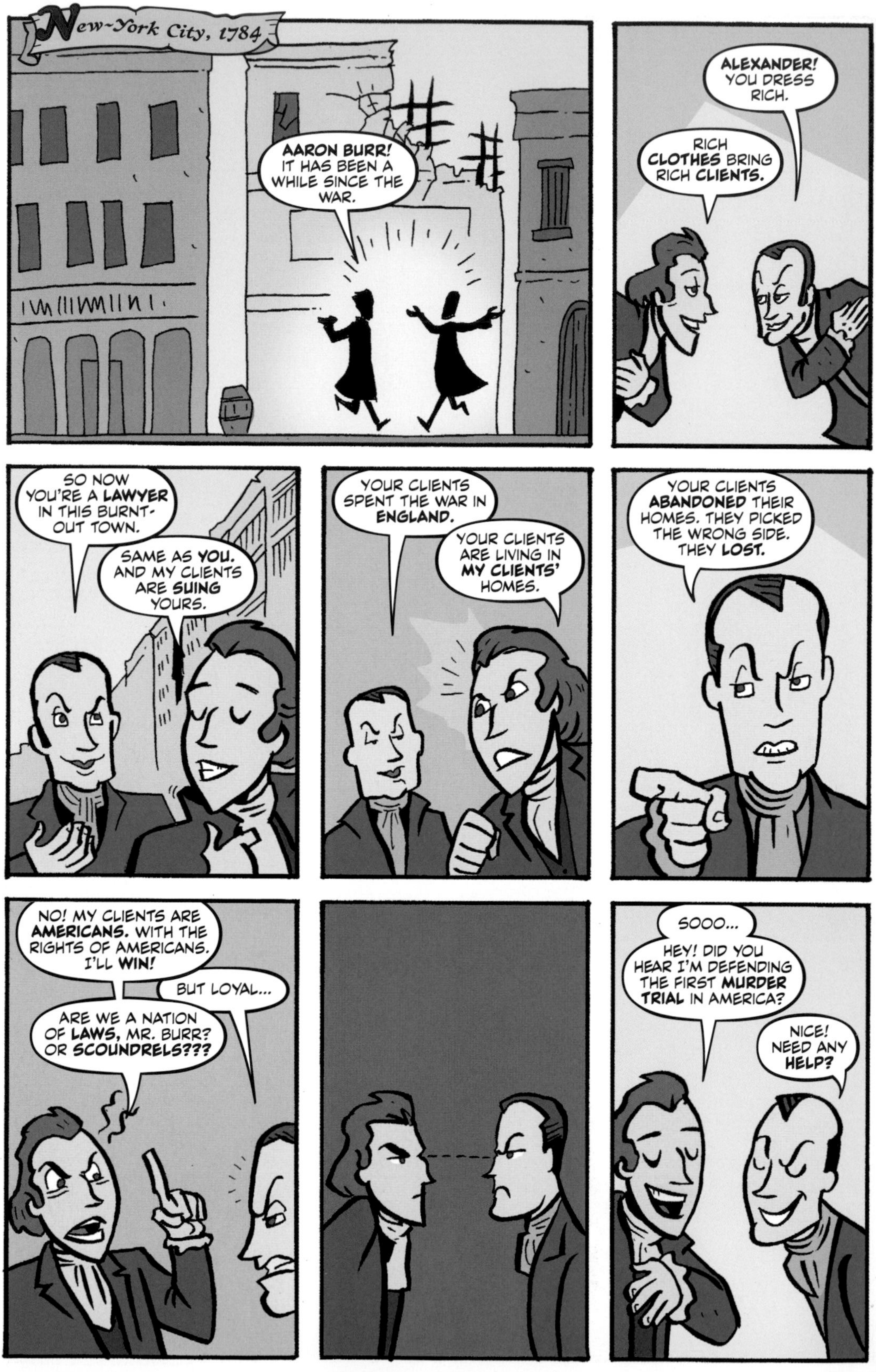
New-York City, 1784
AARON BURR! IT HAS BEEN A WHILE SINCE THE WAR.
ALEXANDER! YOU DRESS RICH.
RICH CLOTHES BRING RICH CLIENTS.
SO NOW YOU'RE A LAWYER IN THIS BURNT-OUT TOWN.
SAME AS YOU. AND MY CLIENTS ARE SUING YOURS.
YOUR CLIENTS SPENT THE WAR IN ENGLAND.
YOUR CLIENTS ARE LIVING IN MY CLIENTS' HOMES.
YOUR CLIENTS ABANDONED THEIR HOMES. THEY PICKED THE WRONG SIDE. THEY LOST.
NO! MY CLIENTS ARE AMERICANS. WITH THE RIGHTS OF AMERICANS. I'LL WIN!
BUT LOYAL...
ARE WE A NATION OF LAWS, MR. BURR? OR SCOUNDRELS???
SOOO...
HEY! DID YOU HEAR I'M DEFENDING THE FIRST MURDER TRIAL IN AMERICA?
NICE! NEED ANY HELP?

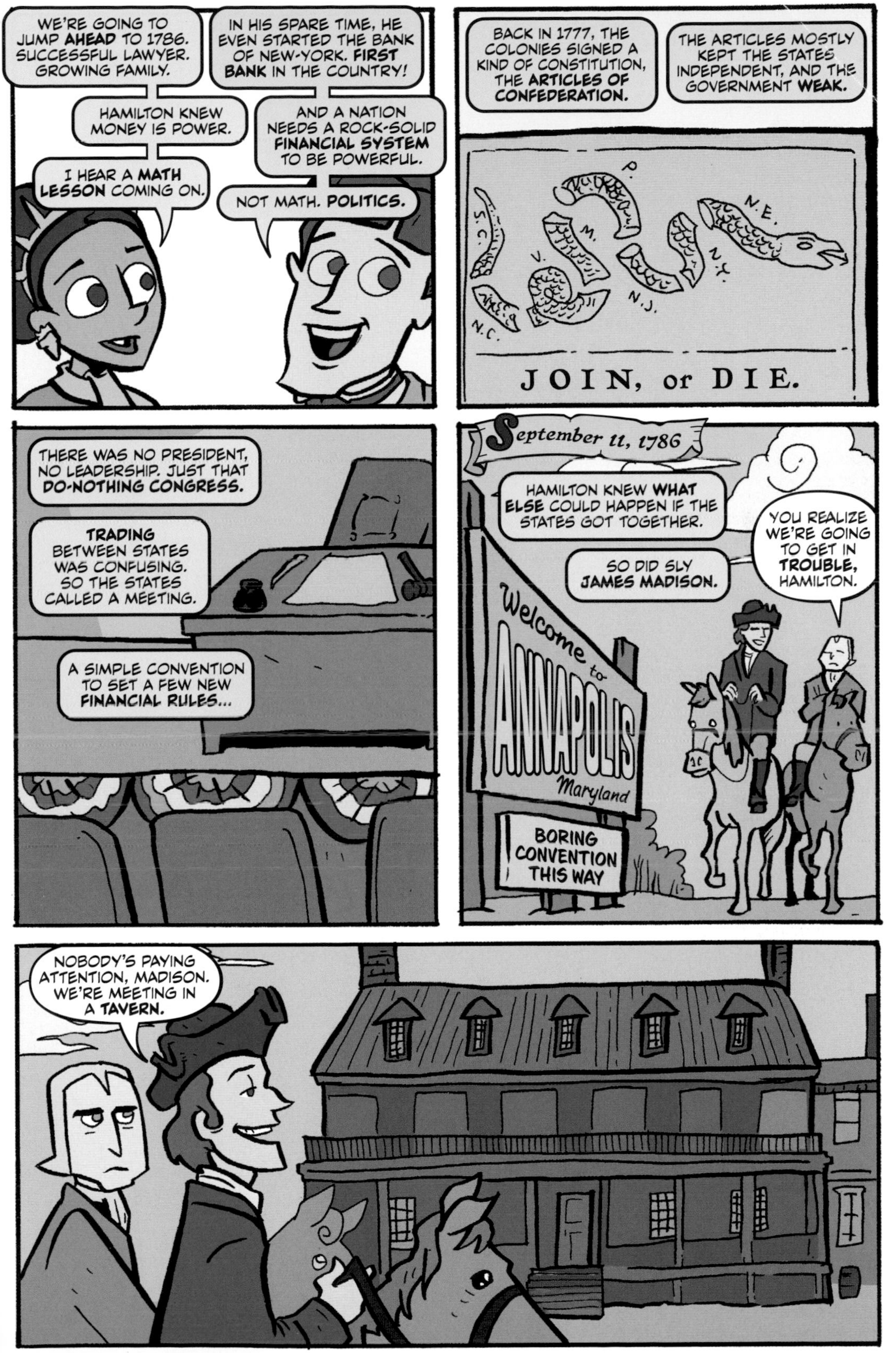
WE'RE GOING TO JUMP AHEAD TO 1786. SUCCESSFUL LAWYER. GROWING FAMILY.
IN HIS SPARE TIME, HE EVEN STARTED THE BANK OF NEW-YORK. FIRST BANK IN THE COUNTRY!
HAMILTON KNEW MONEY IS POWER.
AND A NATION NEEDS A ROCK-SOLID FINANCIAL SYSTEM TO BE POWERFUL.
I HEAR A MATH LESSON COMING ON.
NOT MATH. POLITICS.
BACK IN 1777, THE COLONIES SIGNED A KIND OF CONSTITUTION, THE ARTICLES OF CONFEDERATION.
THE ARTICLES MOSTLY KEPT THE STATES INDEPENDENT, AND THE GOVERNMENT WEAK.
P.
N.E.
S.C.
M.
V.
N.Y.
N.J.
N.C.
JOIN, or DIE.
THERE WAS NO PRESIDENT, NO LEADERSHIP. JUST THAT DO-NOTHING CONGRESS.
TRADING BETWEEN STATES WAS CONFUSING. SO THE STATES CALLED A MEETING.
A SIMPLE CONVENTION TO SET A FEW NEW FINANCIAL RULES...
September 11, 1786
HAMILTON KNEW WHAT ELSE COULD HAPPEN IF THE STATES GOT TOGETHER.
SO DID SLY JAMES MADISON.
YOU REALIZE WE'RE GOING TO GET IN TROUBLE, HAMILTON.
Welcome to ANNAPOLIS Maryland
BORING CONVENTION THIS WAY
NOBODY'S PAYING ATTENTION, MADISON. WE'RE MEETING IN A TAVERN.

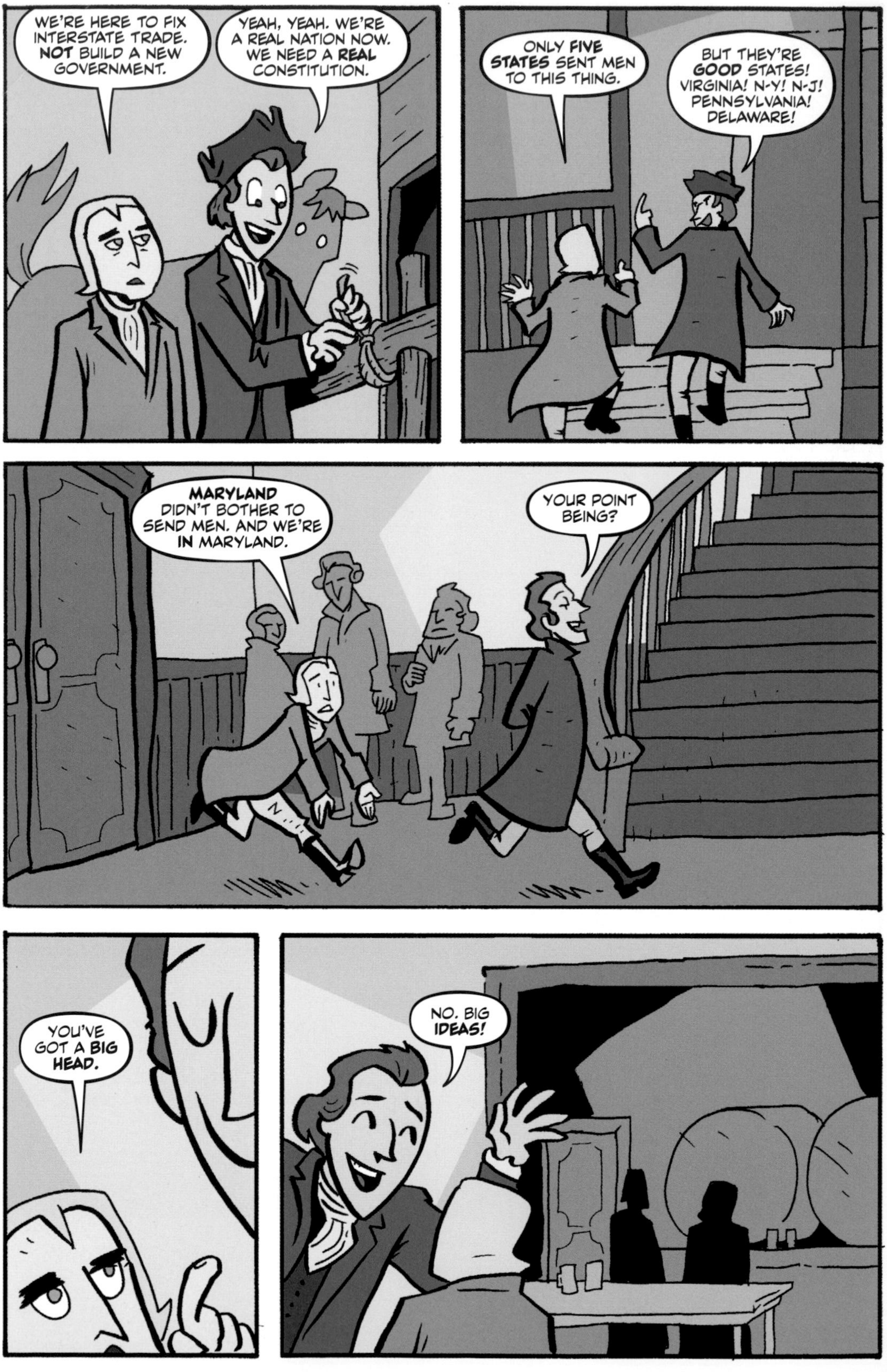
WE'RE HERE TO FIX INTERSTATE TRADE. NOT BUILD A NEW GOVERNMENT.
YEAH, YEAH. WE'RE A REAL NATION NOW. WE NEED A REAL CONSTITUTION.
ONLY FIVE STATES SENT MEN TO THIS THING.
BUT THEY'RE GOOD STATES! VIRGINIA! N-Y! N-J! PENNSYLVANIA! DELAWARE!
MARYLAND DIDN'T BOTHER TO SEND MEN. AND WE'RE IN MARYLAND.
YOUR POINT BEING?
YOU'VE GOT A BIG HEAD.
NO. BIG IDEAS!

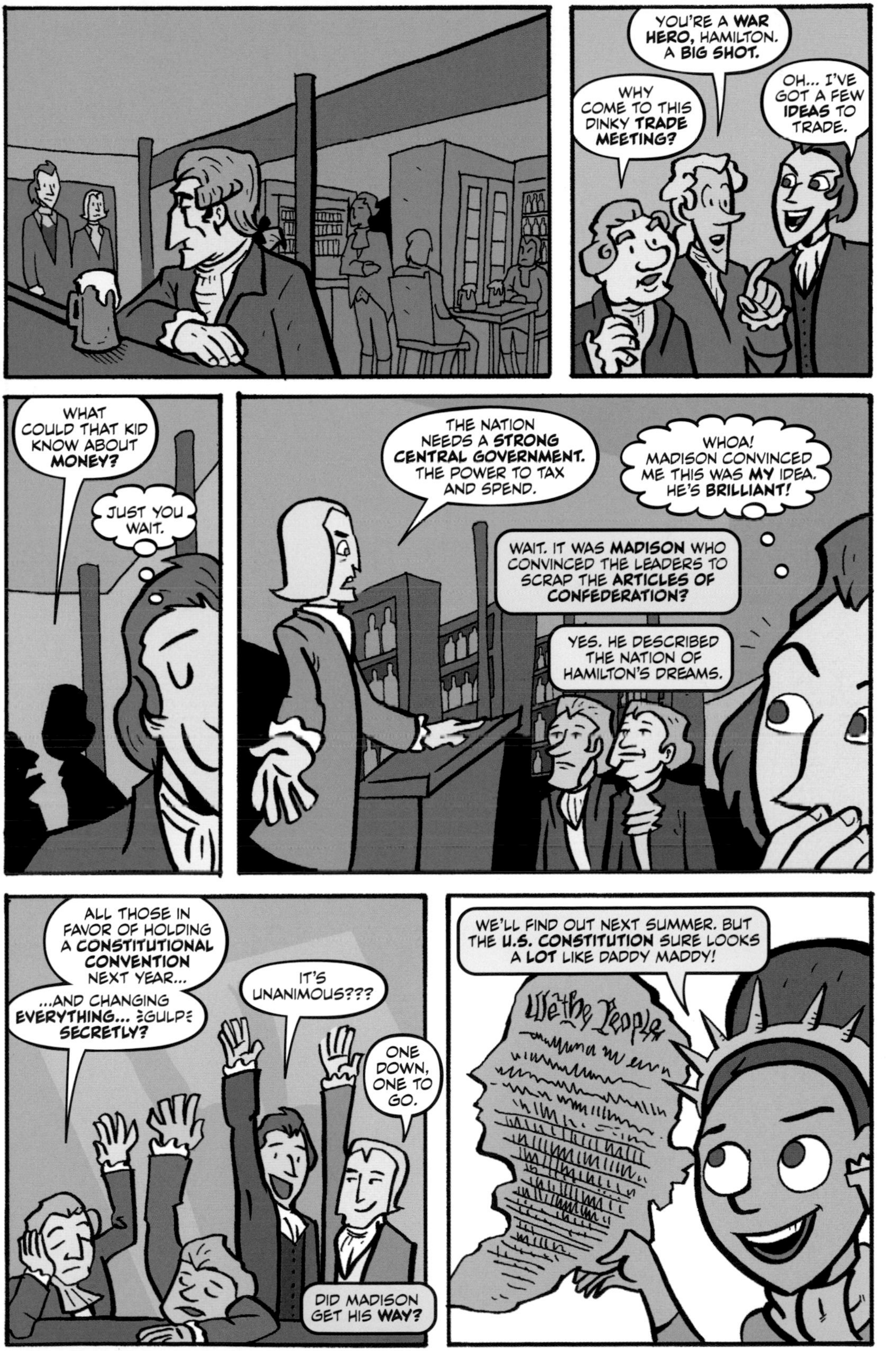

WHY COME TO THIS DINKY TRADE MEETING?
YOU'RE A WAR HERO, HAMILTON. A BIG SHOT.
OH... I'VE GOT A FEW IDEAS TO TRADE.
WHAT COULD THAT KID KNOW ABOUT MONEY?
JUST YOU WAIT.
THE NATION NEEDS A STRONG CENTRAL GOVERNMENT. THE POWER TO TAX AND SPEND.
WHOA! MADISON CONVINCED ME THIS WAS MY IDEA. HE'S BRILLIANT!
WAIT. IT WAS MADISON WHO CONVINCED THE LEADERS TO SCRAP THE ARTICLES OF CONFEDERATION?
YES. HE DESCRIBED THE NATION OF HAMILTON'S DREAMS.
ALL THOSE IN FAVOR OF HOLDING A CONSTITUTIONAL CONVENTION NEXT YEAR...
...AND CHANGING EVERYTHING... GULP SECRETLY?
IT'S UNANIMOUS???
ONE DOWN, ONE TO GO.
DID MADISON GET HIS WAY?
WE'LL FIND OUT NEXT SUMMER. BUT THE U.S. CONSTITUTION SURE LOOKS A LOT LIKE DADDY MADDY!
We the People

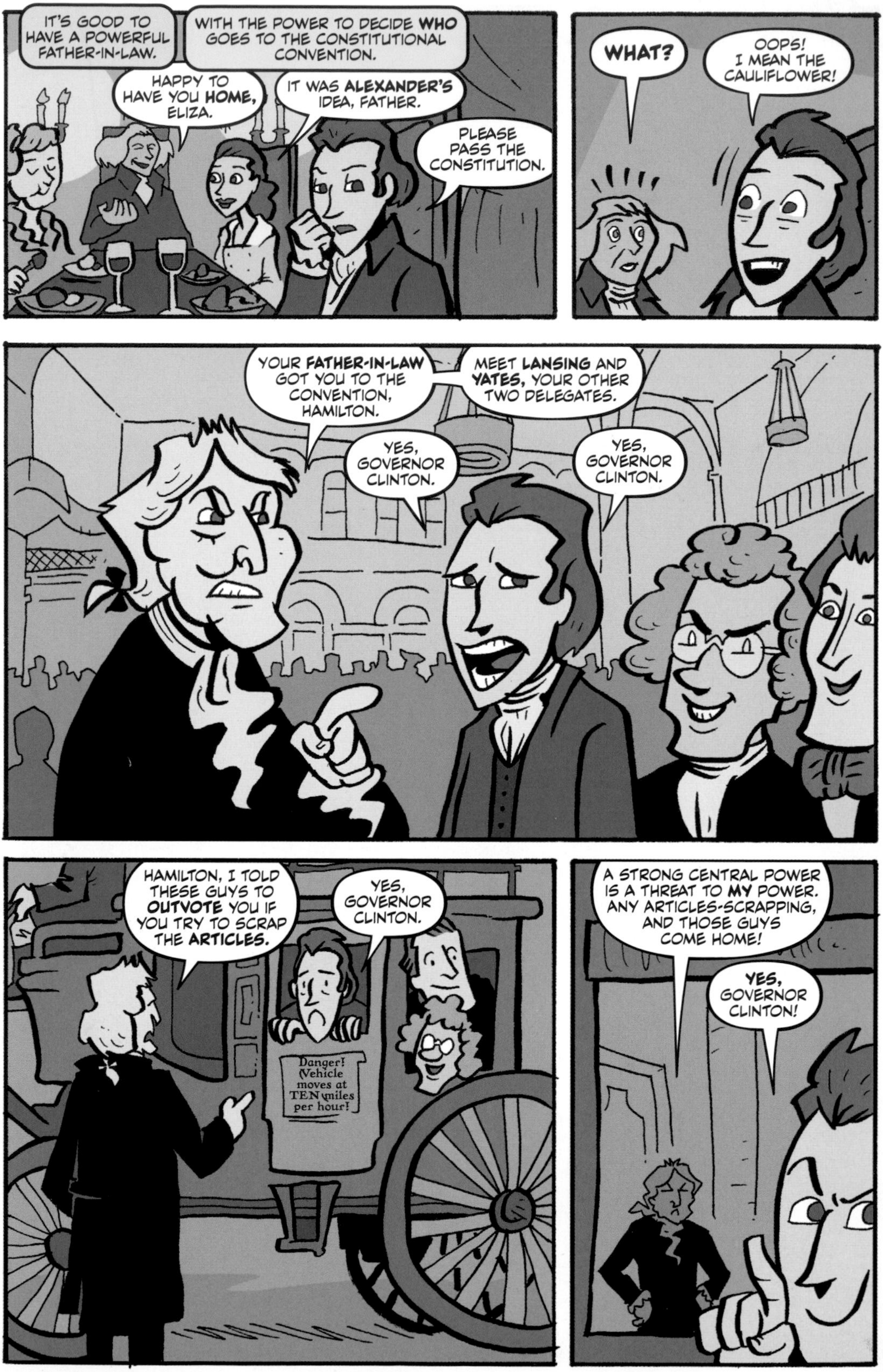
IT'S GOOD TO HAVE A POWERFUL FATHER-IN-LAW.
WITH THE POWER TO DECIDE **WHO** GOES TO THE CONSTITUTIONAL CONVENTION.
HAPPY TO HAVE YOU **HOME,** ELIZA.
IT WAS **ALEXANDER'S** IDEA, FATHER.
PLEASE PASS THE CONSTITUTION.
WHAT?
OOPS! I MEAN THE CAULIFLOWER!
YOUR **FATHER-IN-LAW** GOT YOU TO THE CONVENTION, HAMILTON.
MEET **LANSING** AND **YATES,** YOUR OTHER TWO DELEGATES.
YES, GOVERNOR CLINTON.
YES, GOVERNOR CLINTON.
HAMILTON, I TOLD THESE GUYS TO **OUTVOTE** YOU IF YOU TRY TO SCRAP THE **ARTICLES.**
YES, GOVERNOR CLINTON.
Danger! Vehicle moves at TEN miles per hour!
A STRONG CENTRAL POWER IS A THREAT TO **MY** POWER. ANY ARTICLES-SCRAPPING, AND THOSE GUYS COME HOME!
YES, GOVERNOR CLINTON!

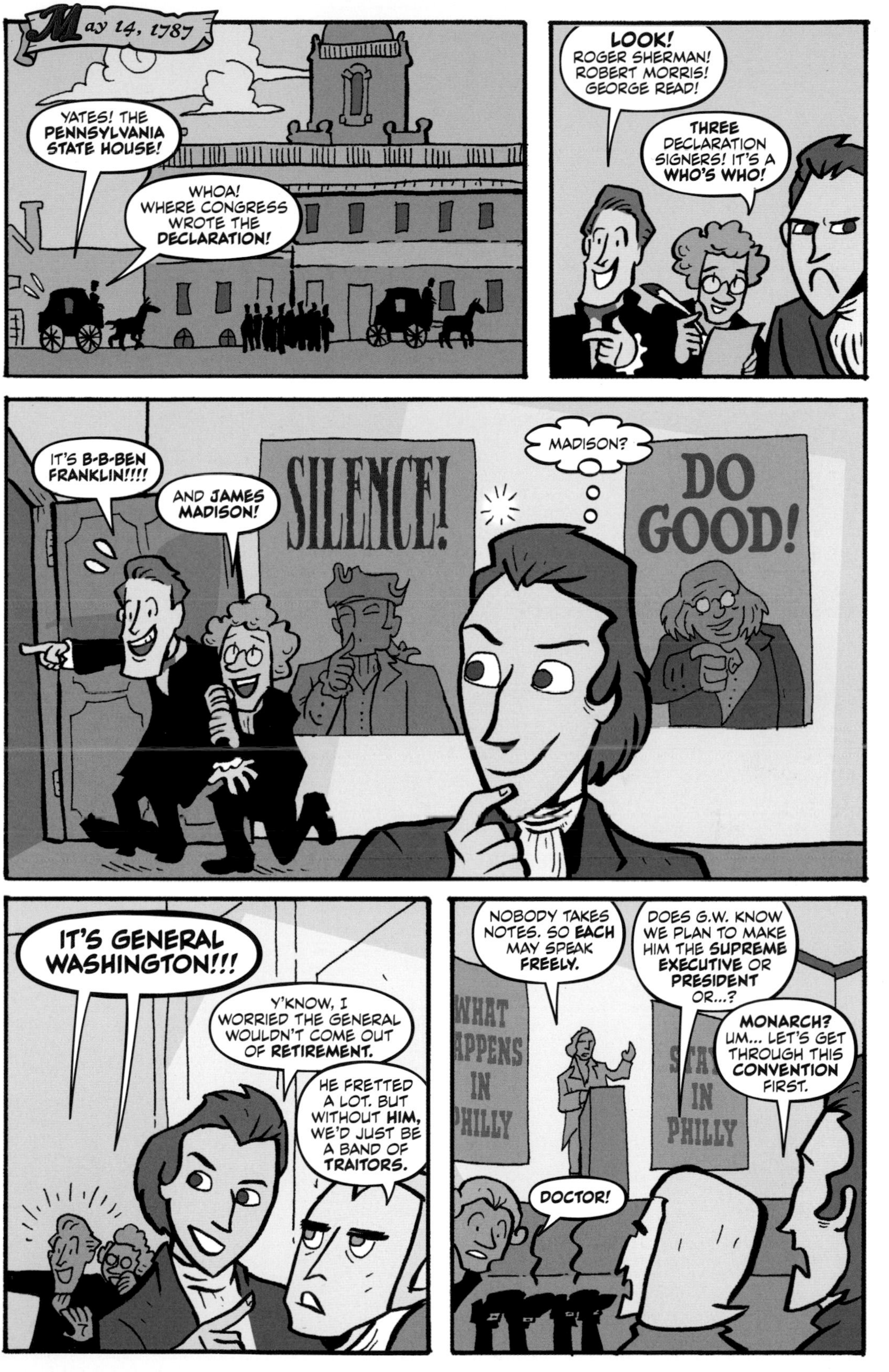
May 14, 1787
YATES! THE PENNSYLVANIA STATE HOUSE!
WHOA! WHERE CONGRESS WROTE THE DECLARATION!
LOOK! ROGER SHERMAN! ROBERT MORRIS! GEORGE READ!
THREE DECLARATION SIGNERS! IT'S A WHO'S WHO!
IT'S B-B-BEN FRANKLIN!!!!
AND JAMES MADISON!
SILENCE!
MADISON?
DO GOOD!
IT'S GENERAL WASHINGTON!!!
Y'KNOW, I WORRIED THE GENERAL WOULDN'T COME OUT OF RETIREMENT.
HE FRETTED A LOT. BUT WITHOUT HIM, WE'D JUST BE A BAND OF TRAITORS.
NOBODY TAKES NOTES. SO EACH MAY SPEAK FREELY.
DOES G.W. KNOW WE PLAN TO MAKE HIM THE SUPREME EXECUTIVE OR PRESIDENT OR...?
MONARCH? UM... LET'S GET THROUGH THIS CONVENTION FIRST.
DOCTOR!

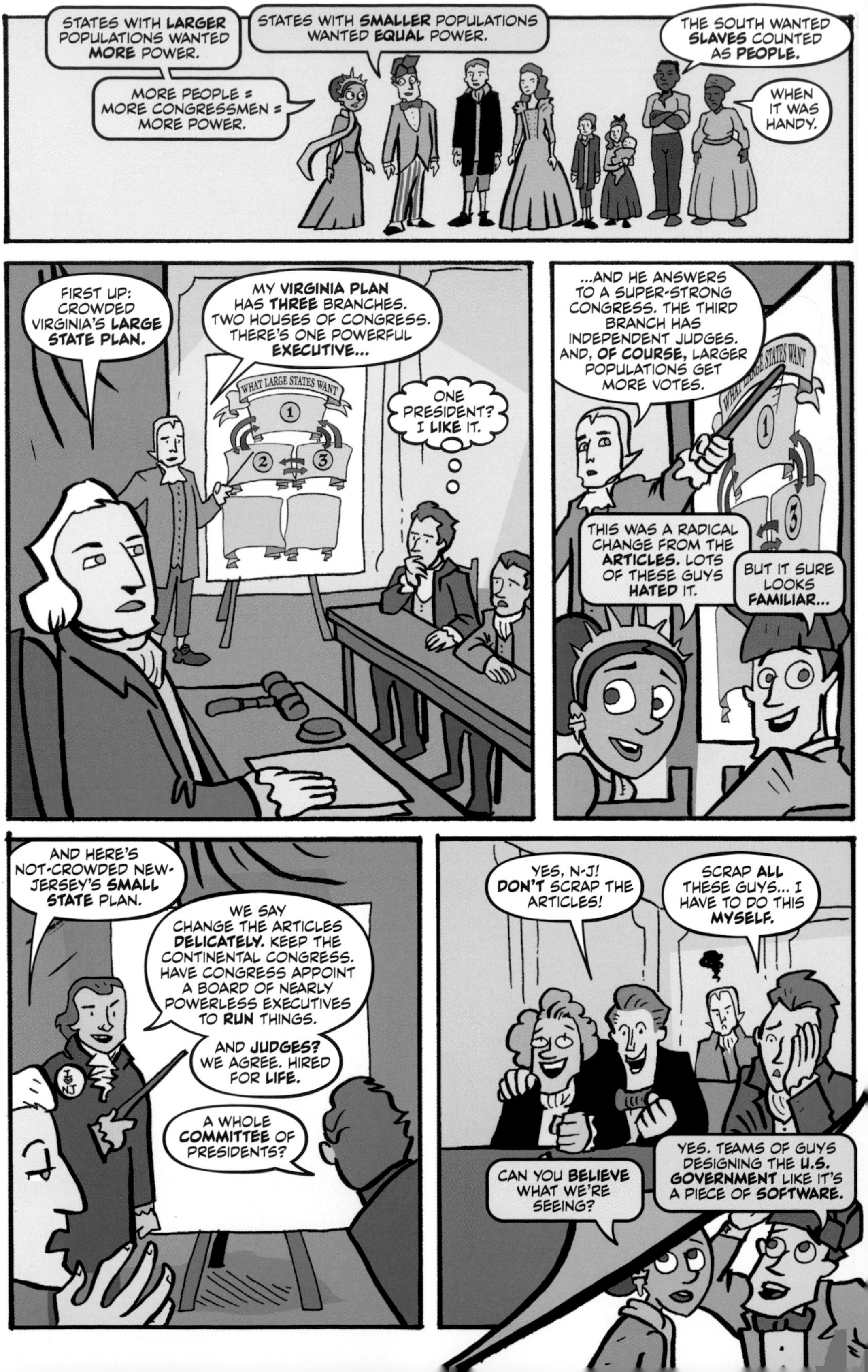

STATES WITH LARGER POPULATIONS WANTED MORE POWER.
MORE PEOPLE = MORE CONGRESSMEN = MORE POWER.
STATES WITH SMALLER POPULATIONS WANTED EQUAL POWER.
THE SOUTH WANTED SLAVES COUNTED AS PEOPLE.
WHEN IT WAS HANDY.
FIRST UP: CROWDED VIRGINIA'S LARGE STATE PLAN.
MY VIRGINIA PLAN HAS THREE BRANCHES. TWO HOUSES OF CONGRESS. THERE'S ONE POWERFUL EXECUTIVE...
WHAT LARGE STATES WANT
ONE PRESIDENT? I LIKE IT.
...AND HE ANSWERS TO A SUPER-STRONG CONGRESS. THE THIRD BRANCH HAS INDEPENDENT JUDGES. AND, OF COURSE, LARGER POPULATIONS GET MORE VOTES.
THIS WAS A RADICAL CHANGE FROM THE ARTICLES. LOTS OF THESE GUYS HATED IT.
BUT IT SURE LOOKS FAMILIAR...
AND HERE'S NOT-CROWDED NEW-JERSEY'S SMALL STATE PLAN.
WE SAY CHANGE THE ARTICLES DELICATELY. KEEP THE CONTINENTAL CONGRESS. HAVE CONGRESS APPOINT A BOARD OF NEARLY POWERLESS EXECUTIVES TO RUN THINGS.
AND JUDGES? WE AGREE. HIRED FOR LIFE.
A WHOLE COMMITTEE OF PRESIDENTS?
YES, N-J! DON'T SCRAP THE ARTICLES!
SCRAP ALL THESE GUYS... I HAVE TO DO THIS MYSELF.
CAN YOU BELIEVE WHAT WE'RE SEEING?
YES. TEAMS OF GUYS DESIGNING THE U.S. GOVERNMENT LIKE IT'S A PIECE OF SOFTWARE.

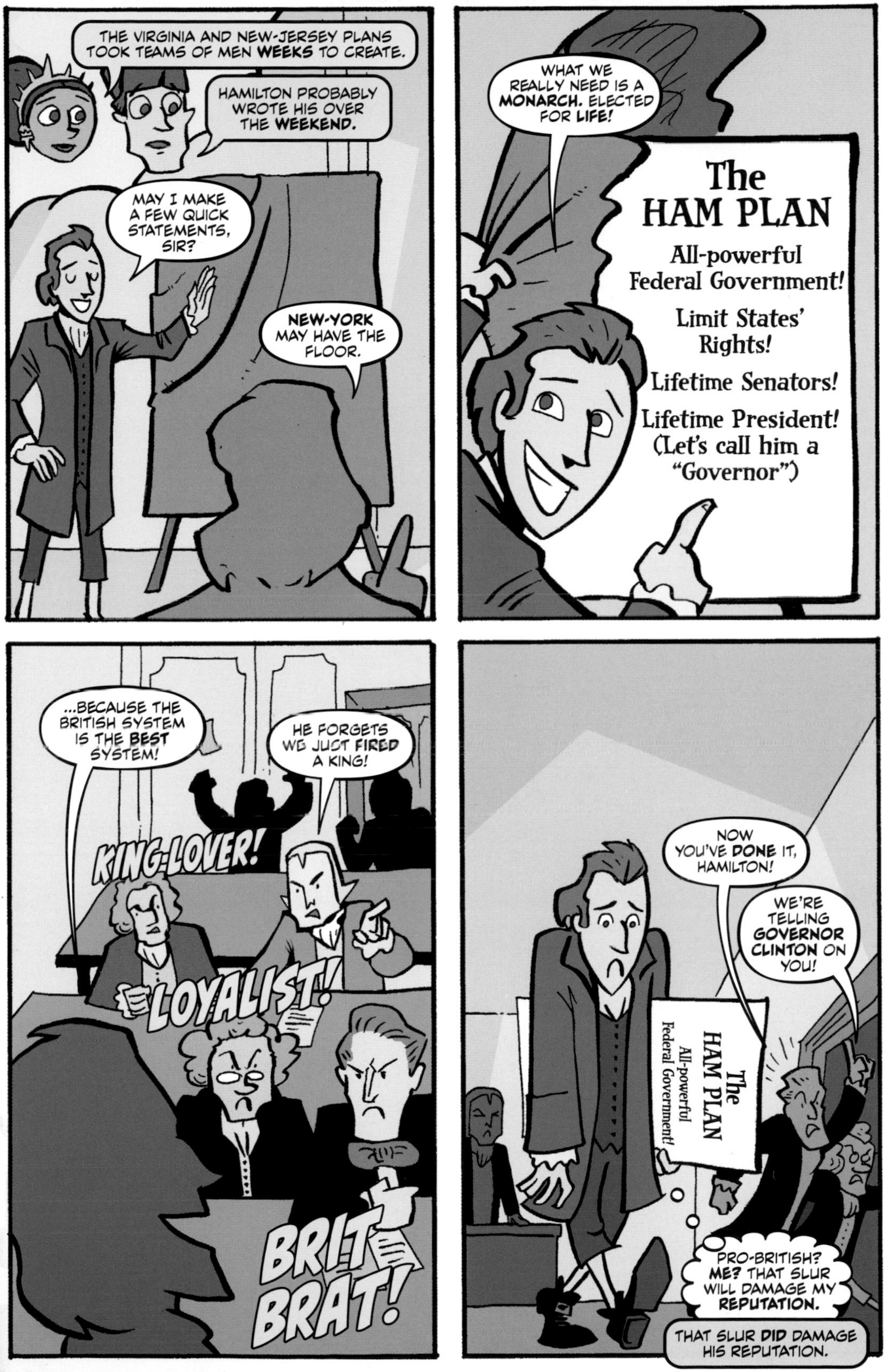
THE VIRGINIA AND NEW-JERSEY PLANS TOOK TEAMS OF MEN WEEKS TO CREATE.
HAMILTON PROBABLY WROTE HIS OVER THE WEEKEND.
MAY I MAKE A FEW QUICK STATEMENTS, SIR?
NEW-YORK MAY HAVE THE FLOOR.
WHAT WE REALLY NEED IS A MONARCH. ELECTED FOR LIFE!
The HAM PLAN
All-powerful Federal Government!
Limit States' Rights!
Lifetime Senators!
Lifetime President! (Let's call him a "Governor")
...BECAUSE THE BRITISH SYSTEM IS THE BEST SYSTEM!
HE FORGETS WE JUST FIRED A KING!
KING-LOVER!
LOYALIST!
BRIT BRAT!
NOW YOU'VE DONE IT, HAMILTON!
WE'RE TELLING GOVERNOR CLINTON ON YOU!
The HAM PLAN
All-powerful Federal Government!
PRO-BRITISH? ME? THAT SLUR WILL DAMAGE MY REPUTATION.
THAT SLUR DID DAMAGE HIS REPUTATION.

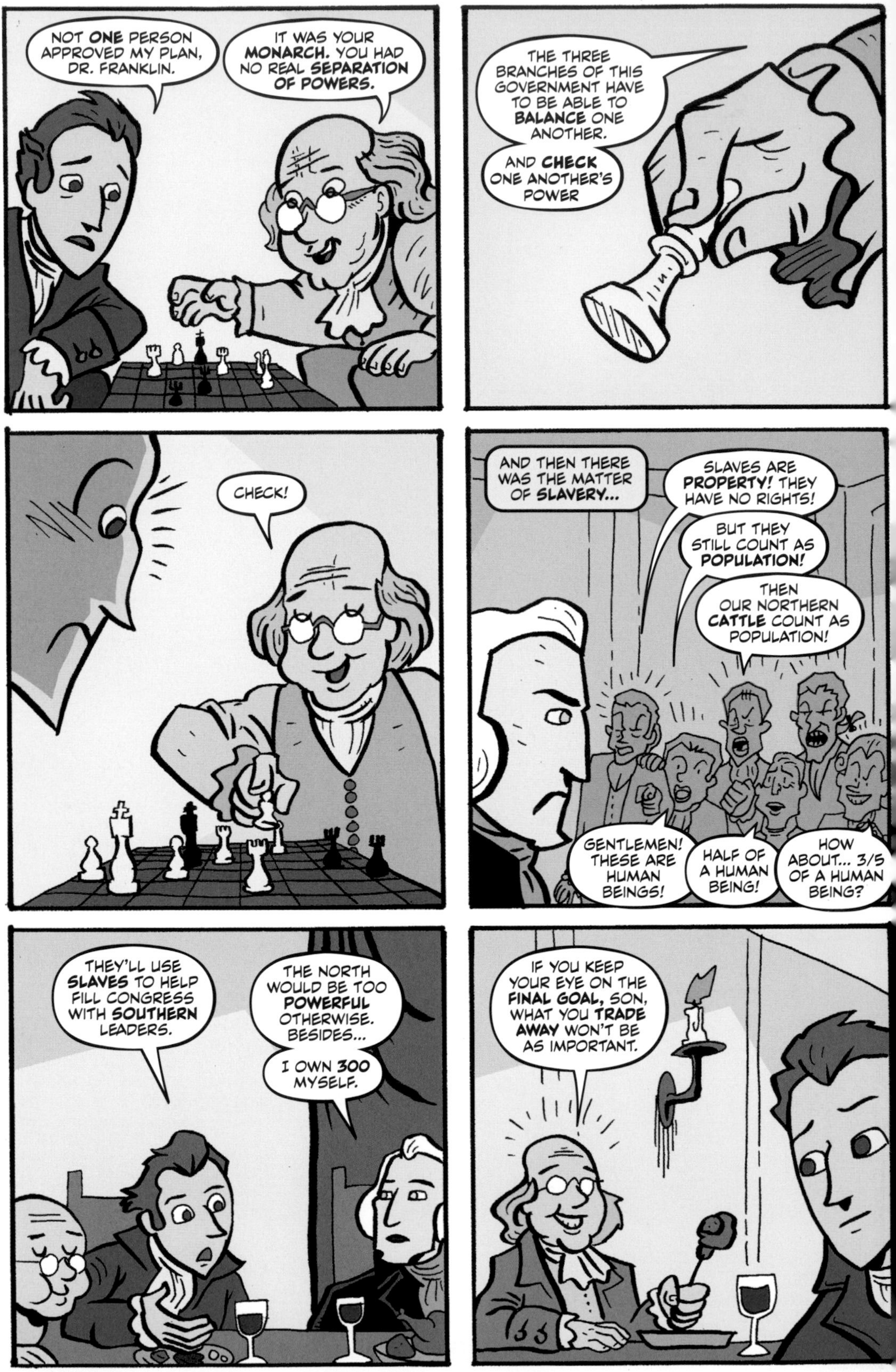
NOT ONE PERSON APPROVED MY PLAN, DR. FRANKLIN.
IT WAS YOUR MONARCH. YOU HAD NO REAL SEPARATION OF POWERS.
THE THREE BRANCHES OF THIS GOVERNMENT HAVE TO BE ABLE TO BALANCE ONE ANOTHER.
AND CHECK ONE ANOTHER'S POWER
CHECK!
AND THEN THERE WAS THE MATTER OF SLAVERY...
SLAVES ARE PROPERTY! THEY HAVE NO RIGHTS!
BUT THEY STILL COUNT AS POPULATION!
THEN OUR NORTHERN CATTLE COUNT AS POPULATION!
GENTLEMEN! THESE ARE HUMAN BEINGS!
HALF OF A HUMAN BEING!
HOW ABOUT... 3/5 OF A HUMAN BEING?
THEY'LL USE SLAVES TO HELP FILL CONGRESS WITH SOUTHERN LEADERS.
THE NORTH WOULD BE TOO POWERFUL OTHERWISE. BESIDES...
I OWN 300 MYSELF.
IF YOU KEEP YOUR EYE ON THE FINAL GOAL, SON, WHAT YOU TRADE AWAY WON'T BE AS IMPORTANT.

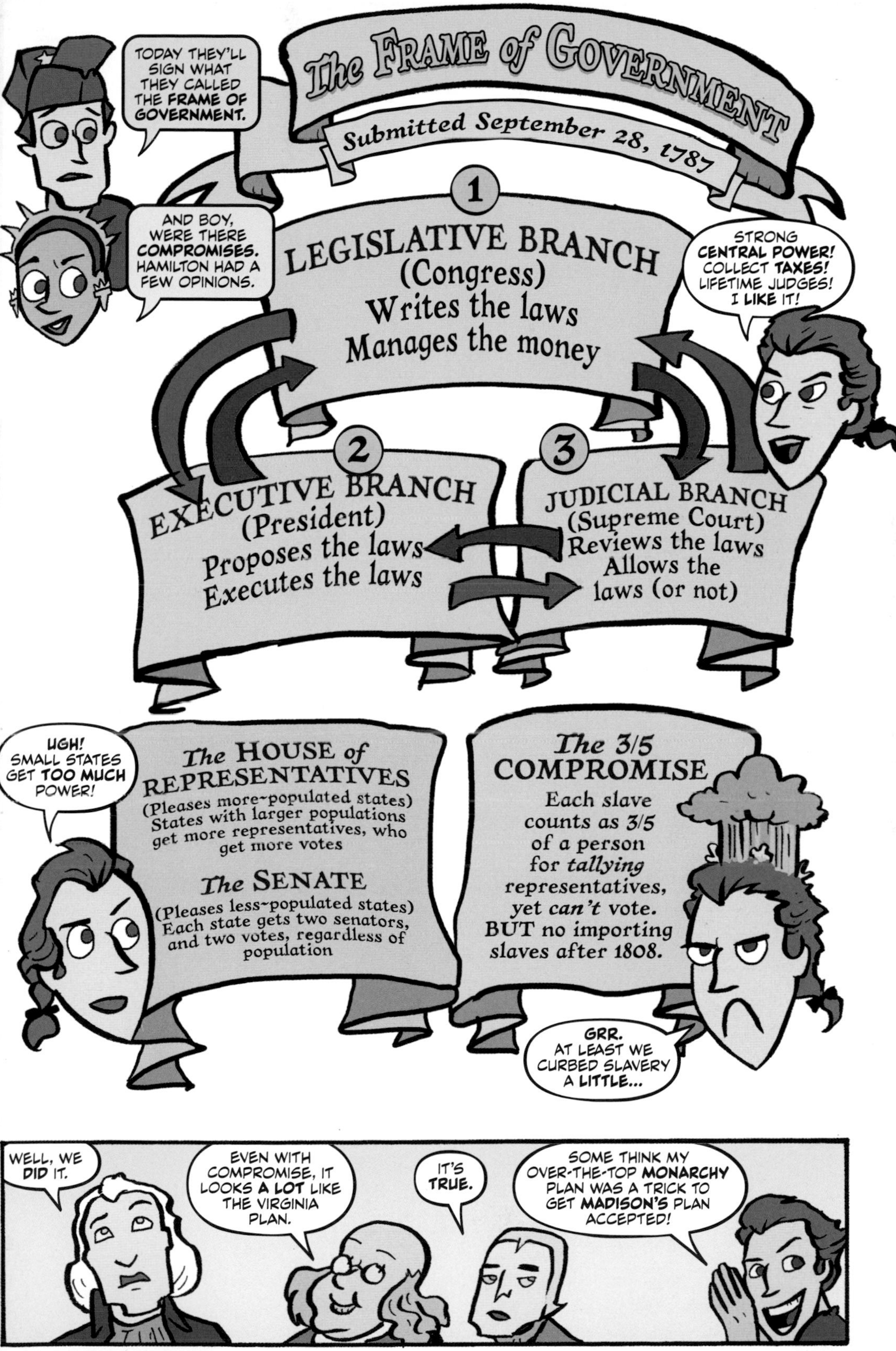

TODAY THEY'LL SIGN WHAT THEY CALLED THE FRAME OF GOVERNMENT.
The FRAME of GOVERNMENT
Submitted September 28, 1787
AND BOY, WERE THERE COMPROMISES. HAMILTON HAD A FEW OPINIONS.
1
LEGISLATIVE BRANCH
(Congress)
Writes the laws
Manages the money
STRONG CENTRAL POWER! COLLECT TAXES! LIFETIME JUDGES! I LIKE IT!
2
EXECUTIVE BRANCH
(President)
Proposes the laws
Executes the laws
3
JUDICIAL BRANCH
(Supreme Court)
Reviews the laws
Allows the laws (or not)
UGH! SMALL STATES GET TOO MUCH POWER!
The HOUSE of REPRESENTATIVES
(Pleases more~populated states) States with larger populations get more representatives, who get more votes
The SENATE
(Pleases less~populated states) Each state gets two senators, and two votes, regardless of population
The 3/5 COMPROMISE
Each slave counts as 3/5 of a person for tallying representatives, yet can't vote. BUT no importing slaves after 1808.
GRR. AT LEAST WE CURBED SLAVERY A LITTLE...
WELL, WE DID IT.
EVEN WITH COMPROMISE, IT LOOKS A LOT LIKE THE VIRGINIA PLAN.
IT'S TRUE.
SOME THINK MY OVER-THE-TOP MONARCHY PLAN WAS A TRICK TO GET MADISON'S PLAN ACCEPTED!

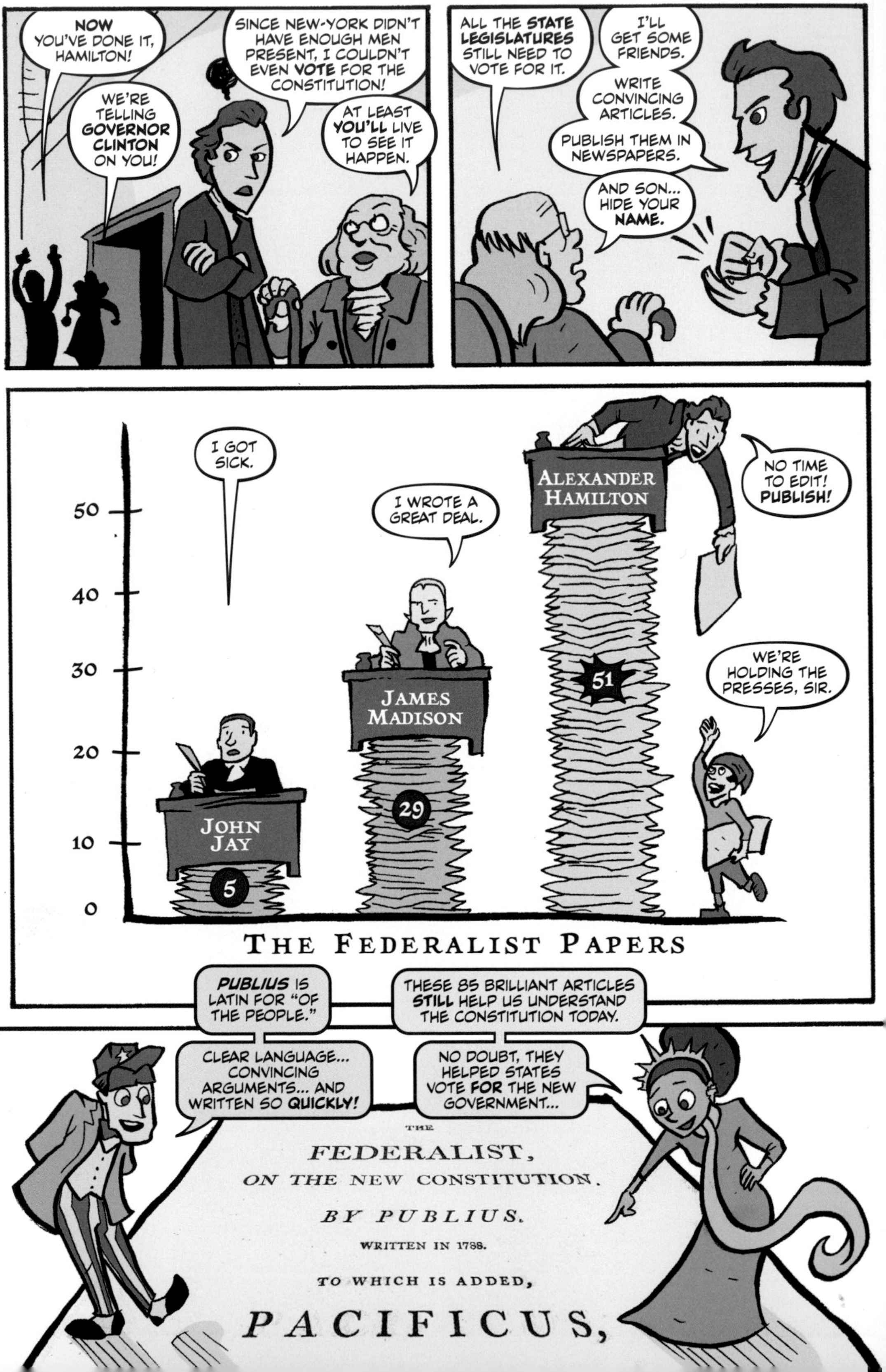
NOW YOU'VE DONE IT, HAMILTON!
WE'RE TELLING GOVERNOR CLINTON ON YOU!
SINCE NEW-YORK DIDN'T HAVE ENOUGH MEN PRESENT, I COULDN'T EVEN VOTE FOR THE CONSTITUTION!
AT LEAST YOU'LL LIVE TO SEE IT HAPPEN.
ALL THE STATE LEGISLATURES STILL NEED TO VOTE FOR IT.
I'LL GET SOME FRIENDS.
WRITE CONVINCING ARTICLES.
PUBLISH THEM IN NEWSPAPERS.
AND SON... HIDE YOUR NAME.
I GOT SICK.
I WRITE A GREAT DEAL.
ALEXANDER HAMILTON
NO TIME TO EDIT! PUBLISH!
50
40
30
20
10
0
JAMES MADISON
29
51
WE'RE HOLDING THE PRESSES, SIR.
JOHN JAY
5
THE FEDERALIST PAPERS
PUBLIUS IS LATIN FOR "OF THE PEOPLE."
CLEAR LANGUAGE... CONVINCING ARGUMENTS... AND WRITTEN SO QUICKLY!
THESE 85 BRILLIANT ARTICLES STILL HELP US UNDERSTAND THE CONSTITUTION TODAY.
NO DOUBT, THEY HELPED STATES VOTE FOR THE NEW GOVERNMENT...
THE
FEDERALIST,
ON THE NEW CONSTITUTION.
BY PUBLIUS.
WRITTEN IN 1788.
TO WHICH IS ADDED,
PACIFICUS,

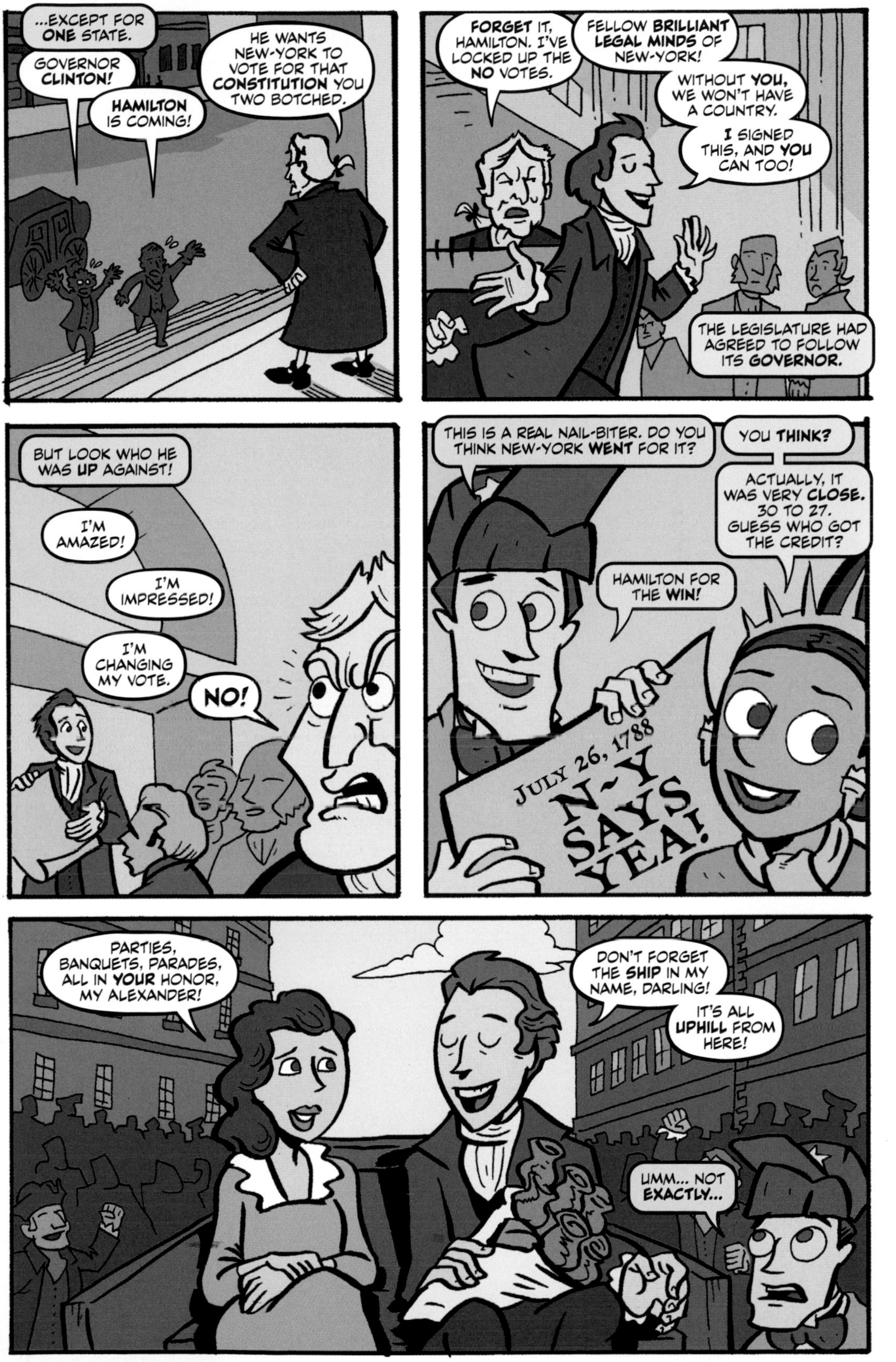
...EXCEPT FOR ONE STATE.
GOVERNOR CLINTON!
HAMILTON IS COMING!
HE WANTS NEW-YORK TO VOTE FOR THAT CONSTITUTION YOU TWO BOTCHED.
FORGET IT, HAMILTON. I'VE LOCKED UP THE NO VOTES.
FELLOW BRILLIANT LEGAL MINDS OF NEW-YORK!
WITHOUT YOU, WE WON'T HAVE A COUNTRY.
I SIGNED THIS, AND YOU CAN TOO!
THE LEGISLATURE HAD AGREED TO FOLLOW ITS GOVERNOR.
BUT LOOK WHO HE WAS UP AGAINST!
I'M AMAZED!
I'M IMPRESSED!
I'M CHANGING MY VOTE.
NO!
THIS IS A REAL NAIL-BITER. DO YOU THINK NEW-YORK WENT FOR IT?
YOU THINK?
ACTUALLY, IT WAS VERY CLOSE. 30 TO 27. GUESS WHO GOT THE CREDIT?
HAMILTON FOR THE WIN!
JULY 26, 1788
N-Y SAYS YEA!
PARTIES, BANQUETS, PARADES, ALL IN YOUR HONOR, MY ALEXANDER!
DON'T FORGET THE SHIP IN MY NAME, DARLING!
IT'S ALL UPHILL FROM HERE!
UMM... NOT EXACTLY...

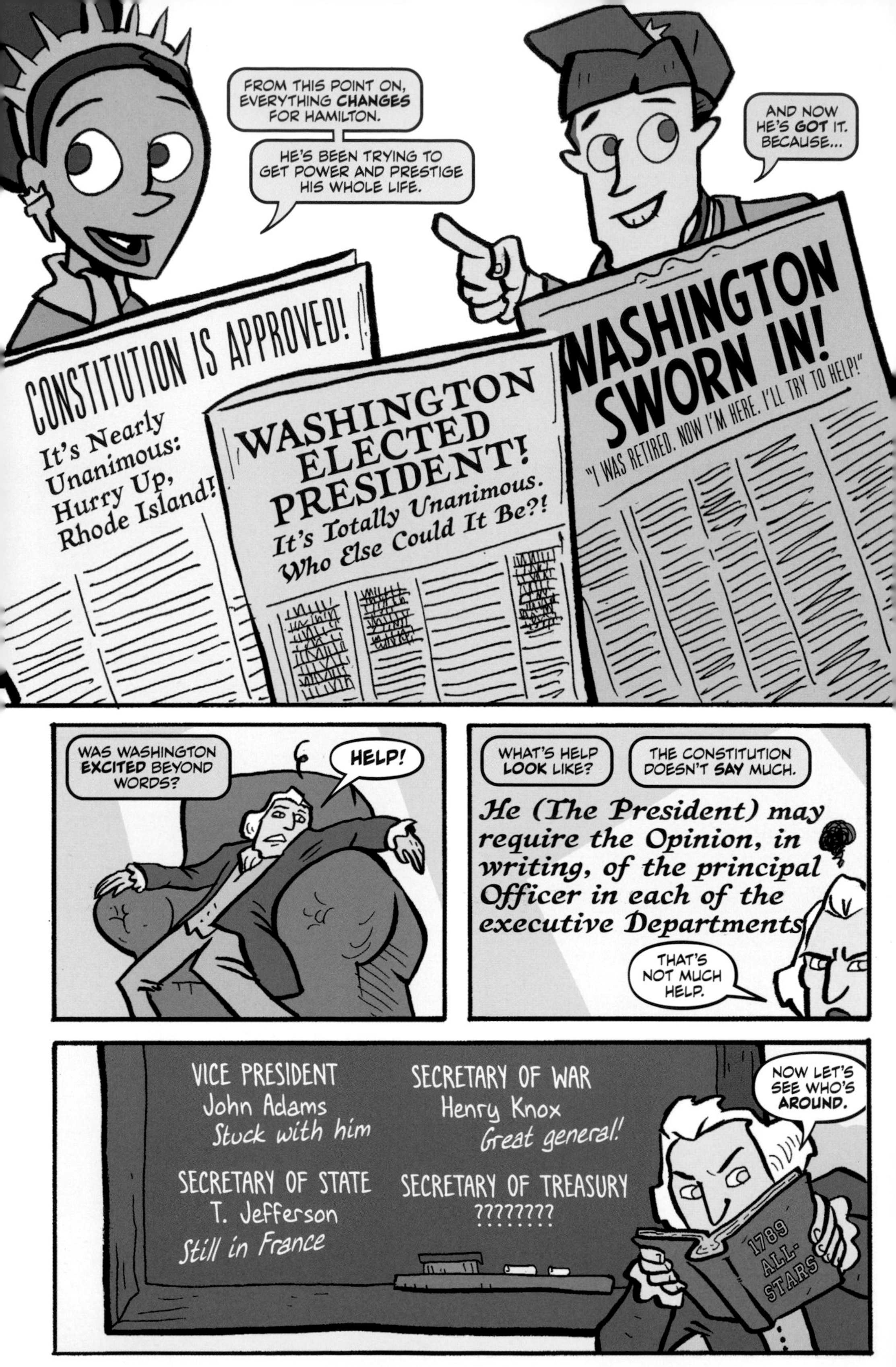
FROM THIS POINT ON, EVERYTHING CHANGES FOR HAMILTON.
HE'S BEEN TRYING TO GET POWER AND PRESTIGE HIS WHOLE LIFE.
AND NOW HE'S GOT IT. BECAUSE...
CONSTITUTION IS APPROVED!
It's Nearly Unanimous: Hurry Up, Rhode Island!
WASHINGTON ELECTED PRESIDENT!
It's Totally Unanimous. Who Else Could It Be?!
WASHINGTON SWORN IN!
"I WAS RETIRED. NOW I'M HERE. I'LL TRY TO HELP!"
WAS WASHINGTON EXCITED BEYOND WORDS?
HELP!
WHAT'S HELP LOOK LIKE?
THE CONSTITUTION DOESN'T SAY MUCH.
He (The President) may require the Opinion, in writing, of the principal Officer in each of the executive Departments
THAT'S NOT MUCH HELP.
VICE PRESIDENT
John Adams
Stuck with him
SECRETARY OF WAR
Henry Knox
Great general!
SECRETARY OF STATE
T. Jefferson
Still in France
SECRETARY OF TREASURY
????????
NOW LET'S SEE WHO'S AROUND.
1789 ALL-STARS

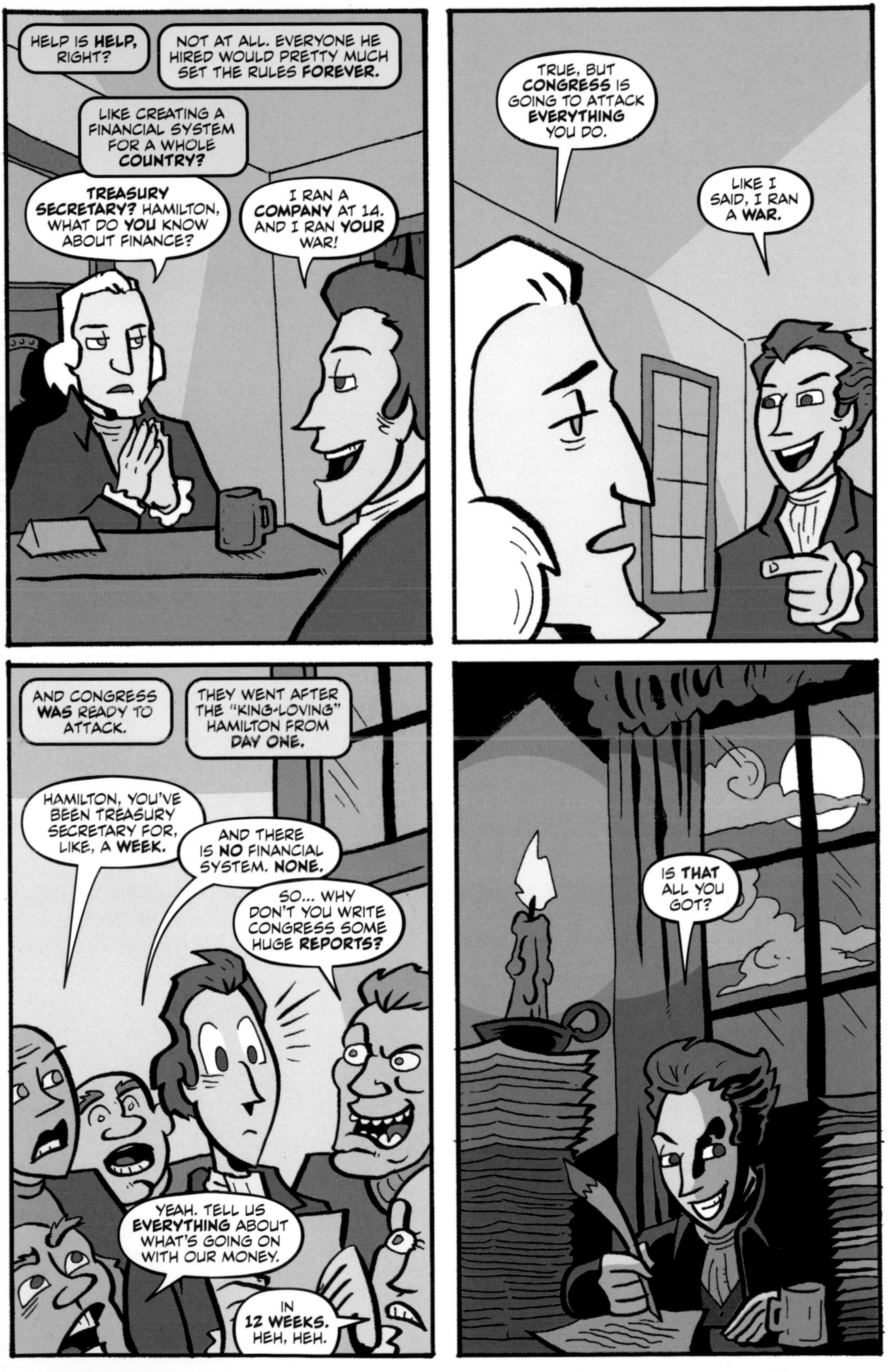
HELP IS **HELP,** RIGHT?
NOT AT ALL. EVERYONE HE HIRED WOULD PRETTY MUCH SET THE RULES **FOREVER.**
LIKE CREATING A FINANCIAL SYSTEM FOR A WHOLE **COUNTRY?**
TREASURY SECRETARY? HAMILTON, WHAT DO **YOU** KNOW ABOUT FINANCE?
I RAN A **COMPANY** AT 14. AND I RAN **YOUR** WAR!
TRUE, BUT **CONGRESS** IS GOING TO ATTACK **EVERYTHING** YOU DO.
LIKE I SAID, I RAN A **WAR.**
AND CONGRESS **WAS** READY TO ATTACK.
THEY WENT AFTER THE "KING-LOVING" HAMILTON FROM **DAY ONE.**
HAMILTON, YOU'VE BEEN TREASURY SECRETARY FOR, LIKE, A **WEEK.**
AND THERE IS **NO** FINANCIAL SYSTEM. **NONE.**
SO... WHY DON'T YOU WRITE CONGRESS SOME HUGE **REPORTS?**
YEAH. TELL US **EVERYTHING** ABOUT WHAT'S GOING ON WITH OUR MONEY.
IN **12 WEEKS.** HEH, HEH.
IS **THAT** ALL YOU GOT?

TO PUT IT LIGHTLY, MY MAN **HAM** BLEW THEIR MINDS OVER IN CONGRESS.

WHAT??

NO WAY.

I CALL IT THE **REPORT RELATIVE TO A PROVISION FOR THE SUPPORT OF PUBLIC CREDIT.**

SNAPPY, HUH? GOES LIKE THIS:

We owe tons of money to countries, businesses, and people, so...

RAISE MONEY!

Pay taxes on luxuries such as whiskey. And pay a tariff on imports if you don't buy American.

We can't afford to pay everyone at once, and we have to borrow to grow, so...

DON'T PAY OFF THE NATIONAL DEBT!

The more we borrow, the more we're worth. And the interest we pay makes lenders wealthy.

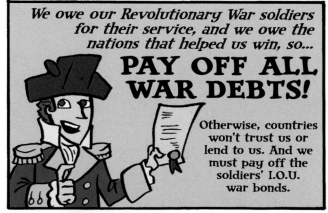

We owe our Revolutionary War soldiers for their service, and we owe the nations that helped us win, so...

PAY OFF ALL WAR DEBTS!

Otherwise, countries won't trust us or lend to us. And we must pay off the soldiers' I.O.U. war bonds.

WHEN YOU ASSUME A DEBT, THAT'S CALLED ASSUMPTION.

I ASSUME THIS IS ALL A JOKE?

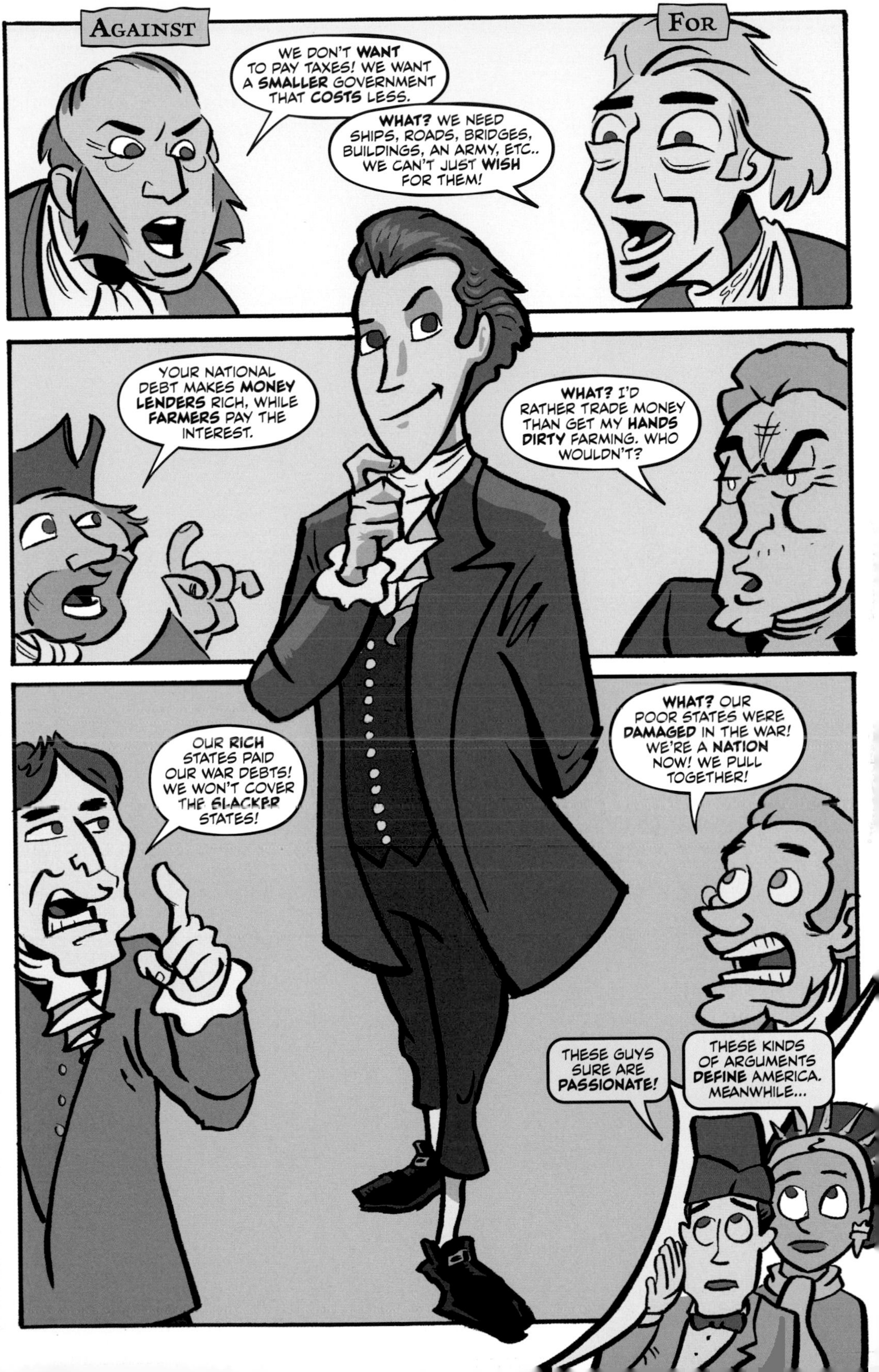
AGAINST
FOR
WE DON'T WANT TO PAY TAXES! WE WANT A SMALLER GOVERNMENT THAT COSTS LESS.
WHAT? WE NEED SHIPS, ROADS, BRIDGES, BUILDINGS, AN ARMY, ETC.. WE CAN'T JUST WISH FOR THEM!
YOUR NATIONAL DEBT MAKES MONEY LENDERS RICH, WHILE FARMERS PAY THE INTEREST.
WHAT? I'D RATHER TRADE MONEY THAN GET MY HANDS DIRTY FARMING. WHO WOULDN'T?
OUR RICH STATES PAID OUR WAR DEBTS! WE WON'T COVER THE SLACKER STATES!
WHAT? OUR POOR STATES WERE DAMAGED IN THE WAR! WE'RE A NATION NOW! WE PULL TOGETHER!
THESE GUYS SURE ARE PASSIONATE!
THESE KINDS OF ARGUMENTS DEFINE AMERICA. MEANWHILE...

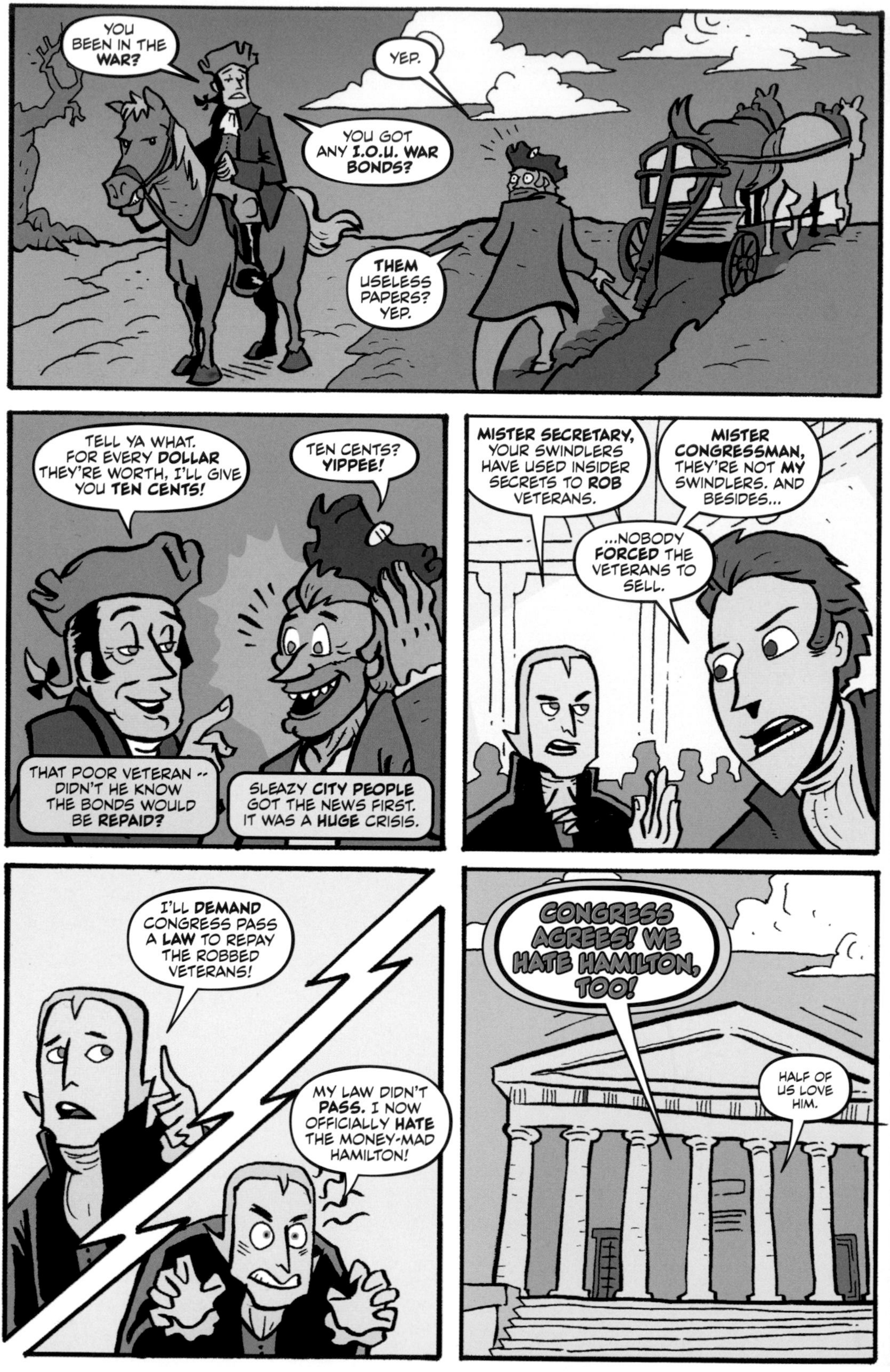

YOU BEEN IN THE **WAR?**
YEP.
YOU GOT ANY **I.O.U. WAR BONDS?**
THEM USELESS PAPERS? YEP.
TELL YA WHAT. FOR EVERY **DOLLAR** THEY'RE WORTH, I'LL GIVE YOU **TEN CENTS!**
TEN CENTS? **YIPPEE!**
THAT POOR VETERAN -- DIDN'T HE KNOW THE BONDS WOULD BE **REPAID?**
SLEAZY **CITY PEOPLE** GOT THE NEWS FIRST. IT WAS A **HUGE** CRISIS.
MISTER SECRETARY, YOUR SWINDLERS HAVE USED INSIDER SECRETS TO **ROB** VETERANS.
MISTER CONGRESSMAN, THEY'RE NOT **MY** SWINDLERS. AND BESIDES...
...NOBODY **FORCED** THE VETERANS TO SELL.
I'LL **DEMAND** CONGRESS PASS A **LAW** TO REPAY THE ROBBED VETERANS!
MY LAW DIDN'T **PASS.** I NOW OFFICIALLY **HATE** THE MONEY-MAD HAMILTON!
CONGRESS AGREES! WE HATE HAMILTON, TOO!
HALF OF US LOVE HIM.

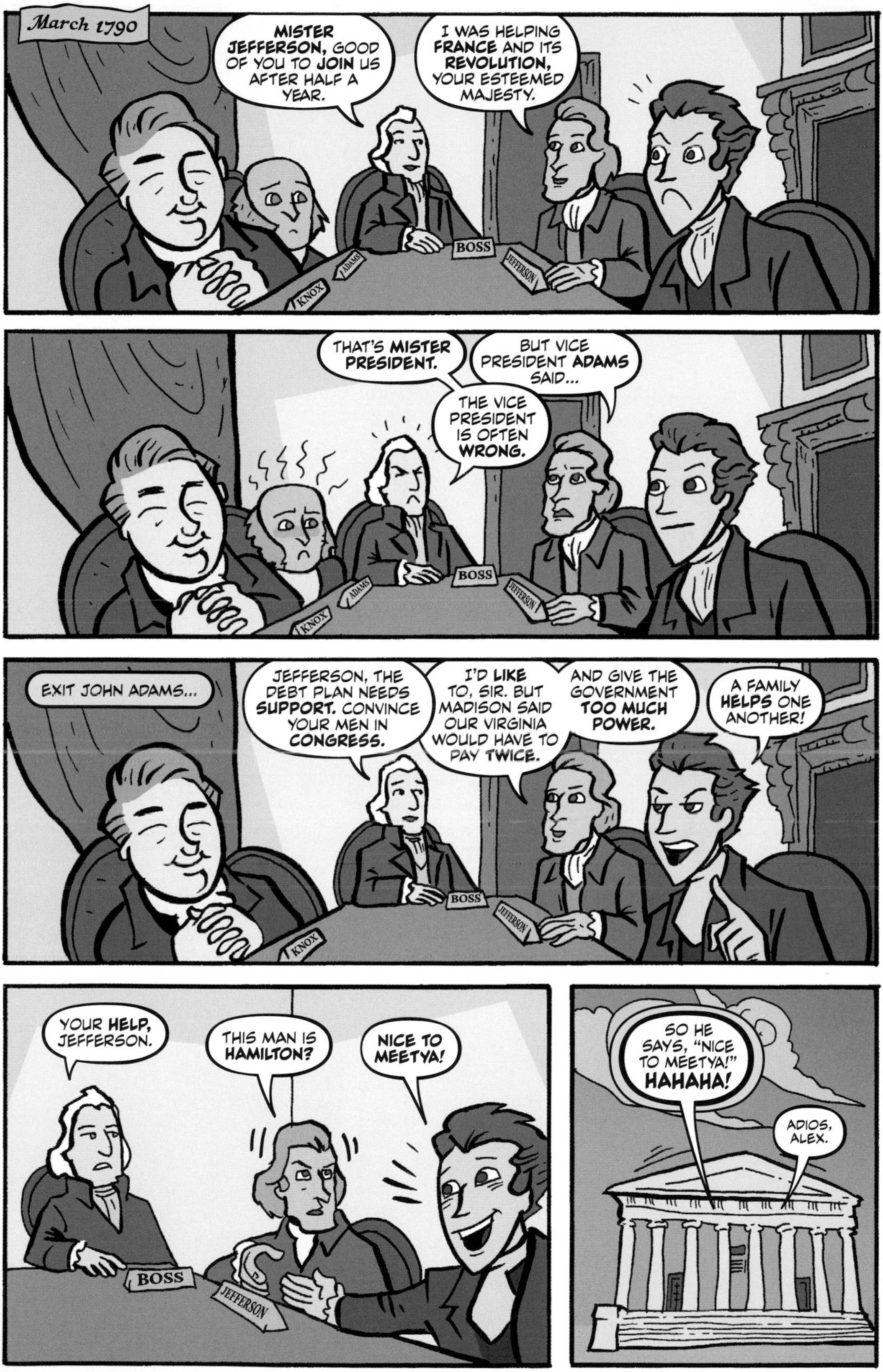
March 1790
MISTER JEFFERSON, GOOD OF YOU TO JOIN US AFTER HALF A YEAR.
I WAS HELPING FRANCE AND ITS REVOLUTION, YOUR ESTEEMED MAJESTY.
KNOX
ADAMS
BOSS
JEFFERSON
THAT'S MISTER PRESIDENT.
BUT VICE PRESIDENT ADAMS SAID...
THE VICE PRESIDENT IS OFTEN WRONG.
EXIT JOHN ADAMS...
JEFFERSON, THE DEBT PLAN NEEDS SUPPORT. CONVINCE YOUR MEN IN CONGRESS.
I'D LIKE TO, SIR. BUT MADISON SAID OUR VIRGINIA WOULD HAVE TO PAY TWICE.
AND GIVE THE GOVERNMENT TOO MUCH POWER.
A FAMILY HELPS ONE ANOTHER!
YOUR HELP, JEFFERSON.
THIS MAN IS HAMILTON?
NICE TO MEETYA!
SO HE SAYS, "NICE TO MEETYA!" HAHAHA!
ADIOS, ALEX.

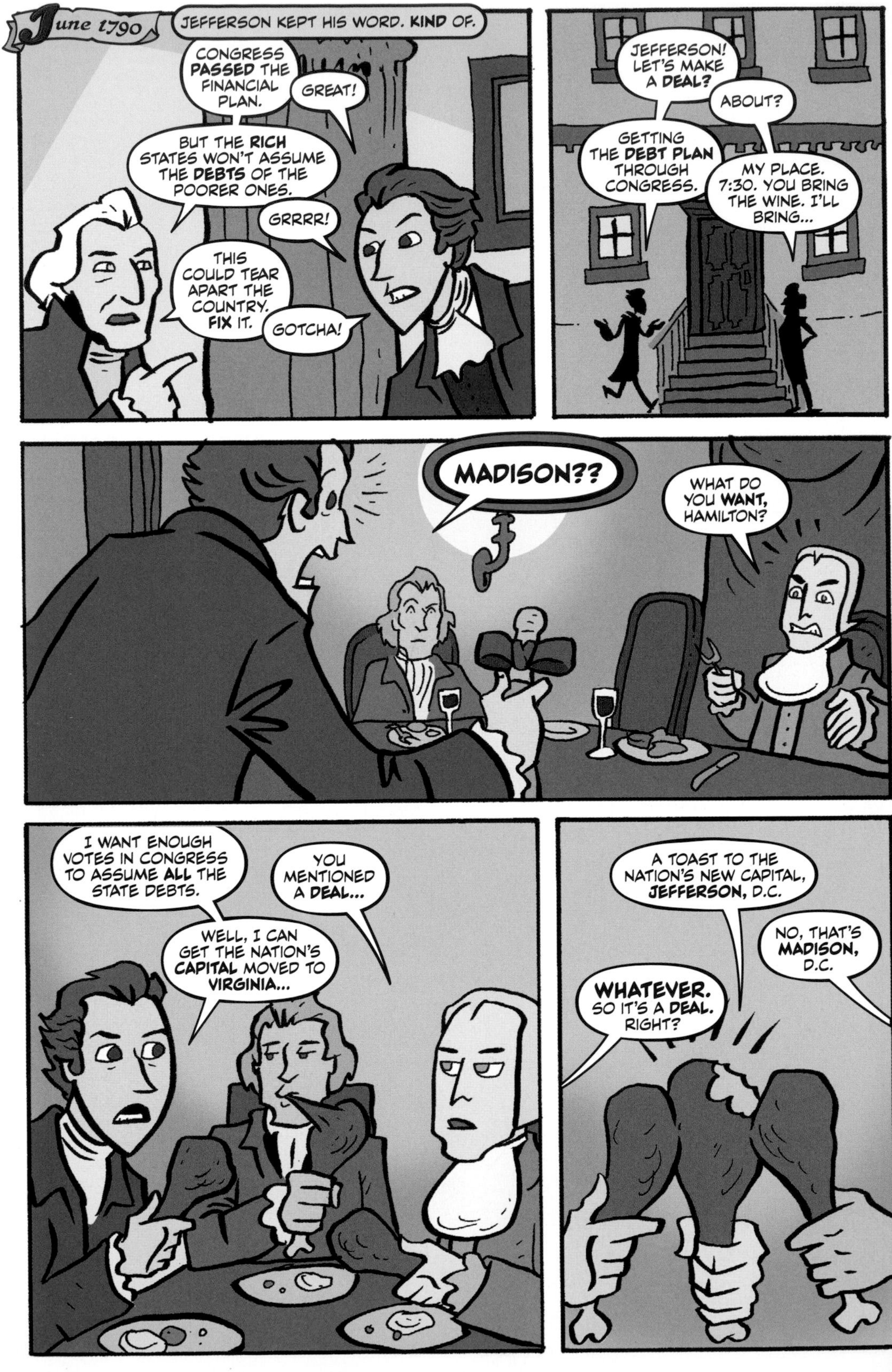
June 1790
JEFFERSON KEPT HIS WORD. KIND OF.
CONGRESS PASSED THE FINANCIAL PLAN.
GREAT!
BUT THE RICH STATES WON'T ASSUME THE DEBTS OF THE POORER ONES.
GRRRR!
THIS COULD TEAR APART THE COUNTRY. FIX IT.
GOTCHA!
JEFFERSON! LET'S MAKE A DEAL?
ABOUT?
GETTING THE DEBT PLAN THROUGH CONGRESS.
MY PLACE. 7:30. YOU BRING THE WINE. I'LL BRING...
MADISON??
WHAT DO YOU WANT, HAMILTON?
I WANT ENOUGH VOTES IN CONGRESS TO ASSUME ALL THE STATE DEBTS.
YOU MENTIONED A DEAL...
WELL, I CAN GET THE NATION'S CAPITAL MOVED TO VIRGINIA...
A TOAST TO THE NATION'S NEW CAPITAL, JEFFERSON, D.C.
NO, THAT'S MADISON, D.C.
WHATEVER. SO IT'S A DEAL. RIGHT?

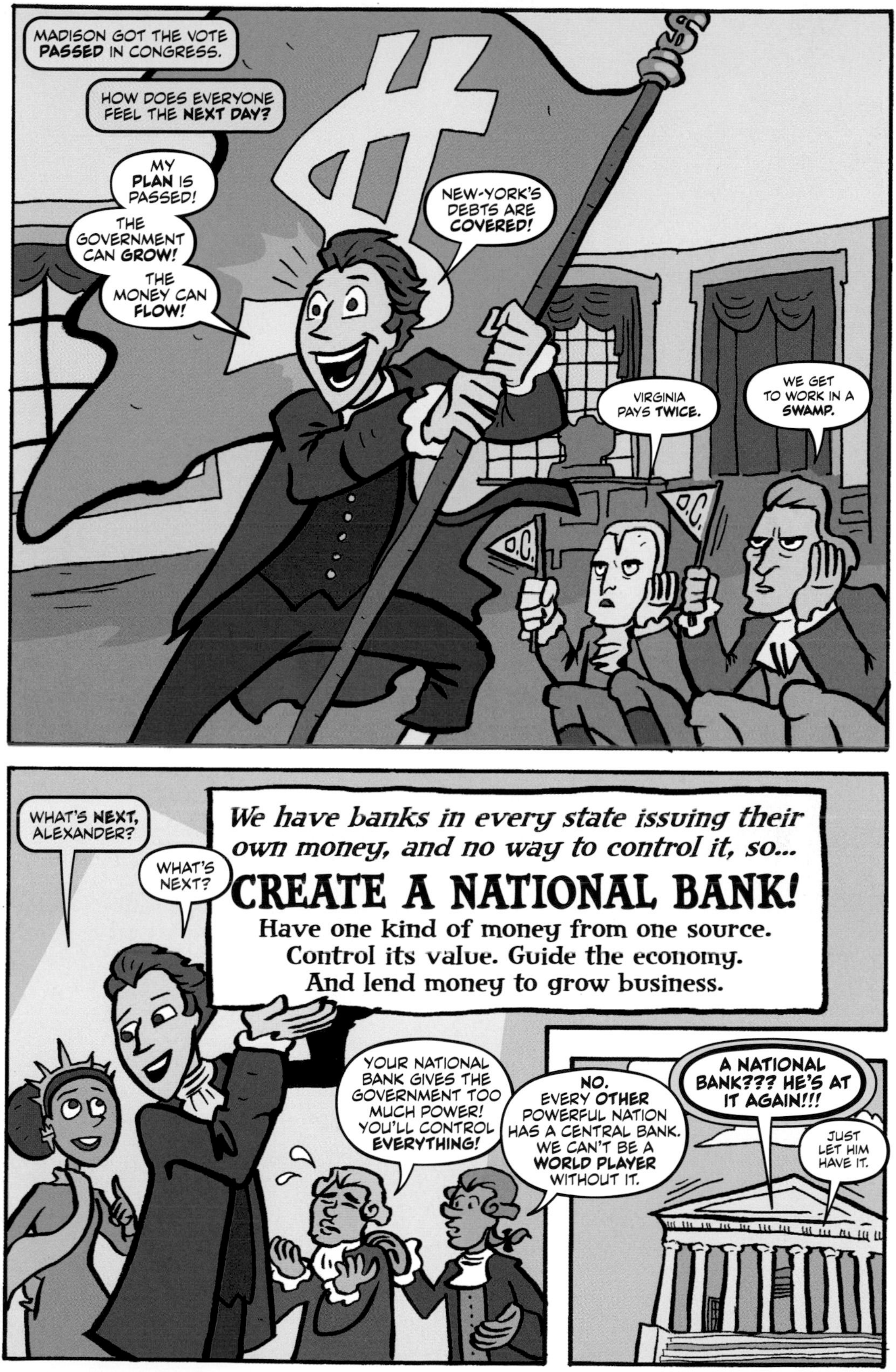
MADISON GOT THE VOTE PASSED IN CONGRESS.
HOW DOES EVERYONE FEEL THE NEXT DAY?
MY PLAN IS PASSED!
THE GOVERNMENT CAN GROW!
THE MONEY CAN FLOW!
NEW-YORK'S DEBTS ARE COVERED!
VIRGINIA PAYS TWICE.
WE GET TO WORK IN A SWAMP.
D.C.
D.C.
WHAT'S NEXT, ALEXANDER?
WHAT'S NEXT?
We have banks in every state issuing their own money, and no way to control it, so...
CREATE A NATIONAL BANK!
Have one kind of money from one source. Control its value. Guide the economy. And lend money to grow business.
YOUR NATIONAL BANK GIVES THE GOVERNMENT TOO MUCH POWER! YOU'LL CONTROL EVERYTHING!
NO. EVERY OTHER POWERFUL NATION HAS A CENTRAL BANK. WE CAN'T BE A WORLD PLAYER WITHOUT IT.
A NATIONAL BANK??? HE'S AT IT AGAIN!!!
JUST LET HIM HAVE IT.

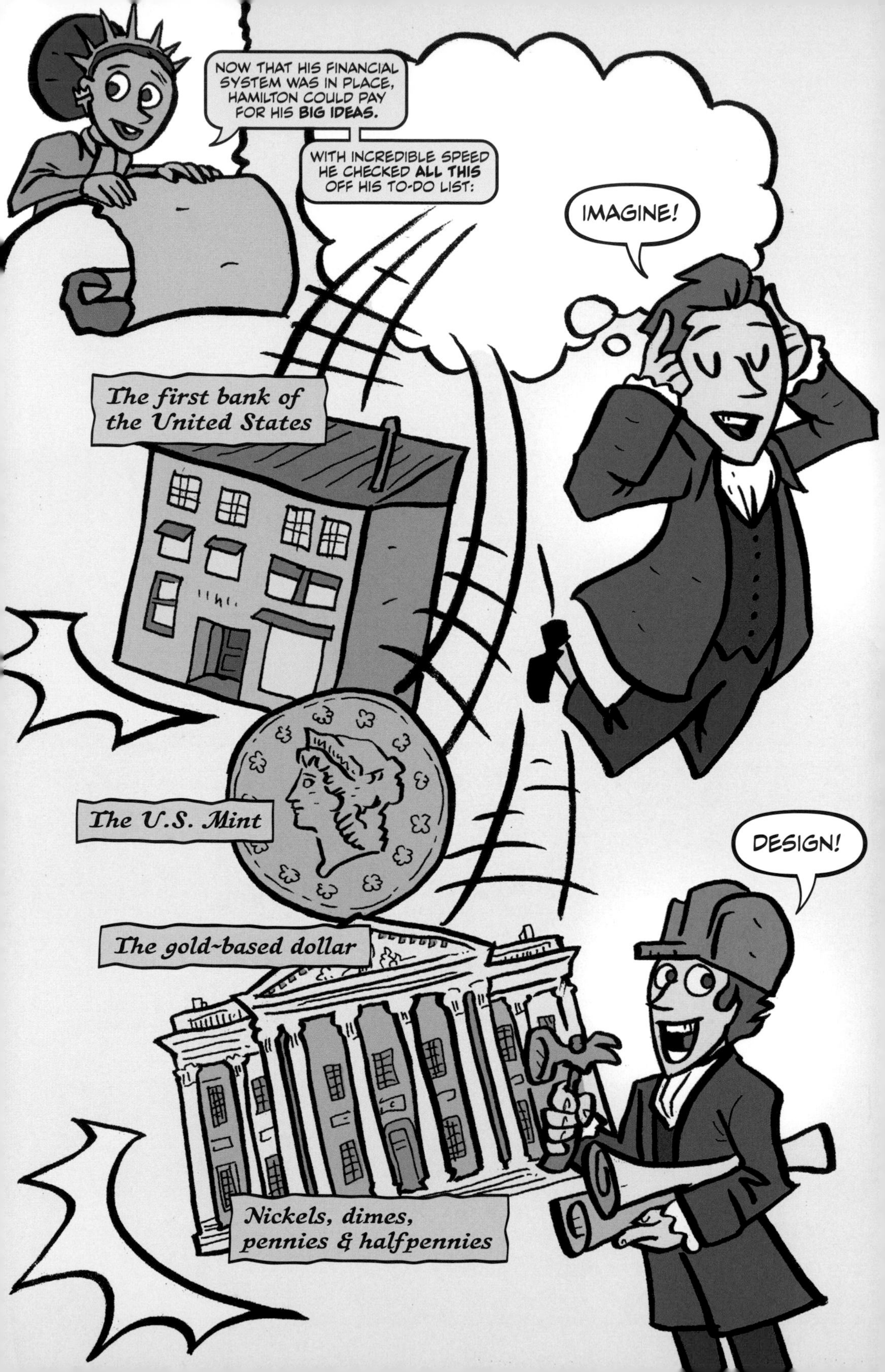

NOW THAT HIS FINANCIAL SYSTEM WAS IN PLACE, HAMILTON COULD PAY FOR HIS BIG IDEAS.
WITH INCREDIBLE SPEED HE CHECKED ALL THIS OFF HIS TO-DO LIST:
IMAGINE!
The first bank of the United States
The U.S. Mint
DESIGN!
The gold-based dollar
Nickels, dimes, pennies & halfpennies

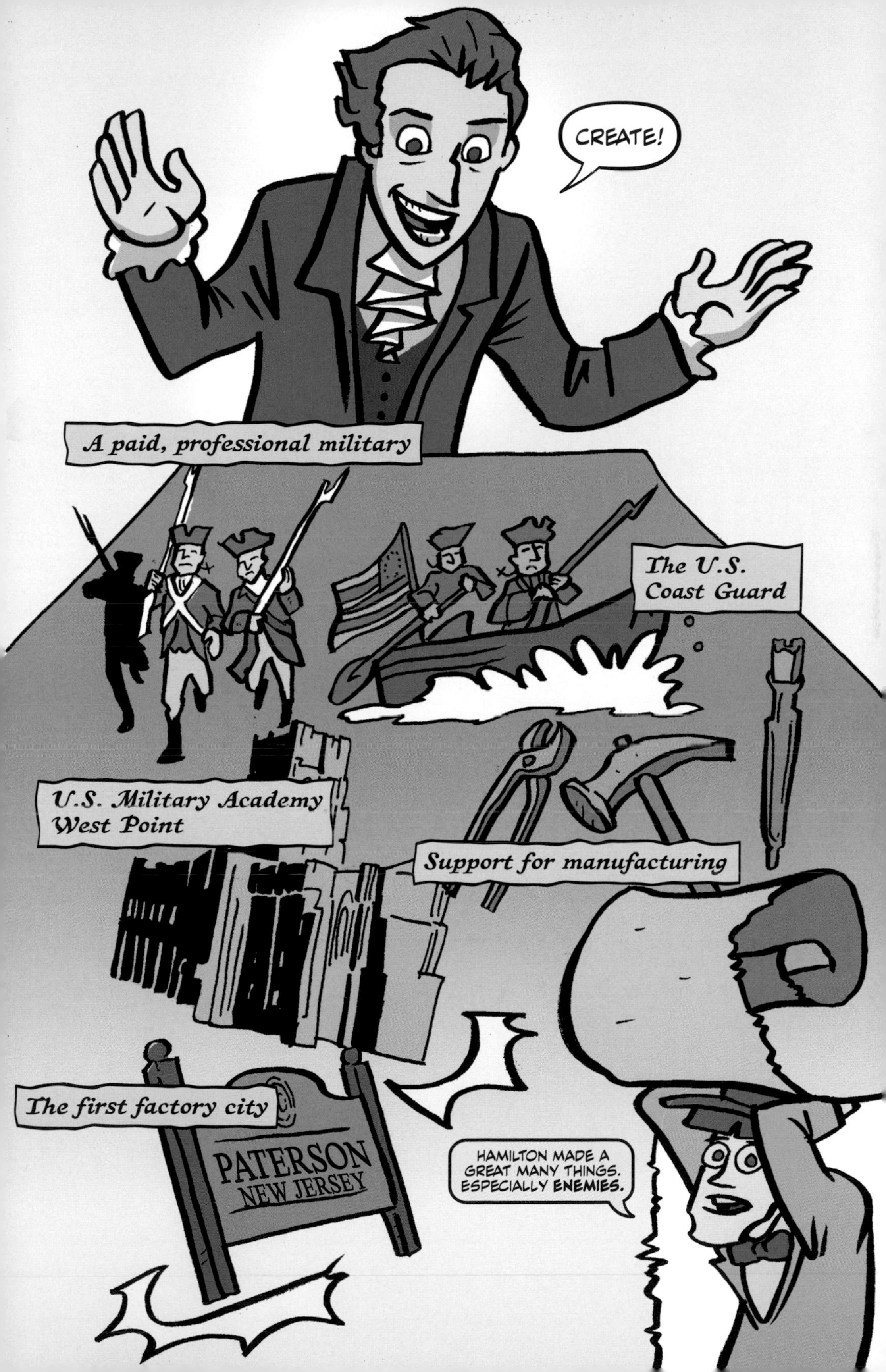
CREATE!
A paid, professional military
The U.S. Coast Guard
U.S. Military Academy West Point
Support for manufacturing
The first factory city
PATERSON
NEW JERSEY
HAMILTON MADE A GREAT MANY THINGS. ESPECIALLY ENEMIES.

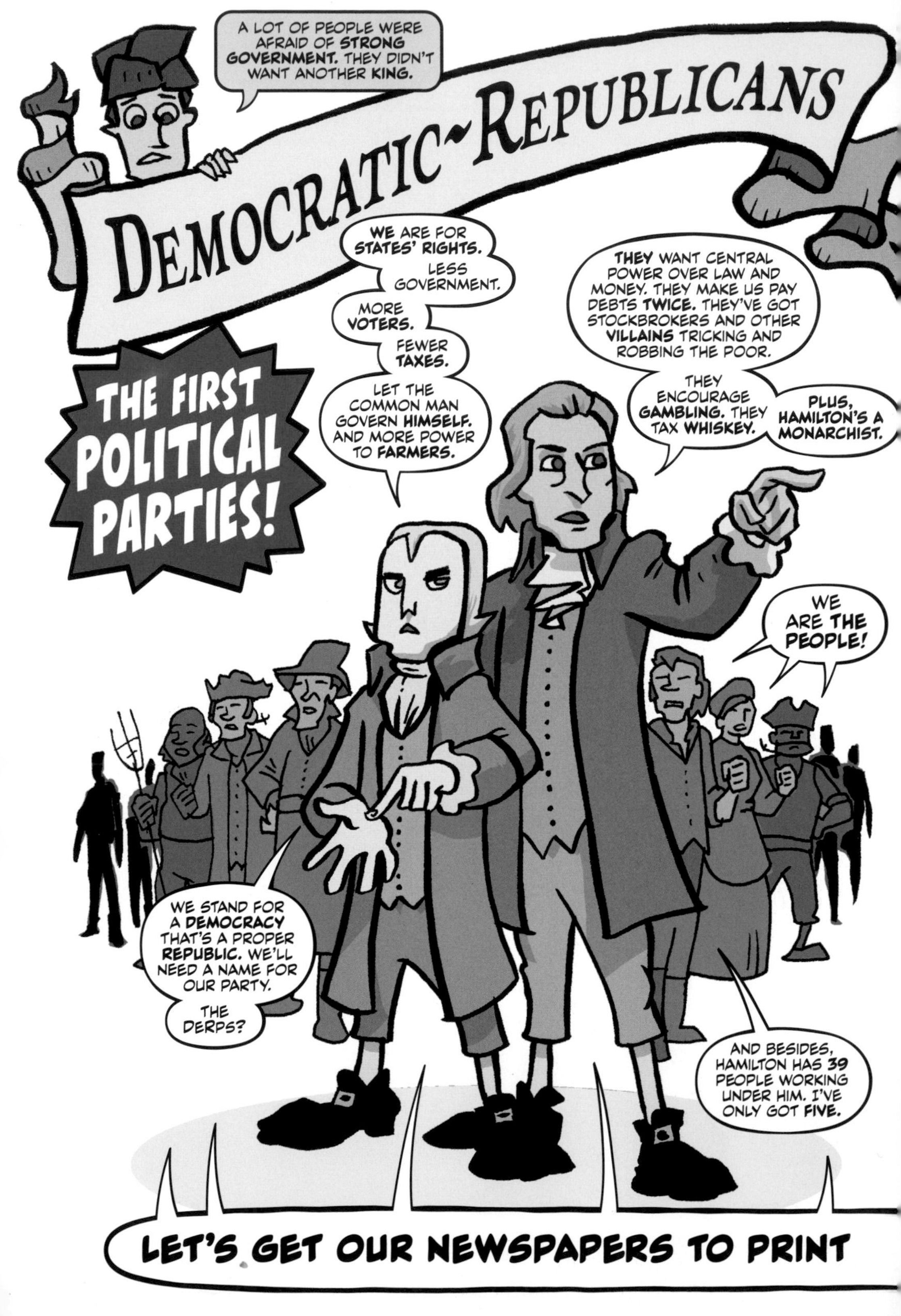
A LOT OF PEOPLE WERE AFRAID OF STRONG GOVERNMENT. THEY DIDN'T WANT ANOTHER KING.
DEMOCRATIC-REPUBLICANS
THE FIRST POLITICAL PARTIES!
WE ARE FOR STATES' RIGHTS.
LESS GOVERNMENT.
MORE VOTERS.
FEWER TAXES.
LET THE COMMON MAN GOVERN HIMSELF. AND MORE POWER TO FARMERS.
THEY WANT CENTRAL POWER OVER LAW AND MONEY. THEY MAKE US PAY DEBTS TWICE. THEY'VE GOT STOCKBROKERS AND OTHER VILLAINS TRICKING AND ROBBING THE POOR.
THEY ENCOURAGE GAMBLING. THEY TAX WHISKEY.
PLUS, HAMILTON'S A MONARCHIST.
WE ARE THE PEOPLE!
WE STAND FOR A DEMOCRACY THAT'S A PROPER REPUBLIC. WE'LL NEED A NAME FOR OUR PARTY.
THE DERPS?
AND BESIDES, HAMILTON HAS 39 PEOPLE WORKING UNDER HIM. I'VE ONLY GOT FIVE.
LET'S GET OUR NEWSPAPERS TO PRINT

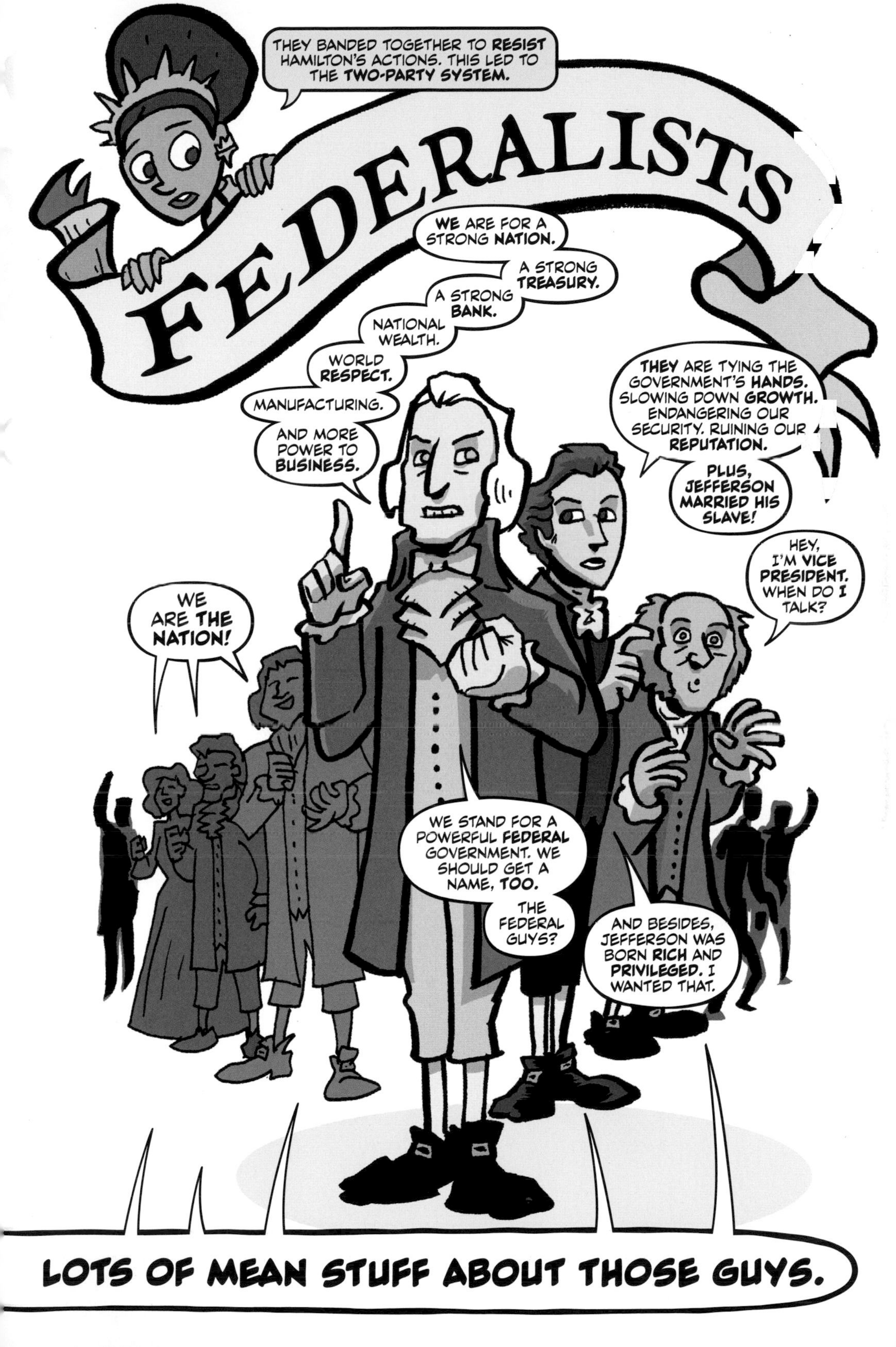
THEY BANDED TOGETHER TO RESIST HAMILTON'S ACTIONS. THIS LED TO THE TWO-PARTY SYSTEM.
FEDERALISTS
WE ARE FOR A STRONG NATION.
A STRONG TREASURY.
A STRONG BANK.
NATIONAL WEALTH.
WORLD RESPECT.
MANUFACTURING.
AND MORE POWER TO BUSINESS.
THEY ARE TYING THE GOVERNMENT'S HANDS. SLOWING DOWN GROWTH. ENDANGERING OUR SECURITY. RUINING OUR REPUTATION.
PLUS, JEFFERSON MARRIED HIS SLAVE!
HEY, I'M VICE PRESIDENT. WHEN DO I TALK?
WE ARE THE NATION!
WE STAND FOR A POWERFUL FEDERAL GOVERNMENT. WE SHOULD GET A NAME, TOO.
THE FEDERAL GUYS?
AND BESIDES, JEFFERSON WAS BORN RICH AND PRIVILEGED. I WANTED THAT.
LOTS OF MEAN STUFF ABOUT THOSE GUYS.

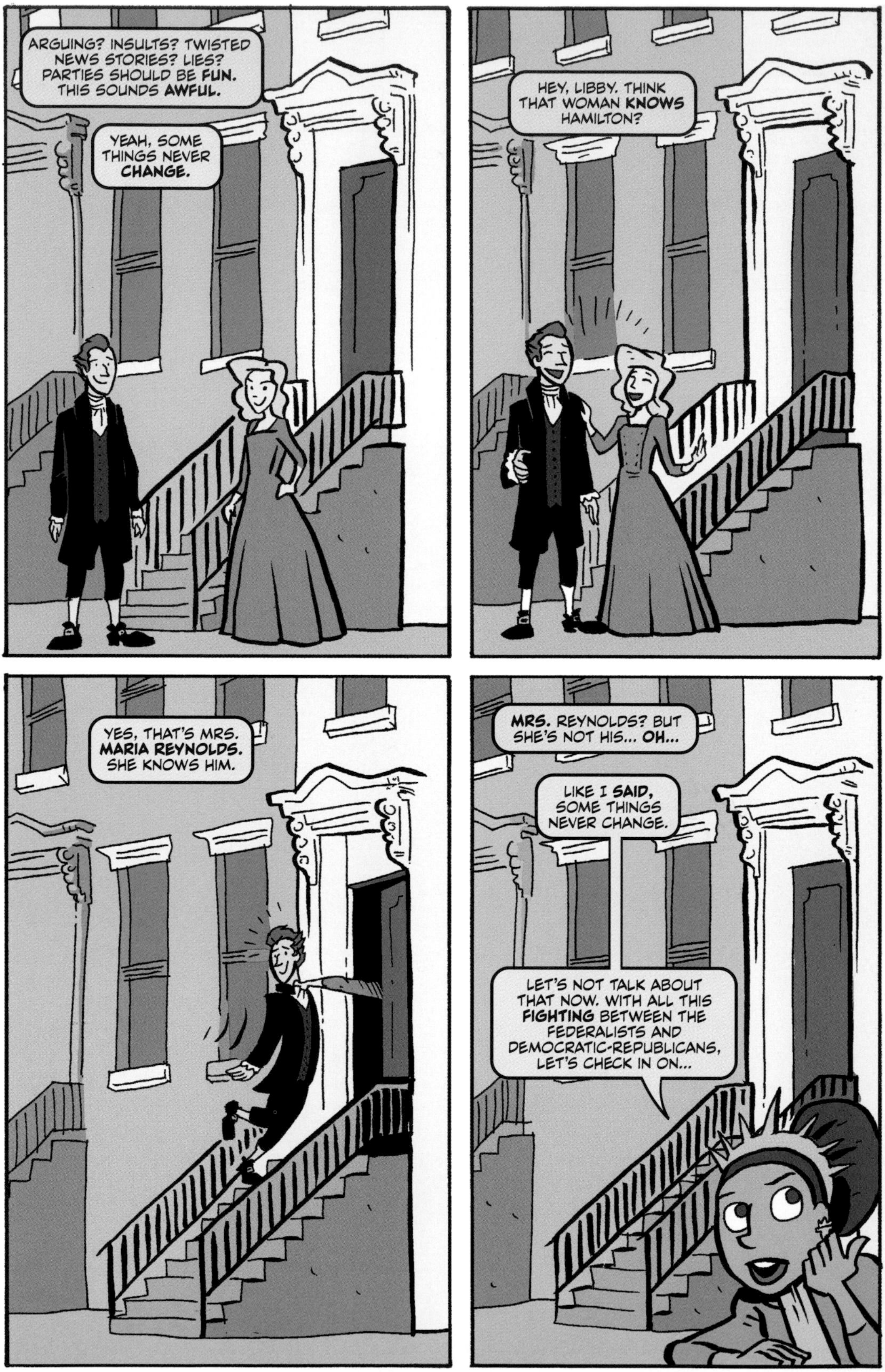
ARGUING? INSULTS? TWISTED NEWS STORIES? LIES? PARTIES SHOULD BE FUN. THIS SOUNDS AWFUL.
YEAH, SOME THINGS NEVER CHANGE.
HEY, LIBBY. THINK THAT WOMAN KNOWS HAMILTON?
YES, THAT'S MRS. MARIA REYNOLDS. SHE KNOWS HIM.
MRS. REYNOLDS? BUT SHE'S NOT HIS... OH...
LIKE I SAID, SOME THINGS NEVER CHANGE.
LET'S NOT TALK ABOUT THAT NOW. WITH ALL THIS FIGHTING BETWEEN THE FEDERALISTS AND DEMOCRATIC-REPUBLICANS, LET'S CHECK IN ON...

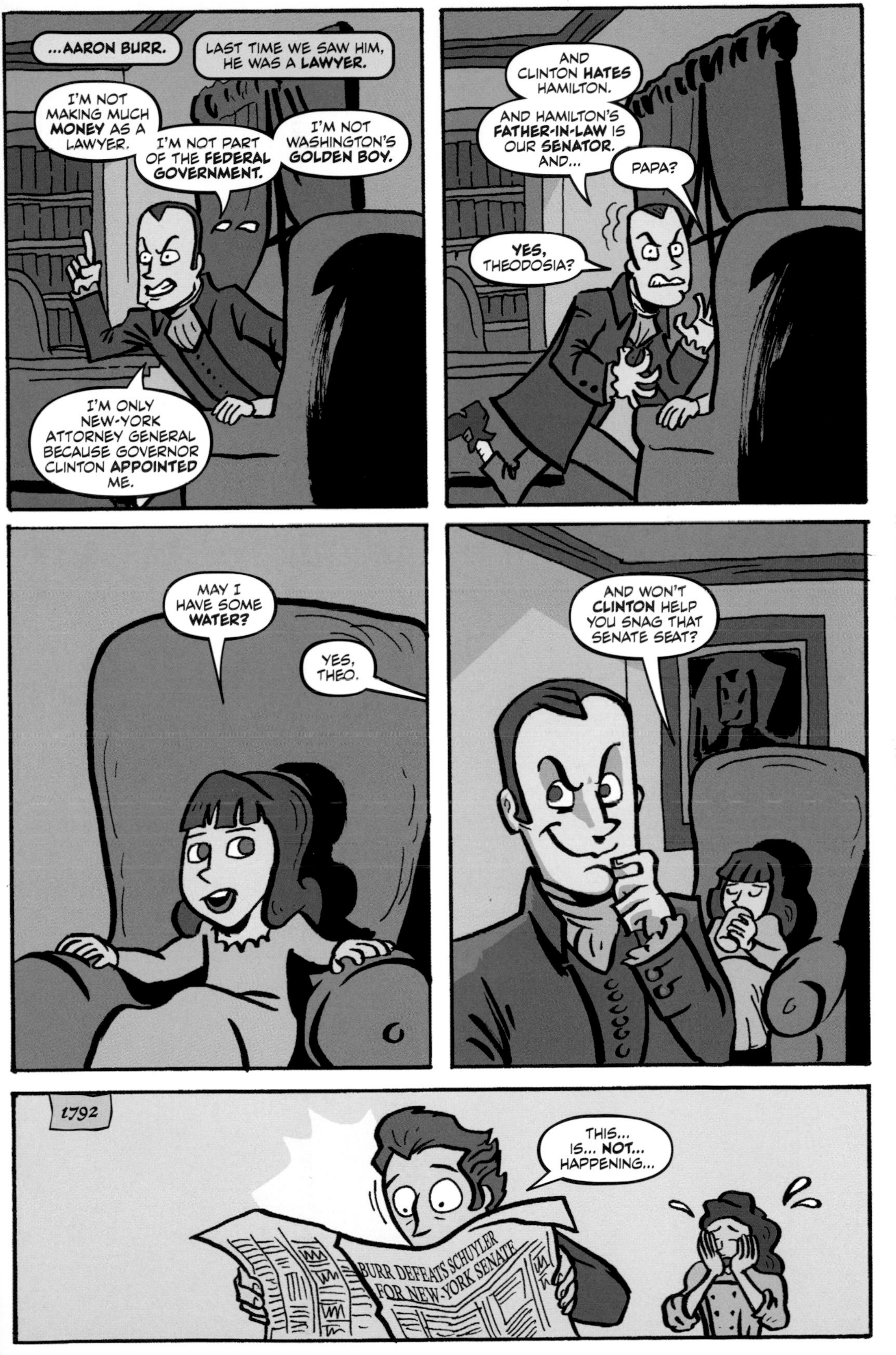
...AARON BURR.
LAST TIME WE SAW HIM, HE WAS A LAWYER.
I'M NOT MAKING MUCH MONEY AS A LAWYER.
I'M NOT PART OF THE FEDERAL GOVERNMENT.
I'M NOT WASHINGTON'S GOLDEN BOY.
I'M ONLY NEW-YORK ATTORNEY GENERAL BECAUSE GOVERNOR CLINTON APPOINTED ME.
AND CLINTON HATES HAMILTON.
AND HAMILTON'S FATHER-IN-LAW IS OUR SENATOR. AND...
PAPA?
YES, THEODOSIA?
MAY I HAVE SOME WATER?
YES, THEO.
AND WON'T CLINTON HELP YOU SNAG THAT SENATE SEAT?
1792
THIS... IS... NOT... HAPPENING...
BURR DEFEATS SCHUYLER FOR NEW-YORK SENATE

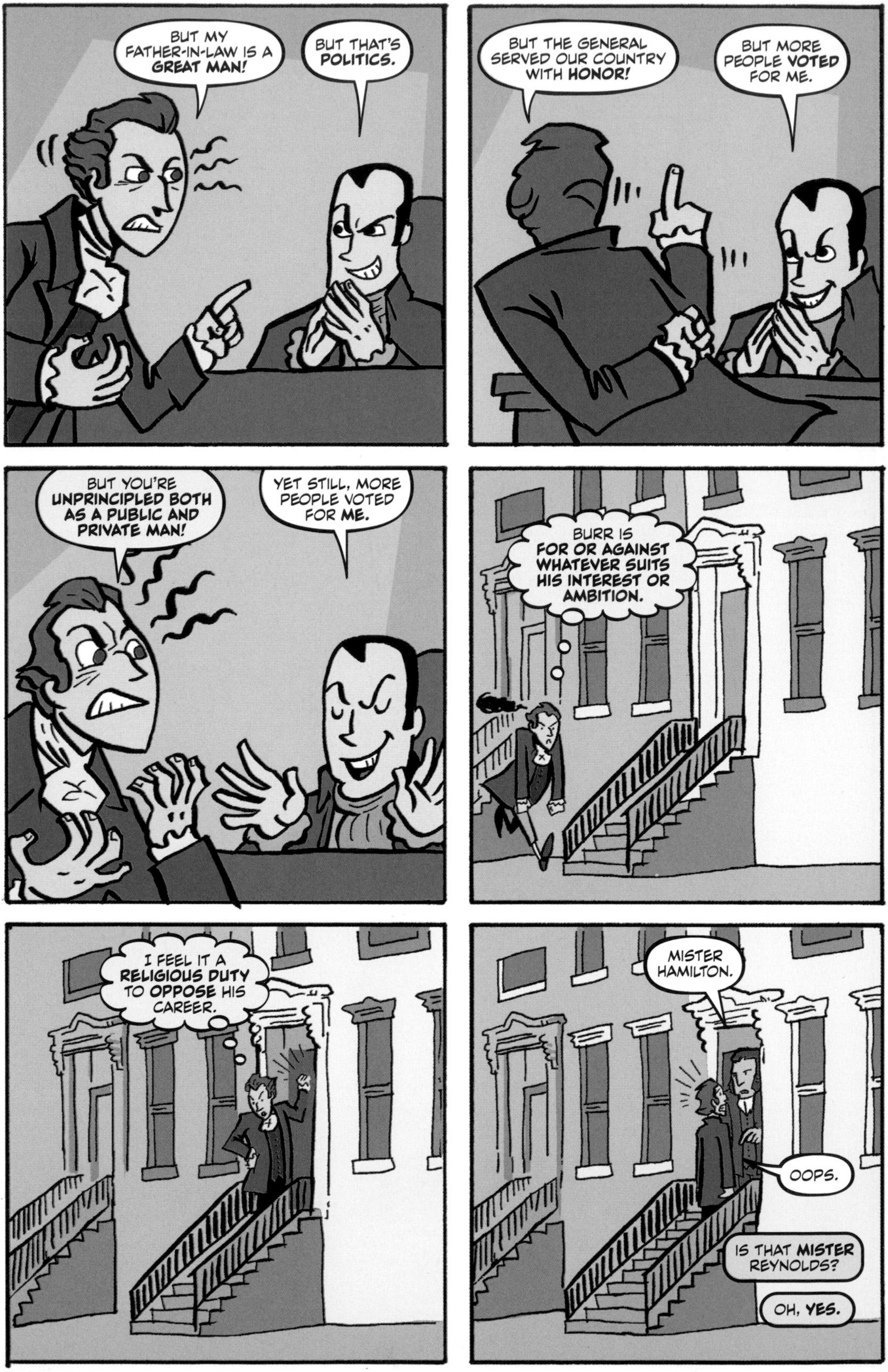
BUT MY FATHER-IN-LAW IS A **GREAT MAN!**
BUT THAT'S **POLITICS.**
BUT THE GENERAL SERVED OUR COUNTRY WITH **HONOR!**
BUT MORE PEOPLE **VOTED** FOR ME.
BUT YOU'RE **UNPRINCIPLED BOTH AS A PUBLIC AND PRIVATE MAN!**
YET STILL, MORE PEOPLE VOTED FOR **ME.**
BURR IS **FOR OR AGAINST WHATEVER SUITS HIS INTEREST OR AMBITION.**
I FEEL IT A **RELIGIOUS DUTY** TO **OPPOSE** HIS CAREER.
MISTER HAMILTON.
OOPS.
IS THAT **MISTER** REYNOLDS?
OH, **YES.**

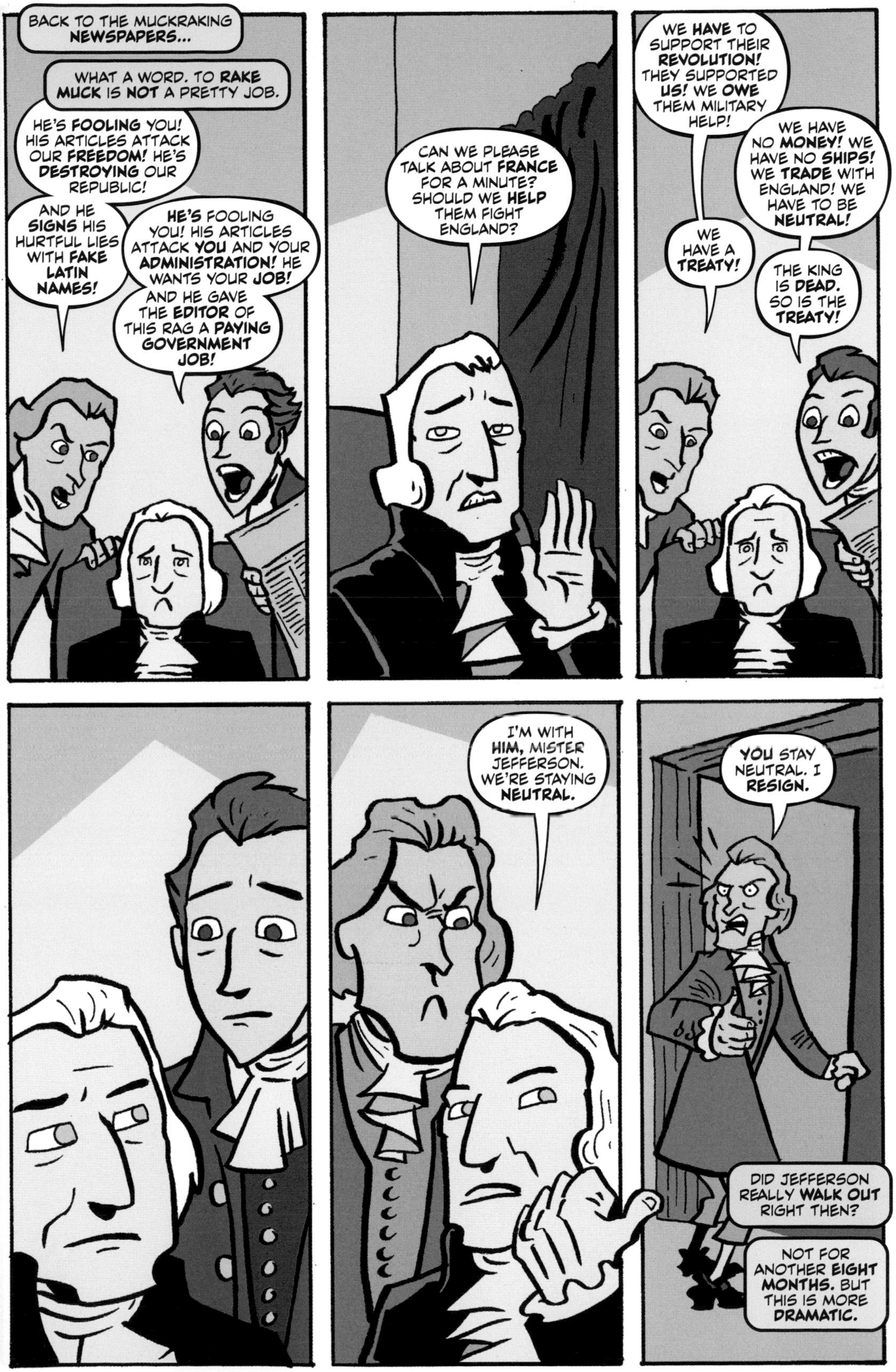
BACK TO THE MUCKRAKING **NEWSPAPERS...**
WHAT A WORD. TO **RAKE MUCK** IS **NOT** A PRETTY JOB.
HE'S **FOOLING** YOU! HIS ARTICLES ATTACK OUR **FREEDOM!** HE'S **DESTROYING** OUR REPUBLIC!
AND HE **SIGNS** HIS HURTFUL LIES WITH **FAKE LATIN NAMES!**
HE'S FOOLING YOU! HIS ARTICLES ATTACK **YOU** AND YOUR **ADMINISTRATION!** HE WANTS YOUR **JOB!**
AND HE GAVE THE **EDITOR** OF THIS RAG A **PAYING GOVERNMENT JOB!**
CAN WE PLEASE TALK ABOUT **FRANCE** FOR A MINUTE? SHOULD WE **HELP** THEM FIGHT ENGLAND?
WE **HAVE** TO SUPPORT THEIR **REVOLUTION!** THEY SUPPORTED **US!** WE **OWE** THEM MILITARY HELP!
WE HAVE NO **MONEY!** WE HAVE NO **SHIPS!** WE **TRADE** WITH ENGLAND! WE HAVE TO BE **NEUTRAL!**
WE HAVE A **TREATY!**
THE KING IS **DEAD.** SO IS THE **TREATY!**
I'M WITH **HIM,** MISTER JEFFERSON. WE'RE STAYING **NEUTRAL.**
YOU STAY NEUTRAL. I **RESIGN.**
DID JEFFERSON REALLY **WALK OUT** RIGHT THEN?
NOT FOR ANOTHER **EIGHT MONTHS.** BUT THIS IS MORE **DRAMATIC.**

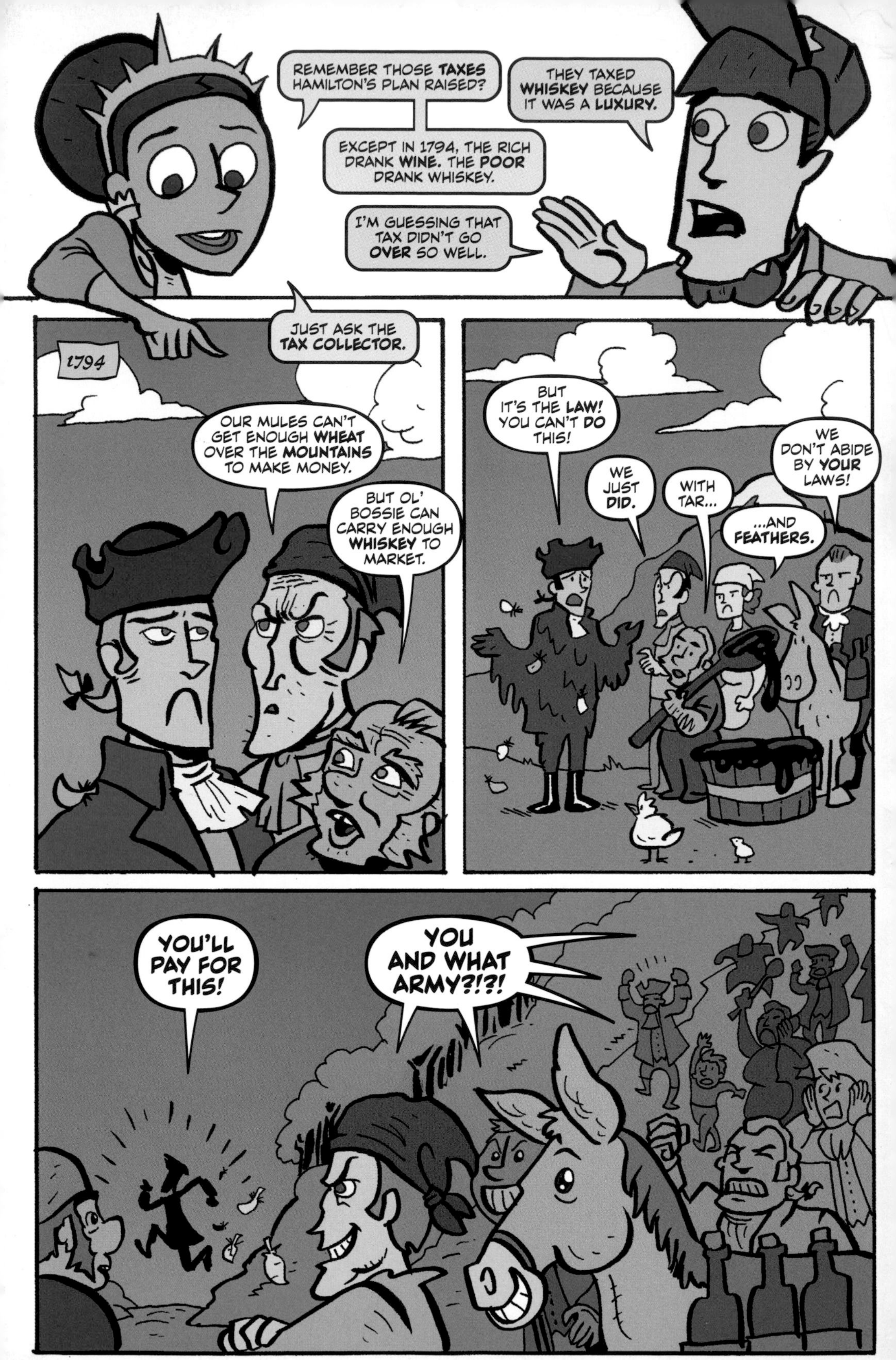

REMEMBER THOSE TAXES HAMILTON'S PLAN RAISED?
THEY TAXED WHISKEY BECAUSE IT WAS A LUXURY.
EXCEPT IN 1794, THE RICH DRANK WINE. THE POOR DRANK WHISKEY.
I'M GUESSING THAT TAX DIDN'T GO OVER SO WELL.
JUST ASK THE TAX COLLECTOR.
1794
OUR MULES CAN'T GET ENOUGH WHEAT OVER THE MOUNTAINS TO MAKE MONEY.
BUT OL' BOSSIE CAN CARRY ENOUGH WHISKEY TO MARKET.
BUT IT'S THE LAW! YOU CAN'T DO THIS!
WE JUST DID.
WITH TAR...
...AND FEATHERS.
WE DON'T ABIDE BY YOUR LAWS!
YOU'LL PAY FOR THIS!
YOU AND WHAT ARMY?!?!

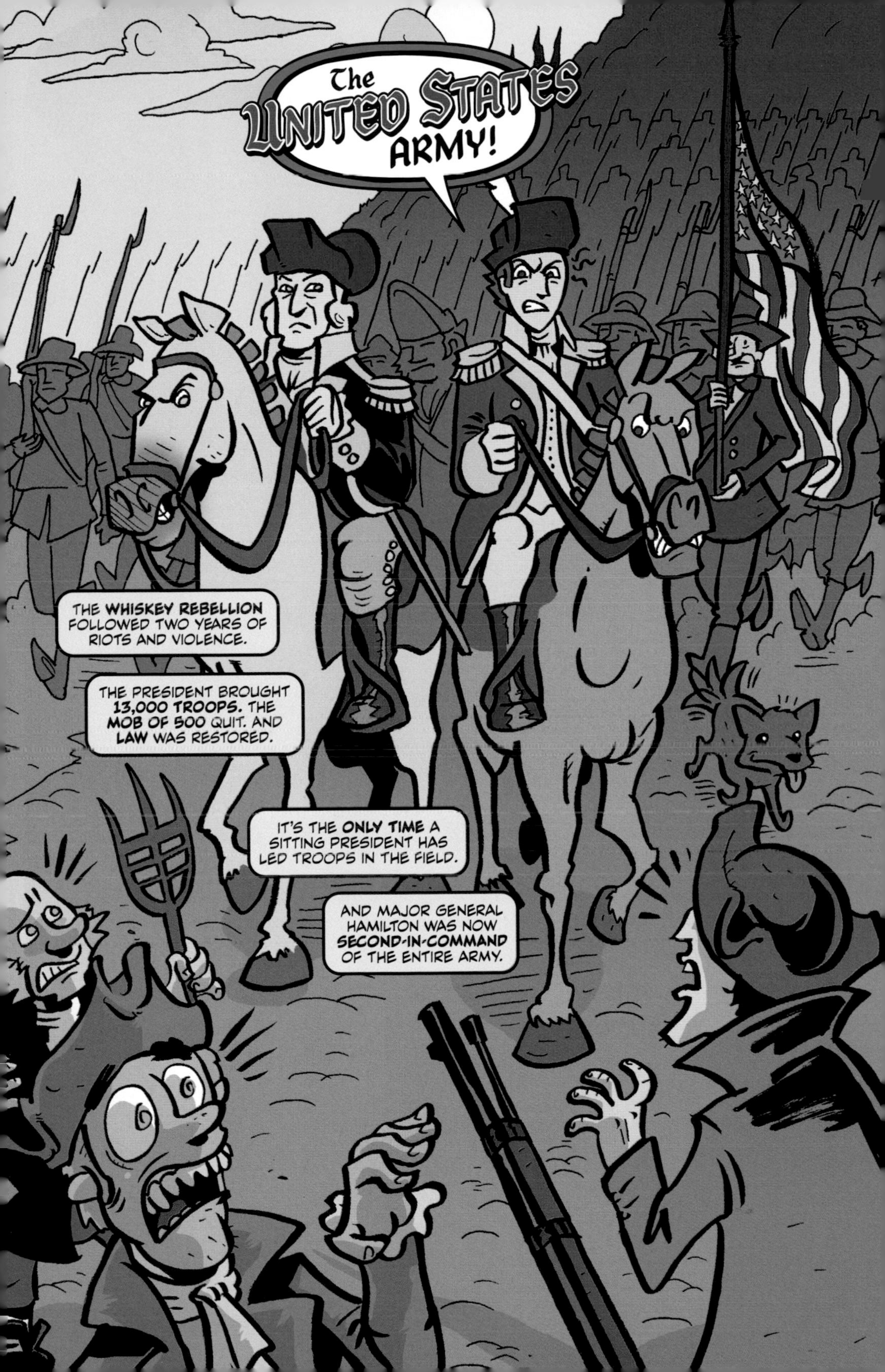

The UNITED STATES ARMY!
THE WHISKEY REBELLION FOLLOWED TWO YEARS OF RIOTS AND VIOLENCE.
THE PRESIDENT BROUGHT 13,000 TROOPS. THE MOB OF 500 QUIT. AND LAW WAS RESTORED.
IT'S THE ONLY TIME A SITTING PRESIDENT HAS LED TROOPS IN THE FIELD.
AND MAJOR GENERAL HAMILTON WAS NOW SECOND-IN-COMMAND OF THE ENTIRE ARMY.

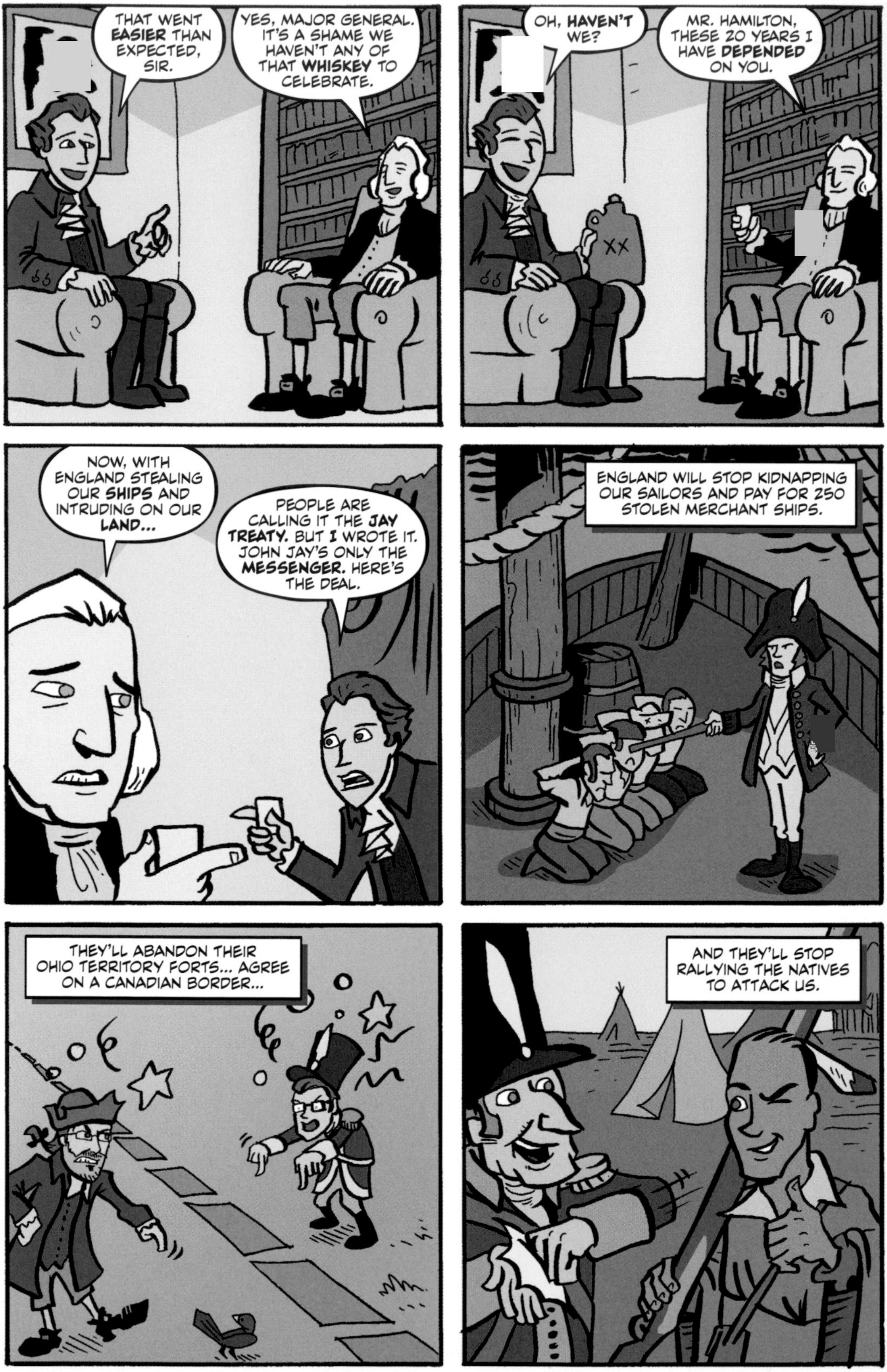
THAT WENT EASIER THAN EXPECTED, SIR.
YES, MAJOR GENERAL. IT'S A SHAME WE HAVEN'T ANY OF THAT WHISKEY TO CELEBRATE.
OH, HAVEN'T WE?
MR. HAMILTON, THESE 20 YEARS I HAVE DEPENDED ON YOU.
XX
NOW, WITH ENGLAND STEALING OUR SHIPS AND INTRUDING ON OUR LAND...
PEOPLE ARE CALLING IT THE JAY TREATY. BUT I WROTE IT. JOHN JAY'S ONLY THE MESSENGER. HERE'S THE DEAL.
ENGLAND WILL STOP KIDNAPPING OUR SAILORS AND PAY FOR 250 STOLEN MERCHANT SHIPS.
THEY'LL ABANDON THEIR OHIO TERRITORY FORTS... AGREE ON A CANADIAN BORDER...
AND THEY'LL STOP RALLYING THE NATIVES TO ATTACK US.

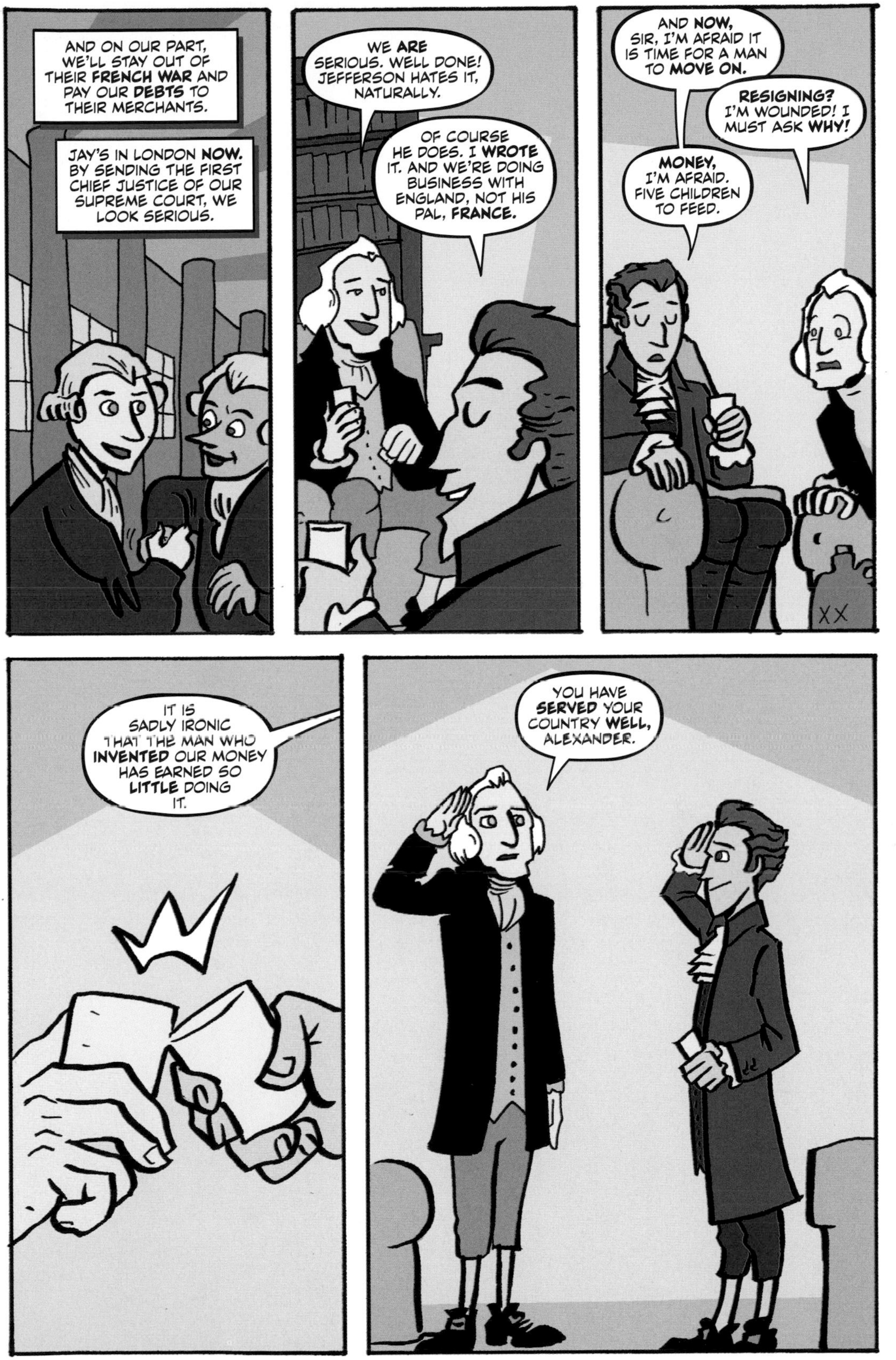
AND ON OUR PART, WE'LL STAY OUT OF THEIR **FRENCH WAR** AND PAY OUR **DEBTS** TO THEIR MERCHANTS.
JAY'S IN LONDON **NOW.** BY SENDING THE FIRST CHIEF JUSTICE OF OUR SUPREME COURT, WE LOOK SERIOUS.
WE **ARE** SERIOUS. WELL DONE! JEFFERSON HATES IT, NATURALLY.
OF COURSE HE DOES. I **WROTE** IT. AND WE'RE DOING BUSINESS WITH ENGLAND, NOT HIS PAL, **FRANCE.**
AND **NOW,** SIR, I'M AFRAID IT IS TIME FOR A MAN TO **MOVE ON.**
RESIGNING? I'M WOUNDED! I MUST ASK **WHY!**
MONEY, I'M AFRAID. FIVE CHILDREN TO FEED.
IT IS SADLY IRONIC THAT THE MAN WHO **INVENTED** OUR MONEY HAS EARNED SO **LITTLE** DOING IT.
YOU HAVE **SERVED** YOUR COUNTRY **WELL,** ALEXANDER.

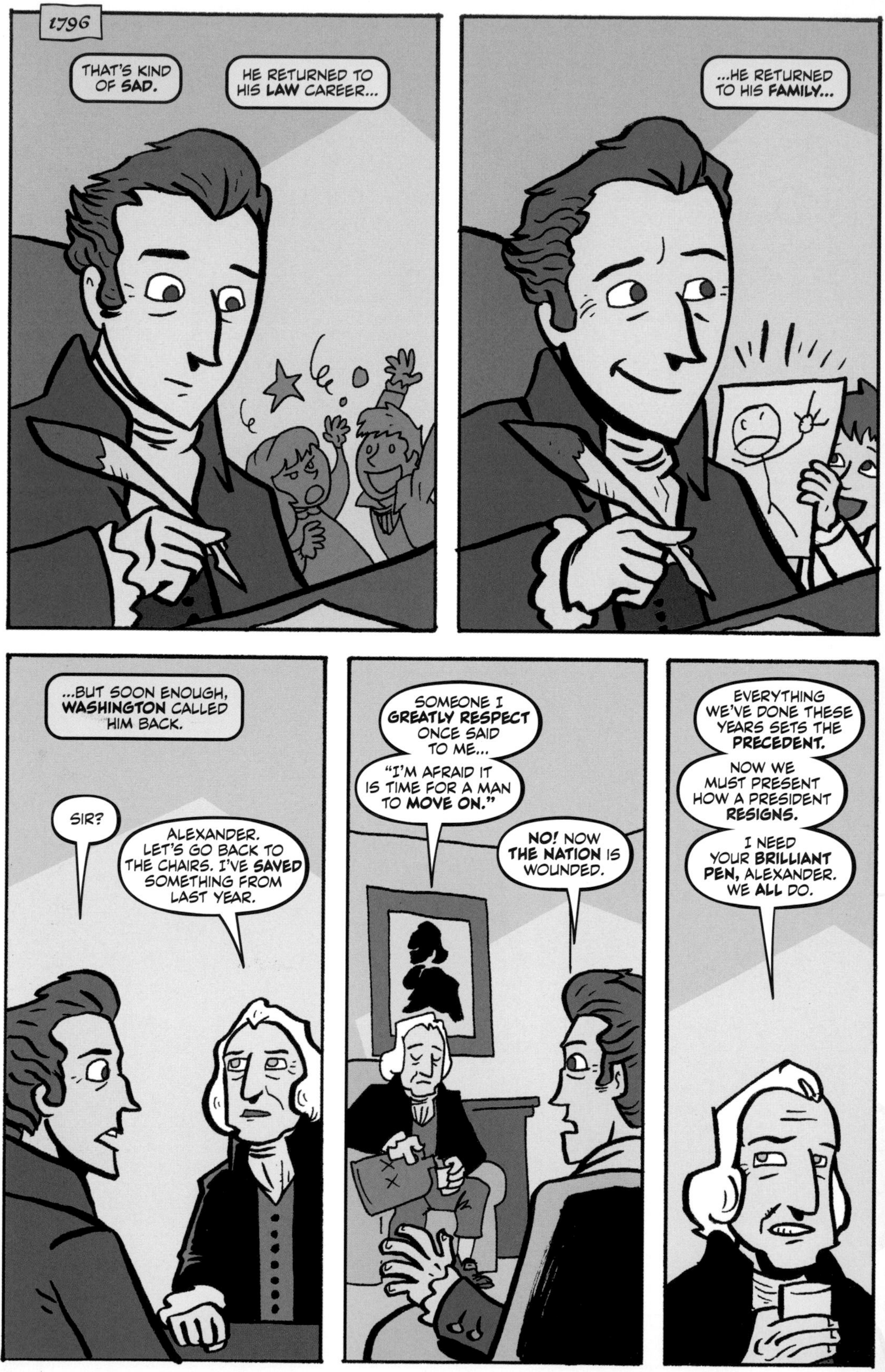
1796
THAT'S KIND OF SAD.
HE RETURNED TO HIS LAW CAREER...
...HE RETURNED TO HIS FAMILY...
...BUT SOON ENOUGH, WASHINGTON CALLED HIM BACK.
SIR?
ALEXANDER. LET'S GO BACK TO THE CHAIRS. I'VE SAVED SOMETHING FROM LAST YEAR.
SOMEONE I GREATLY RESPECT ONCE SAID TO ME...
"I'M AFRAID IT IS TIME FOR A MAN TO MOVE ON."
NO! NOW THE NATION IS WOUNDED.
EVERYTHING WE'VE DONE THESE YEARS SETS THE PRECEDENT.
NOW WE MUST PRESENT HOW A PRESIDENT RESIGNS.
I NEED YOUR BRILLIANT PEN, ALEXANDER. WE ALL DO.

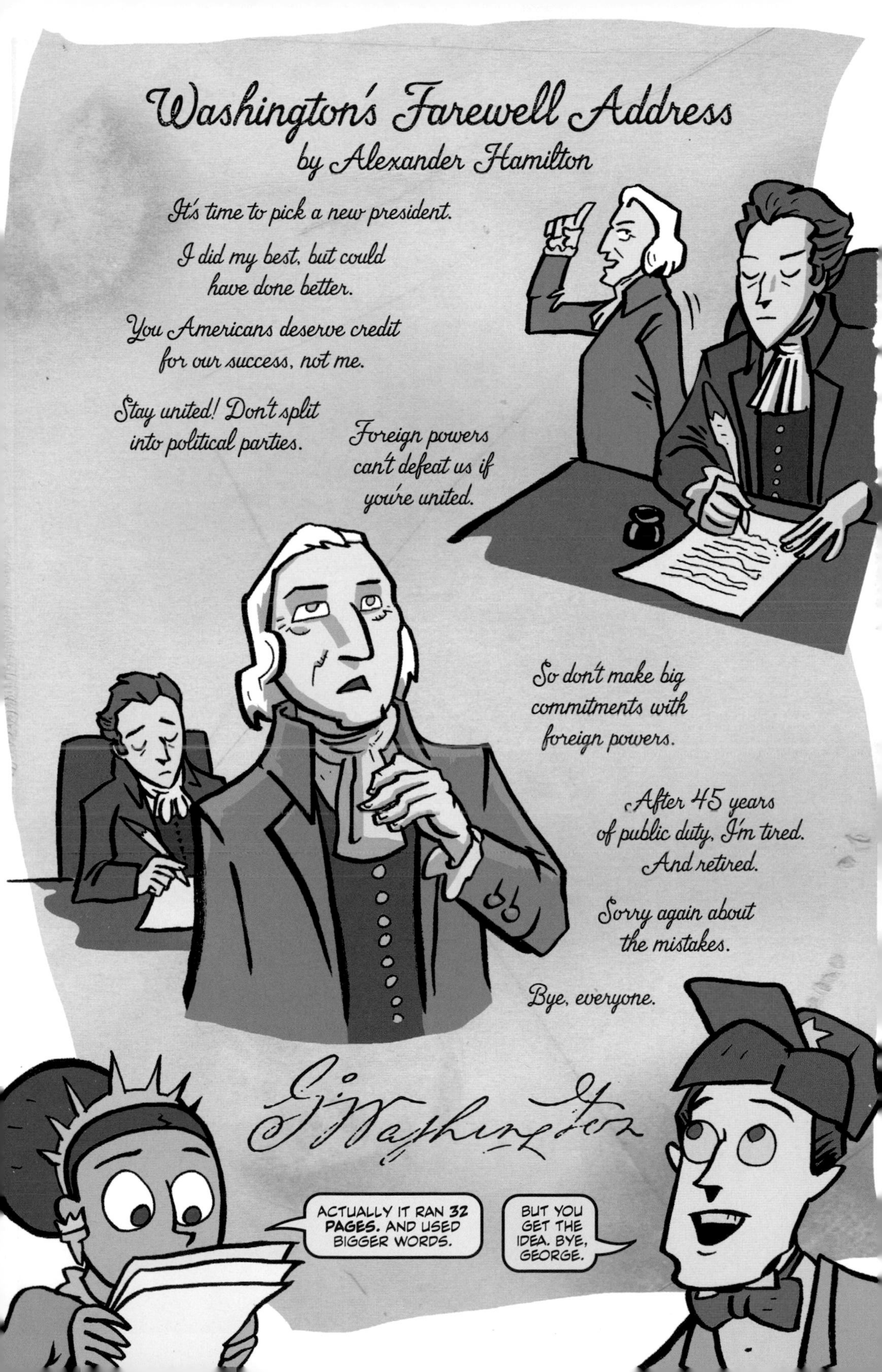
Washington's Farewell Address
by Alexander Hamilton
It's time to pick a new president.
I did my best, but could have done better.
You Americans deserve credit for our success, not me.
Stay united! Don't split into political parties.
Foreign powers can't defeat us if you're united.
So don't make big commitments with foreign powers.
After 45 years of public duty, I'm tired. And retired.
Sorry again about the mistakes.
Bye, everyone.
G. Washington
ACTUALLY IT RAN 32 PAGES. AND USED BIGGER WORDS.
BUT YOU GET THE IDEA. BYE, GEORGE.

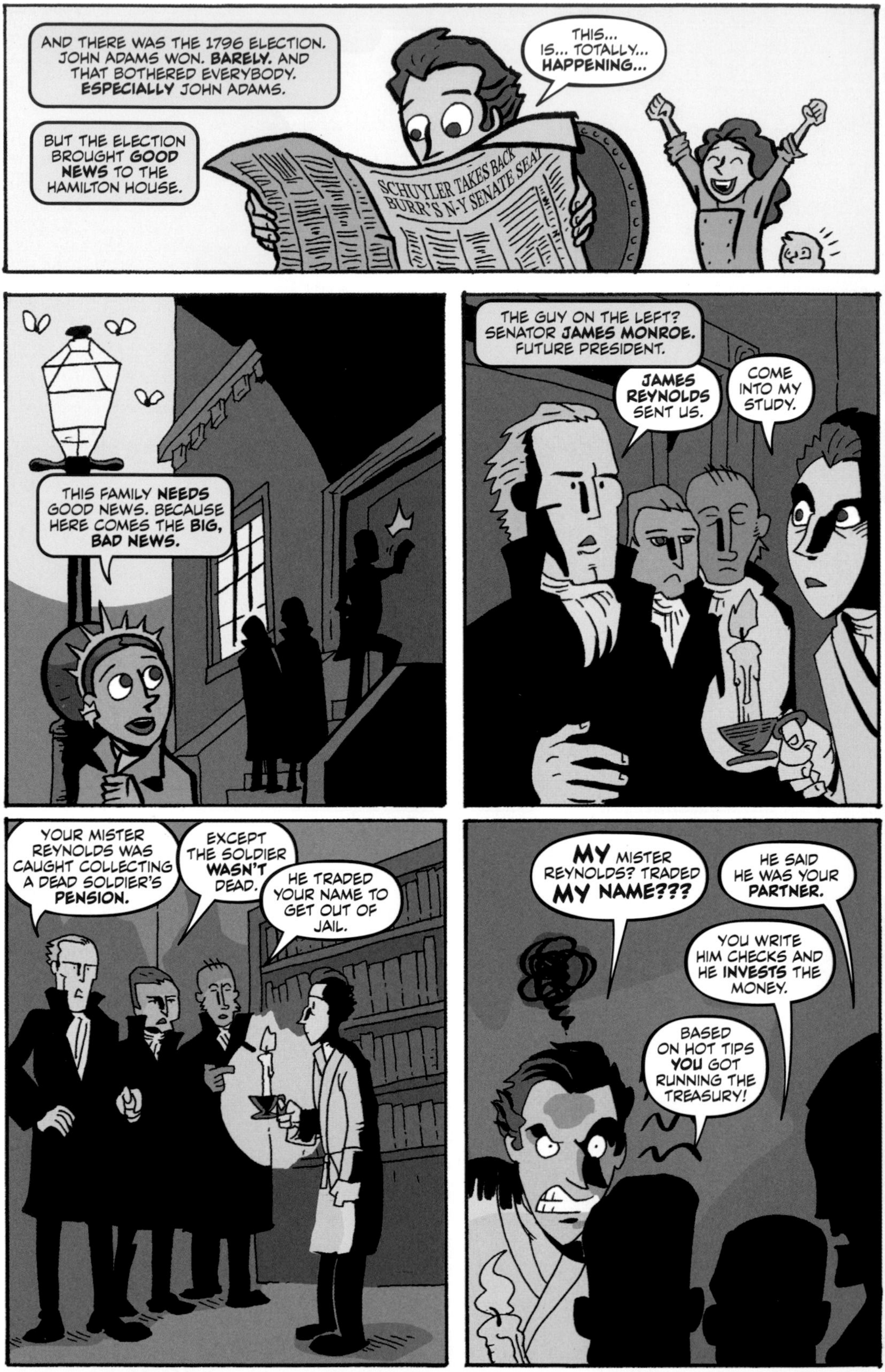

AND THERE WAS THE 1796 ELECTION. JOHN ADAMS WON. **BARELY.** AND THAT BOTHERED EVERYBODY. **ESPECIALLY** JOHN ADAMS.
BUT THE ELECTION BROUGHT **GOOD NEWS** TO THE HAMILTON HOUSE.
SCHUYLER TAKES BACK BURR'S N-Y SENATE SEAT
THIS... IS... TOTALLY... **HAPPENING...**
THIS FAMILY **NEEDS** GOOD NEWS. BECAUSE HERE COMES THE **BIG, BAD NEWS.**
THE GUY ON THE LEFT? SENATOR **JAMES MONROE.** FUTURE PRESIDENT.
JAMES REYNOLDS SENT US.
COME INTO MY STUDY.
YOUR MISTER REYNOLDS WAS CAUGHT COLLECTING A DEAD SOLDIER'S **PENSION.**
EXCEPT THE SOLDIER **WASN'T** DEAD.
HE TRADED YOUR NAME TO GET OUT OF JAIL.
MY MISTER REYNOLDS? TRADED **MY NAME???**
HE SAID HE WAS YOUR **PARTNER.**
YOU WRITE HIM CHECKS AND HE **INVESTS** THE MONEY.
BASED ON HOT TIPS **YOU** GOT RUNNING THE TREASURY!

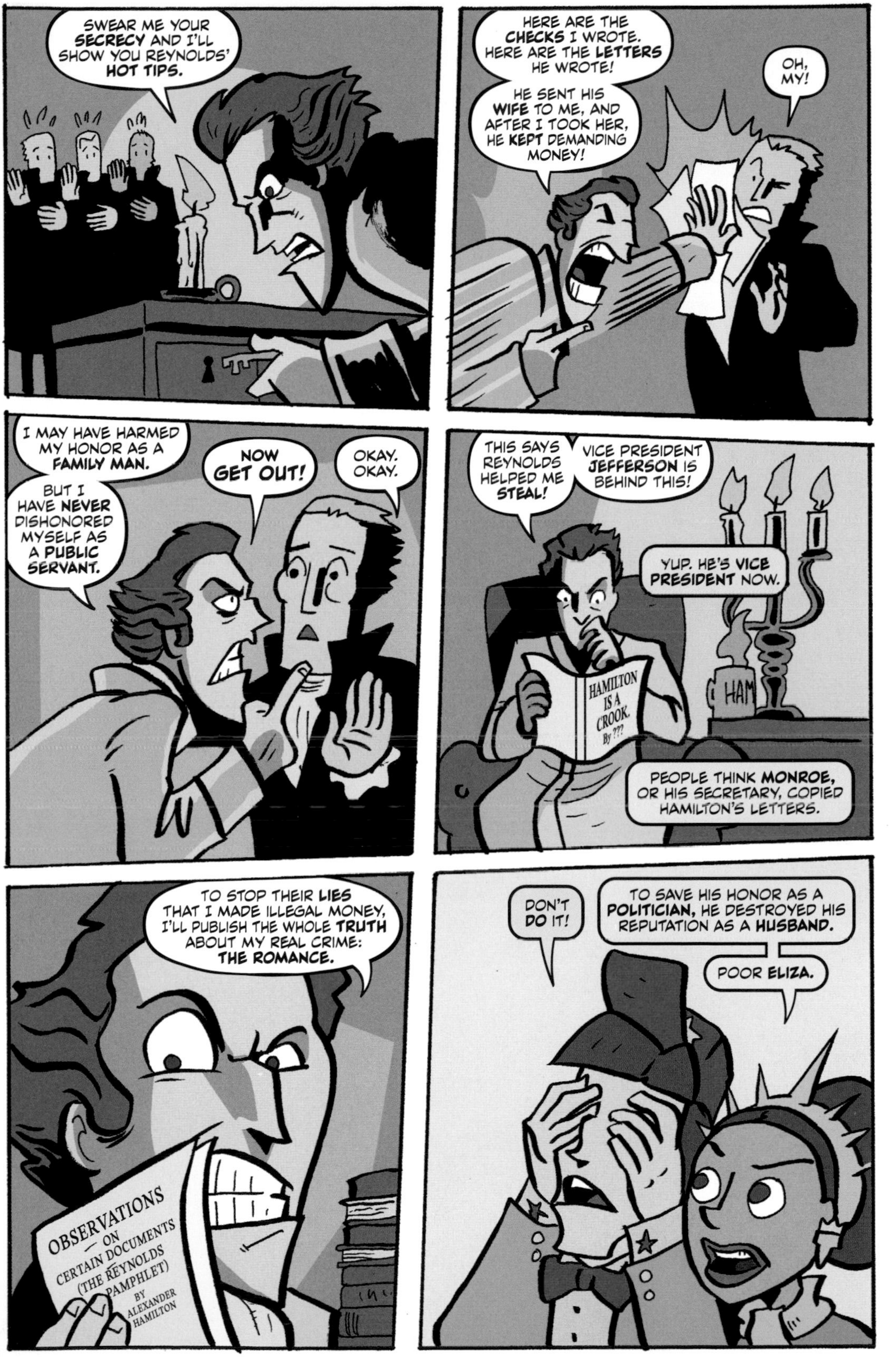
SWEAR ME YOUR SECRECY AND I'LL SHOW YOU REYNOLDS' HOT TIPS.
HERE ARE THE CHECKS I WROTE. HERE ARE THE LETTERS HE WROTE!
HE SENT HIS WIFE TO ME, AND AFTER I TOOK HER, HE KEPT DEMANDING MONEY!
OH, MY!
I MAY HAVE HARMED MY HONOR AS A FAMILY MAN.
BUT I HAVE NEVER DISHONORED MYSELF AS A PUBLIC SERVANT.
NOW GET OUT!
OKAY. OKAY.
THIS SAYS REYNOLDS HELPED ME STEAL!
VICE PRESIDENT JEFFERSON IS BEHIND THIS!
HAMILTON IS A CROOK. By ???
YUP. HE'S VICE PRESIDENT NOW.
HAM
PEOPLE THINK MONROE, OR HIS SECRETARY, COPIED HAMILTON'S LETTERS.
TO STOP THEIR LIES THAT I MADE ILLEGAL MONEY, I'LL PUBLISH THE WHOLE TRUTH ABOUT MY REAL CRIME: THE ROMANCE.
OBSERVATIONS ON CERTAIN DOCUMENTS (THE REYNOLDS PAMPHLET) BY ALEXANDER HAMILTON
DON'T DO IT!
TO SAVE HIS HONOR AS A POLITICIAN, HE DESTROYED HIS REPUTATION AS A HUSBAND.
POOR ELIZA.

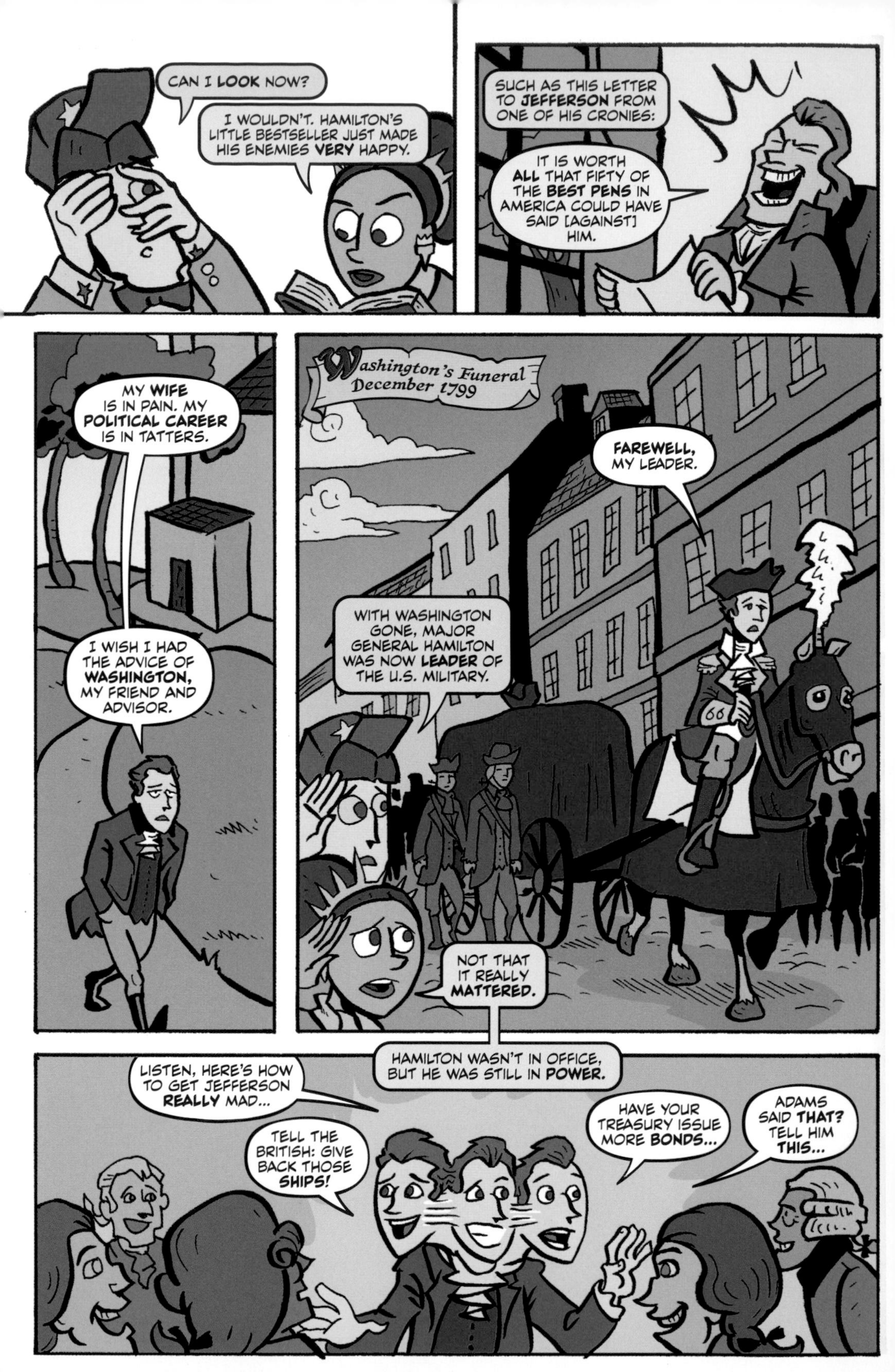
CAN I LOOK NOW?
I WOULDN'T. HAMILTON'S LITTLE BESTSELLER JUST MADE HIS ENEMIES VERY HAPPY.
SUCH AS THIS LETTER TO JEFFERSON FROM ONE OF HIS CRONIES:
IT IS WORTH ALL THAT FIFTY OF THE BEST PENS IN AMERICA COULD HAVE SAID [AGAINST] HIM.
MY WIFE IS IN PAIN. MY POLITICAL CAREER IS IN TATTERS.
I WISH I HAD THE ADVICE OF WASHINGTON, MY FRIEND AND ADVISOR.
Washington's Funeral December 1799
FAREWELL, MY LEADER.
WITH WASHINGTON GONE, MAJOR GENERAL HAMILTON WAS NOW LEADER OF THE U.S. MILITARY.
NOT THAT IT REALLY MATTERED.
HAMILTON WASN'T IN OFFICE, BUT HE WAS STILL IN POWER.
LISTEN, HERE'S HOW TO GET JEFFERSON REALLY MAD...
TELL THE BRITISH: GIVE BACK THOSE SHIPS!
HAVE YOUR TREASURY ISSUE MORE BONDS...
ADAMS SAID THAT? TELL HIM THIS...

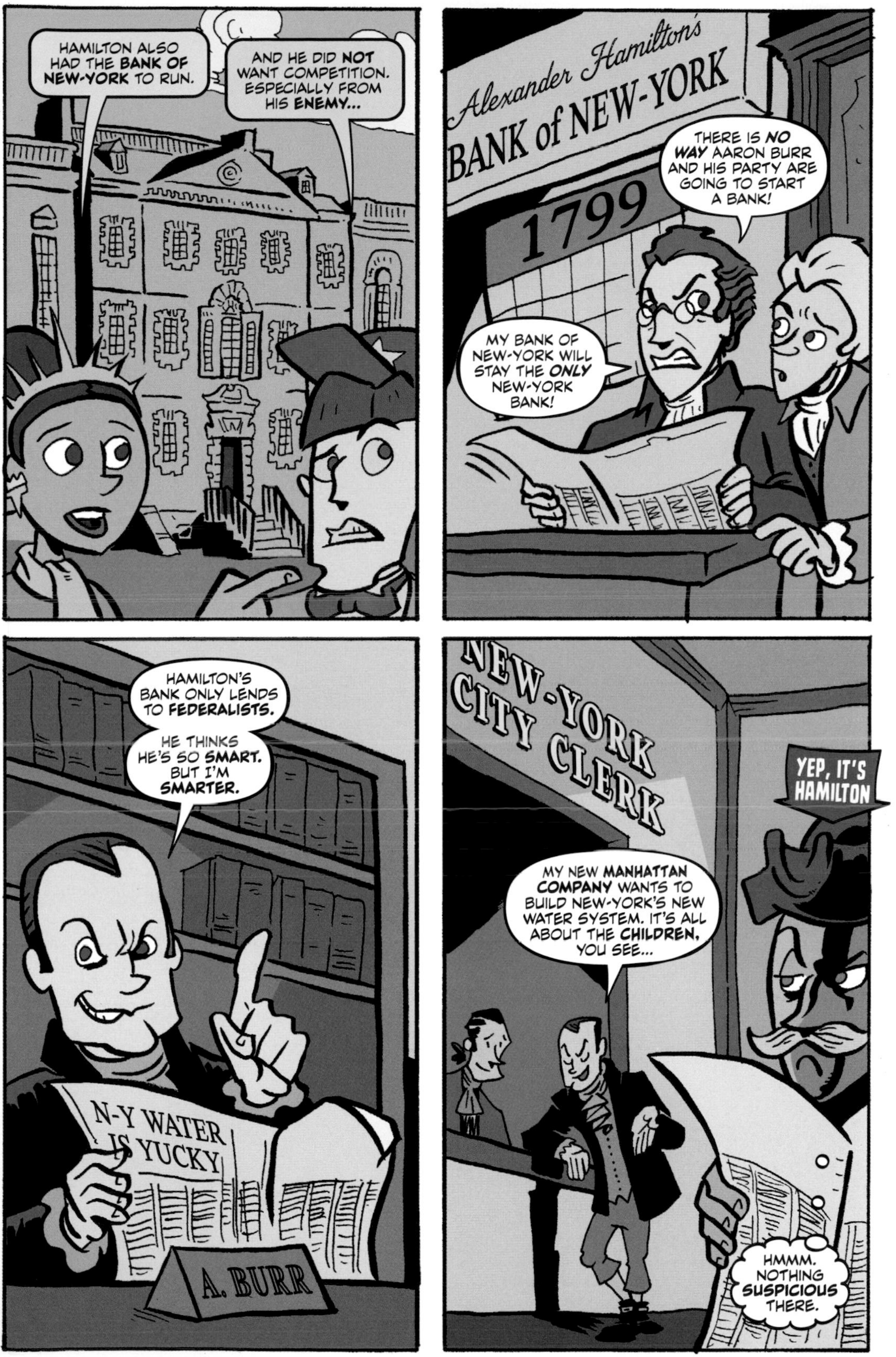
HAMILTON ALSO HAD THE BANK OF NEW-YORK TO RUN.
AND HE DID NOT WANT COMPETITION. ESPECIALLY FROM HIS ENEMY...
Alexander Hamilton's BANK of NEW-YORK
1799
THERE IS NO WAY AARON BURR AND HIS PARTY ARE GOING TO START A BANK!
MY BANK OF NEW-YORK WILL STAY THE ONLY NEW-YORK BANK!
HAMILTON'S BANK ONLY LENDS TO FEDERALISTS.
HE THINKS HE'S SO SMART. BUT I'M SMARTER.
N-Y WATER IS YUCKY
A. BURR
NEW-YORK CITY CLERK
YEP, IT'S HAMILTON
MY NEW MANHATTAN COMPANY WANTS TO BUILD NEW-YORK'S NEW WATER SYSTEM. IT'S ALL ABOUT THE CHILDREN, YOU SEE...
HMMM. NOTHING SUSPICIOUS THERE.

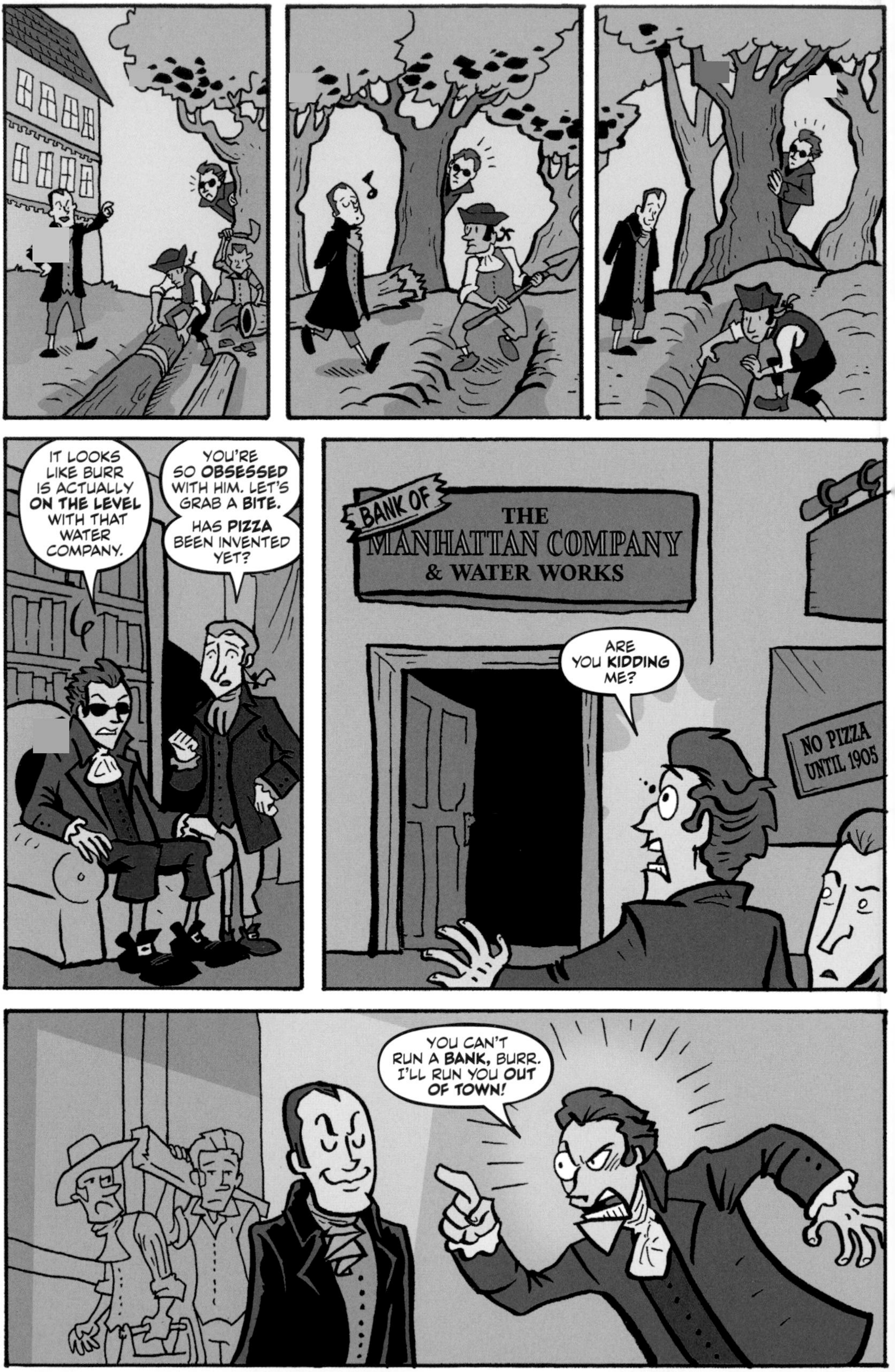
IT LOOKS LIKE BURR IS ACTUALLY ON THE LEVEL WITH THAT WATER COMPANY.
YOU'RE SO OBSESSED WITH HIM. LET'S GRAB A BITE.
HAS PIZZA BEEN INVENTED YET?
BANK OF
THE MANHATTAN COMPANY & WATER WORKS
ARE YOU KIDDING ME?
NO PIZZA UNTIL 1905
YOU CAN'T RUN A BANK, BURR. I'LL RUN YOU OUT OF TOWN!

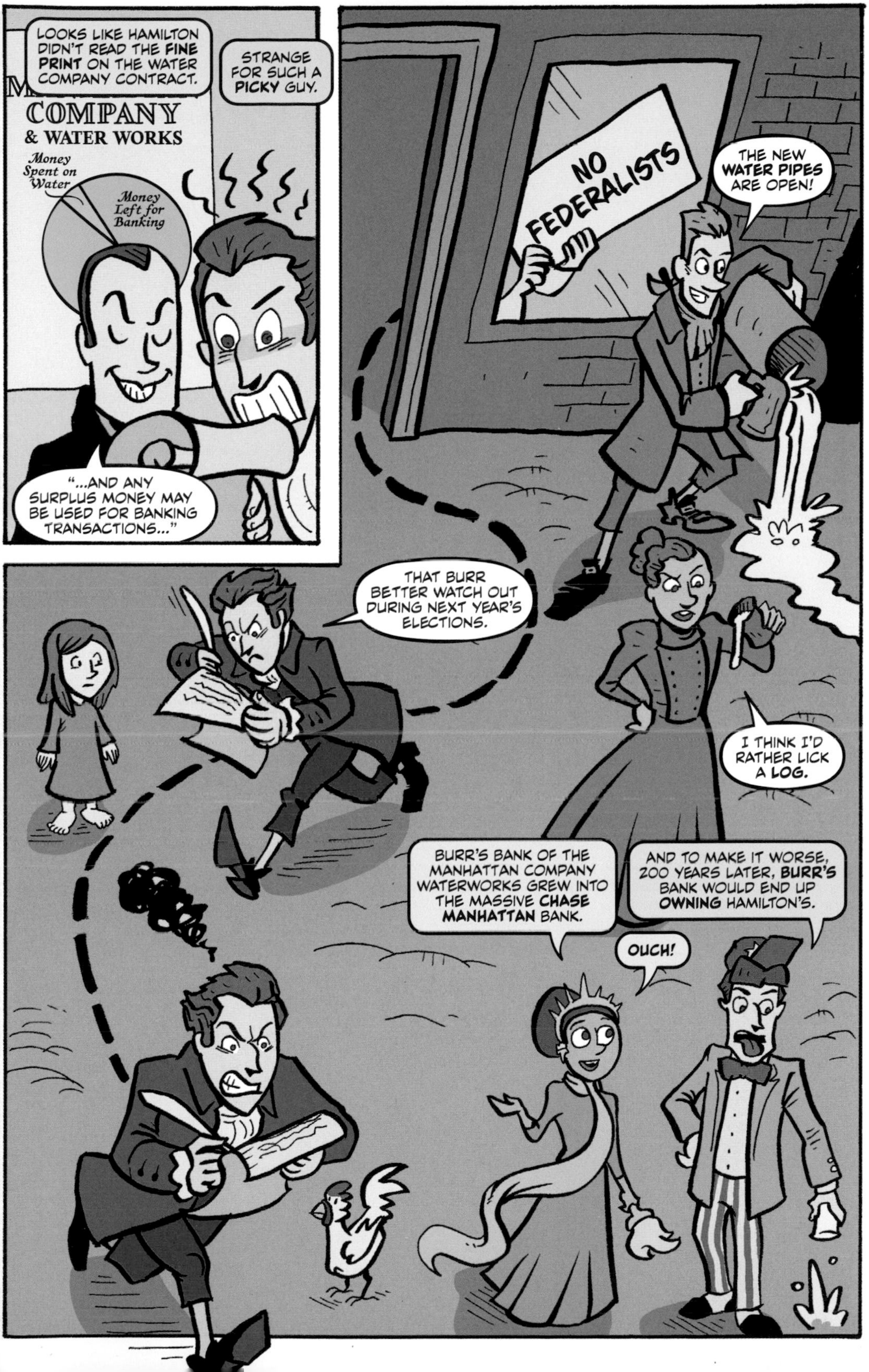

LOOKS LIKE HAMILTON DIDN'T READ THE **FINE PRINT** ON THE WATER COMPANY CONTRACT.
STRANGE FOR SUCH A **PICKY** GUY.
COMPANY & WATER WORKS
Money Spent on Water
Money Left for Banking
"...AND ANY SURPLUS MONEY MAY BE USED FOR BANKING TRANSACTIONS..."
NO FEDERALISTS
THE NEW **WATER PIPES** ARE OPEN!
THAT BURR BETTER WATCH OUT DURING NEXT YEAR'S ELECTIONS.
I THINK I'D RATHER LICK A **LOG.**
BURR'S BANK OF THE MANHATTAN COMPANY WATERWORKS GREW INTO THE MASSIVE **CHASE MANHATTAN** BANK.
AND TO MAKE IT WORSE, 200 YEARS LATER, **BURR'S** BANK WOULD END UP **OWNING** HAMILTON'S.
OUCH!

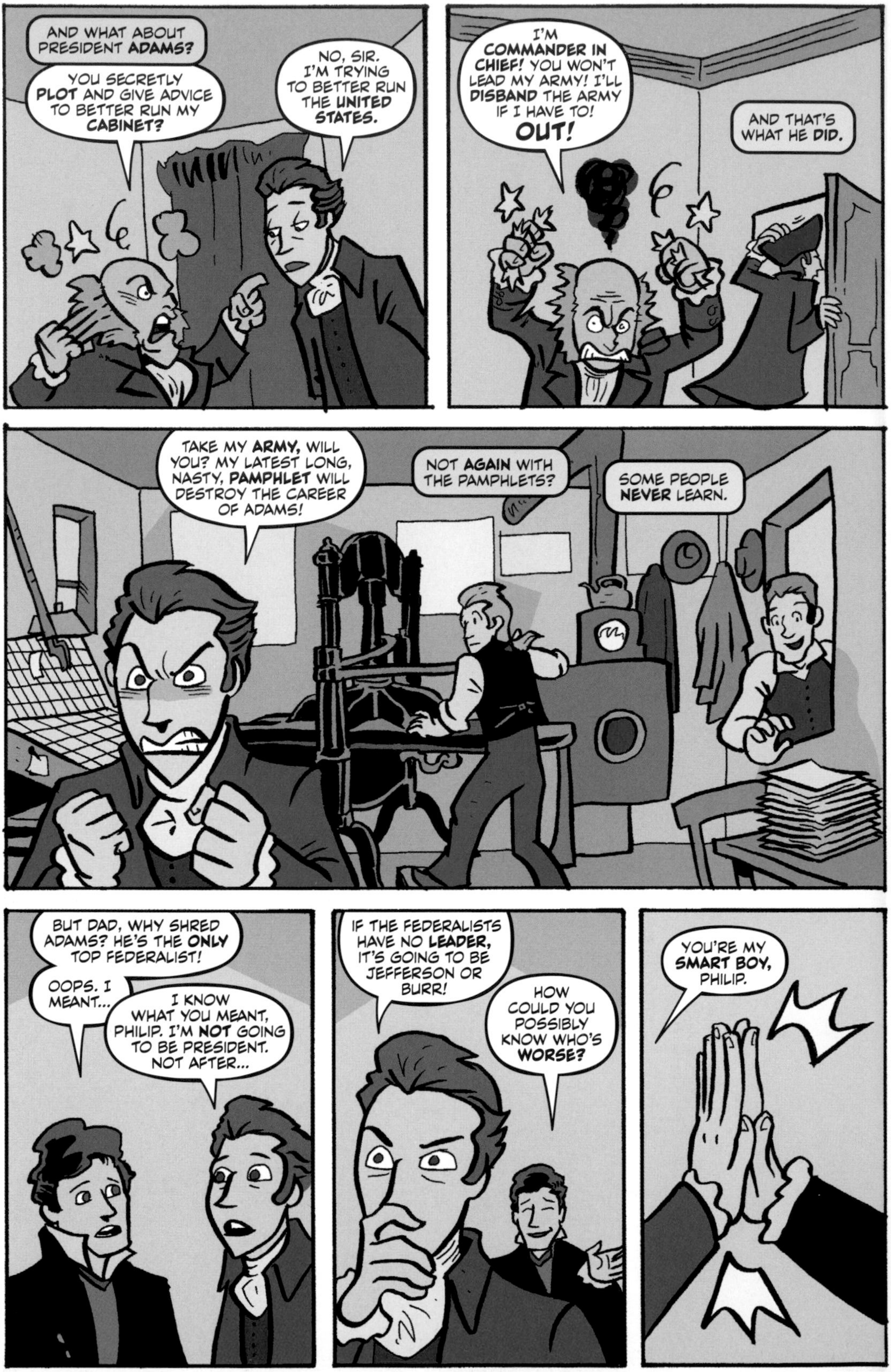
AND WHAT ABOUT PRESIDENT ADAMS?
YOU SECRETLY PLOT AND GIVE ADVICE TO BETTER RUN MY CABINET?
NO, SIR. I'M TRYING TO BETTER RUN THE UNITED STATES.
I'M COMMANDER IN CHIEF! YOU WON'T LEAD MY ARMY! I'LL DISBAND THE ARMY IF I HAVE TO! OUT!
AND THAT'S WHAT HE DID.
TAKE MY ARMY, WILL YOU? MY LATEST LONG, NASTY, PAMPHLET WILL DESTROY THE CAREER OF ADAMS!
NOT AGAIN WITH THE PAMPHLETS?
SOME PEOPLE NEVER LEARN.
BUT DAD, WHY SHRED ADAMS? HE'S THE ONLY TOP FEDERALIST!
OOPS. I MEANT...
I KNOW WHAT YOU MEANT, PHILIP. I'M NOT GOING TO BE PRESIDENT. NOT AFTER...
IF THE FEDERALISTS HAVE NO LEADER, IT'S GOING TO BE JEFFERSON OR BURR!
HOW COULD YOU POSSIBLY KNOW WHO'S WORSE?
YOU'RE MY SMART BOY, PHILIP.

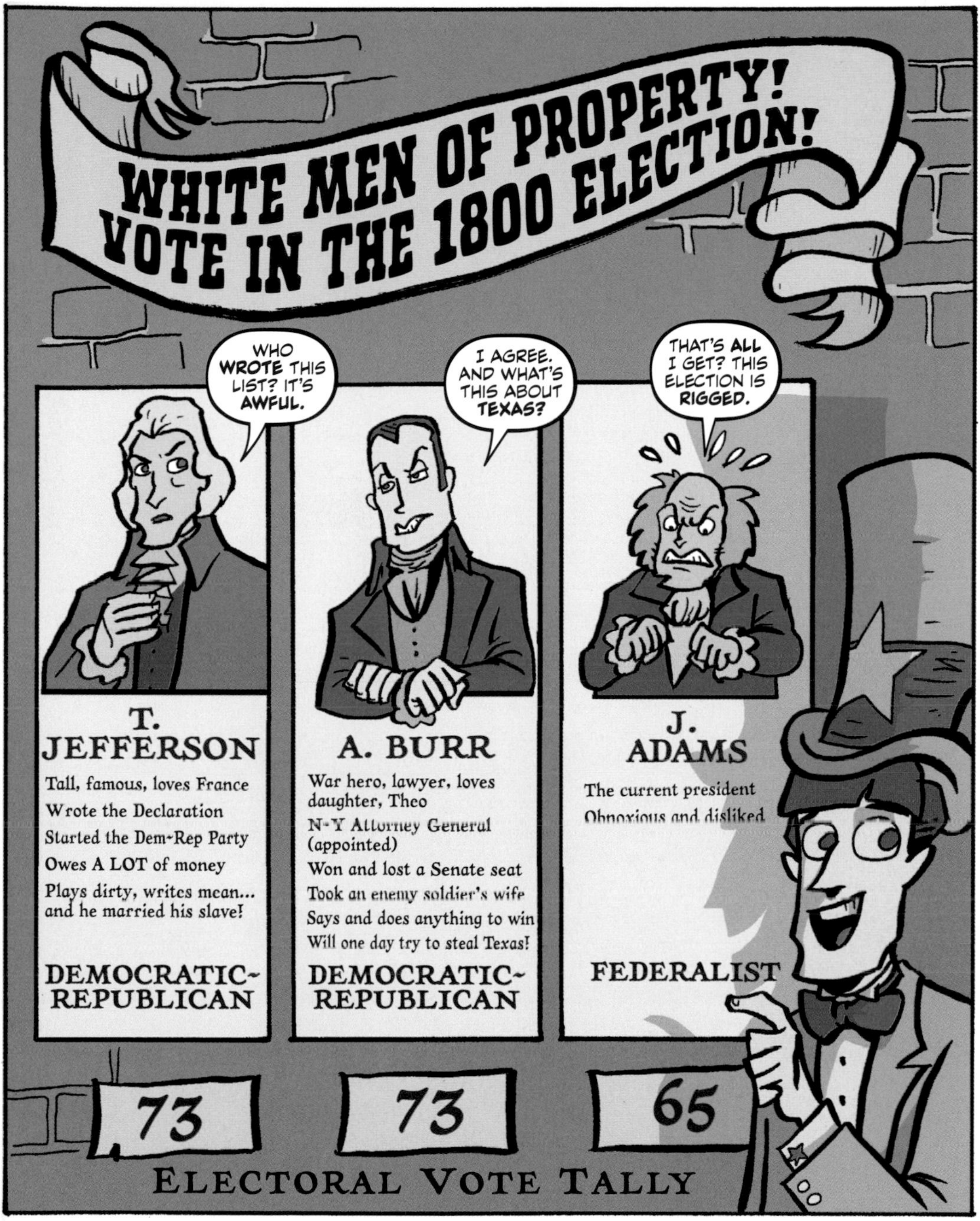
WHITE MEN OF PROPERTY! VOTE IN THE 1800 ELECTION!
WHO WROTE THIS LIST? IT'S AWFUL.
I AGREE. AND WHAT'S THIS ABOUT TEXAS?
THAT'S ALL I GET? THIS ELECTION IS RIGGED.
T. JEFFERSON
Tall, famous, loves France
Wrote the Declaration
Started the Dem-Rep Party
Owes A LOT of money
Plays dirty, writes mean... and he married his slave!
DEMOCRATIC-REPUBLICAN
A. BURR
War hero, lawyer, loves daughter, Theo
N-Y Attorney General (appointed)
Won and lost a Senate seat
Took an enemy soldier's wife
Says and does anything to win
Will one day try to steal Texas!
DEMOCRATIC-REPUBLICAN
J. ADAMS
The current president
Obnoxious and disliked
FEDERALIST
73
73
65
ELECTORAL VOTE TALLY

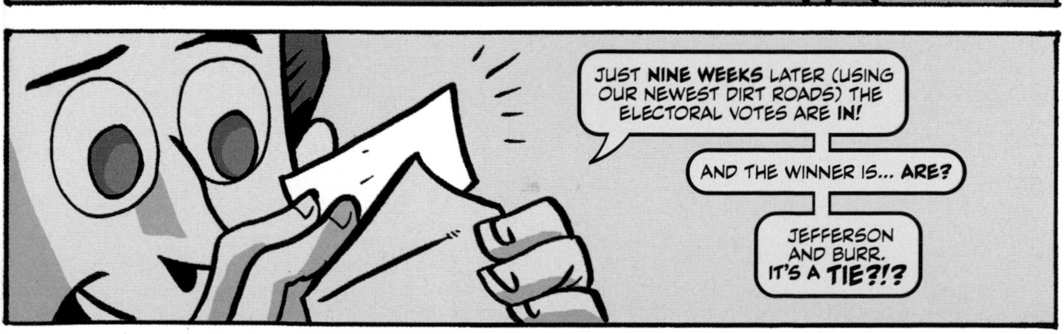
JUST NINE WEEKS LATER (USING OUR NEWEST DIRT ROADS) THE ELECTORAL VOTES ARE IN!
AND THE WINNER IS... ARE?
JEFFERSON AND BURR. IT'S A TIE?!?

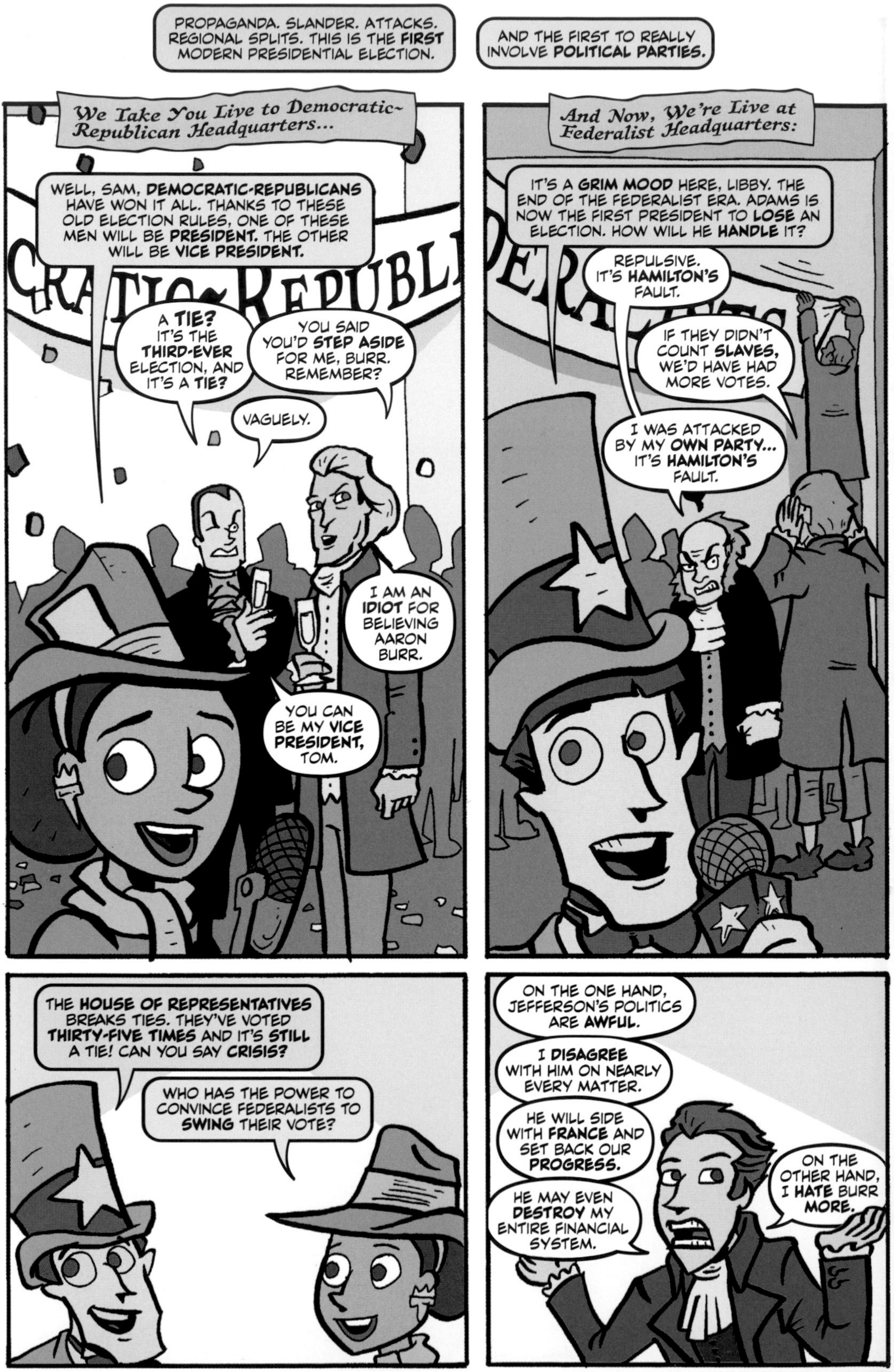
PROPAGANDA. SLANDER. ATTACKS. REGIONAL SPLITS. THIS IS THE FIRST MODERN PRESIDENTIAL ELECTION.
AND THE FIRST TO REALLY INVOLVE POLITICAL PARTIES.
We Take You Live to Democratic-Republican Headquarters...
WELL, SAM, DEMOCRATIC-REPUBLICANS HAVE WON IT ALL. THANKS TO THESE OLD ELECTION RULES, ONE OF THESE MEN WILL BE PRESIDENT. THE OTHER WILL BE VICE PRESIDENT.
A TIE? IT'S THE THIRD-EVER ELECTION, AND IT'S A TIE?
YOU SAID YOU'D STEP ASIDE FOR ME, BURR. REMEMBER?
VAGUELY.
I AM AN IDIOT FOR BELIEVING AARON BURR.
YOU CAN BE MY VICE PRESIDENT, TOM.
And Now, We're Live at Federalist Headquarters:
IT'S A GRIM MOOD HERE, LIBBY. THE END OF THE FEDERALIST ERA. ADAMS IS NOW THE FIRST PRESIDENT TO LOSE AN ELECTION. HOW WILL HE HANDLE IT?
REPULSIVE. IT'S HAMILTON'S FAULT.
IF THEY DIDN'T COUNT SLAVES, WE'D HAVE HAD MORE VOTES.
I WAS ATTACKED BY MY OWN PARTY... IT'S HAMILTON'S FAULT.
THE HOUSE OF REPRESENTATIVES BREAKS TIES. THEY'VE VOTED THIRTY-FIVE TIMES AND IT'S STILL A TIE! CAN YOU SAY CRISIS?
WHO HAS THE POWER TO CONVINCE FEDERALISTS TO SWING THEIR VOTE?
ON THE ONE HAND, JEFFERSON'S POLITICS ARE AWFUL.
I DISAGREE WITH HIM ON NEARLY EVERY MATTER.
HE WILL SIDE WITH FRANCE AND SET BACK OUR PROGRESS.
HE MAY EVEN DESTROY MY ENTIRE FINANCIAL SYSTEM.
ON THE OTHER HAND, I HATE BURR MORE.

Daily News-Post

JEFFERSON ELECTED PRESIDENT
BURR BECOMES VICE PRESIDENT

Adams sneaks away in the night unseen

WHY, THEO? WHY WOULD HAMILTON PLOT AGAINST ME?

GEE, DAD, YOU DID TAKE HIS FATHER-IN-LAW'S SENATE SEAT.

CAN WE GET BACK TO MY WEDDING NOW?

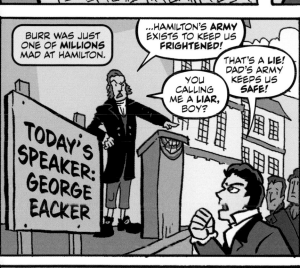

BURR WAS JUST ONE OF MILLIONS MAD AT HAMILTON.

...HAMILTON'S ARMY EXISTS TO KEEP US FRIGHTENED!

THAT'S A LIE! DAD'S ARMY KEEPS US SAFE!

YOU CALLING ME A LIAR, BOY?

TODAY'S SPEAKER: GEORGE EACKER

A DUEL? OVER ME? I'M HONORED, PHILIP, BUT YOU SHOULDN'T HAVE ACCEPTED.

BUT I HAVE TO DUEL THAT APE, FATHER. IT'S A MATTER OF HONOR.

IF SO, SHOOT IN THE AIR.

A GENTLEMAN WILL DO THE SAME.

I HAVE NO WORDS.

PHILIP SCHUYLER HAMILTON
22 Jan 1782 -
23 Nov 1801
(aged 19)

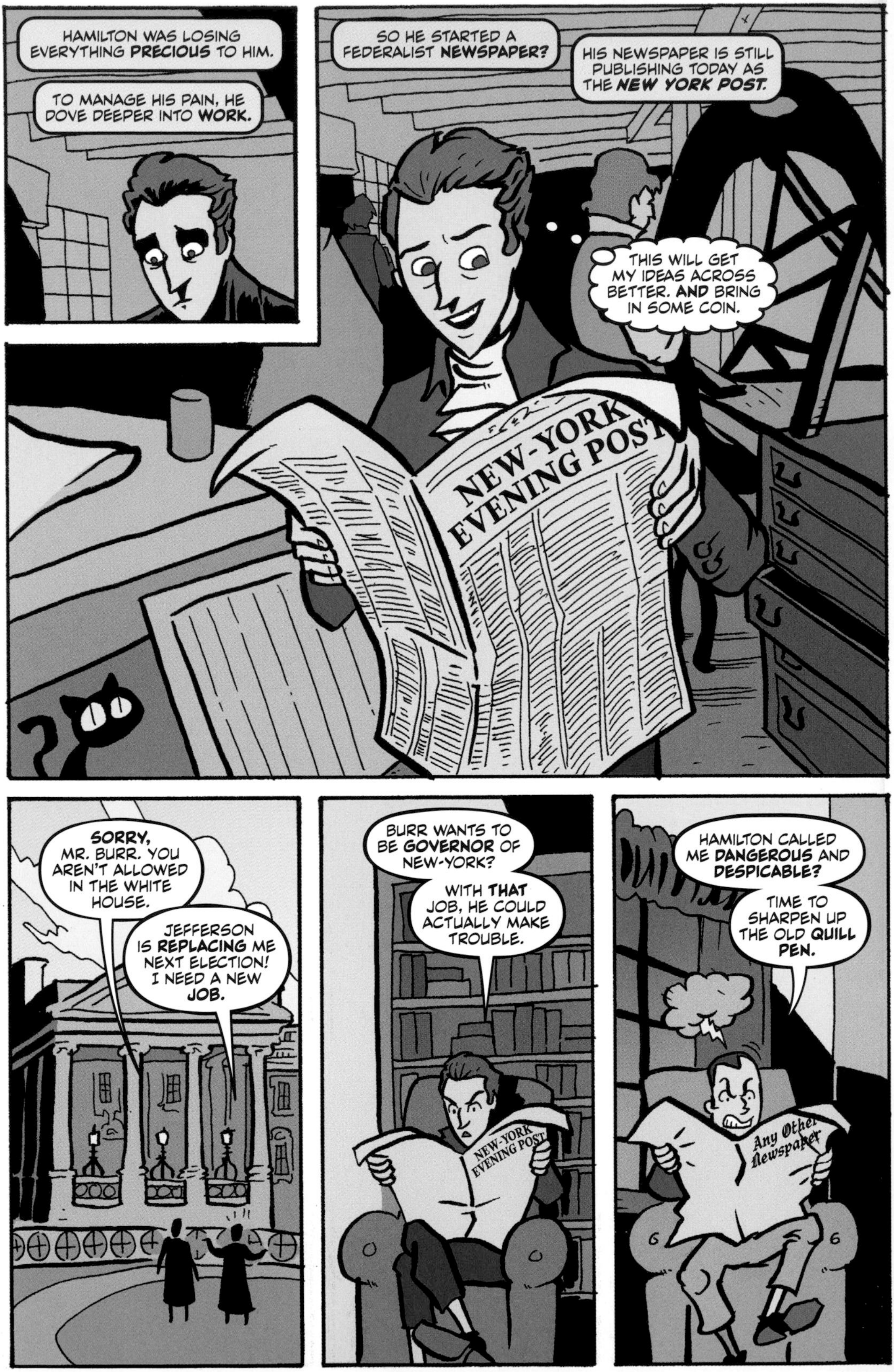
HAMILTON WAS LOSING EVERYTHING **PRECIOUS** TO HIM.
TO MANAGE HIS PAIN, HE DOVE DEEPER INTO **WORK.**
SO HE STARTED A FEDERALIST **NEWSPAPER?**
HIS NEWSPAPER IS STILL PUBLISHING TODAY AS THE ***NEW YORK POST.***
THIS WILL GET MY IDEAS ACROSS BETTER. **AND** BRING IN SOME COIN.
NEW-YORK EVENING POST
SORRY, MR. BURR. YOU AREN'T ALLOWED IN THE WHITE HOUSE.
JEFFERSON IS **REPLACING** ME NEXT ELECTION! I NEED A NEW **JOB.**
BURR WANTS TO BE **GOVERNOR** OF NEW-YORK?
WITH **THAT** JOB, HE COULD ACTUALLY MAKE TROUBLE.
NEW-YORK EVENING POST
HAMILTON CALLED ME **DANGEROUS** AND **DESPICABLE?**
TIME TO SHARPEN UP THE OLD **QUILL PEN.**
Any Other Newspaper

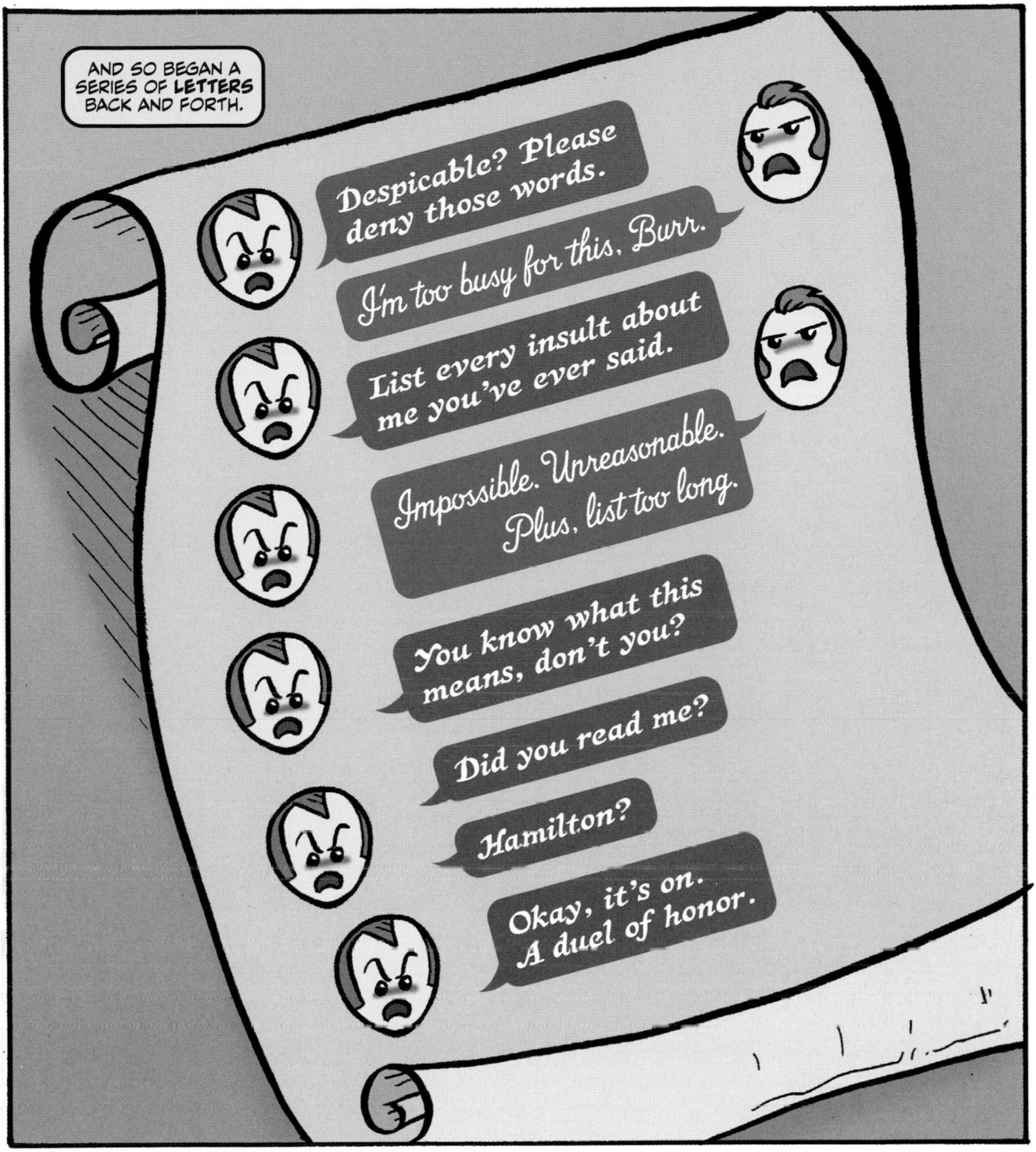
AND SO BEGAN A SERIES OF **LETTERS** BACK AND FORTH.
Despicable? Please deny those words.
I'm too busy for this, Burr.
List every insult about me you've ever said.
Impossible. Unreasonable. Plus, list too long.
You know what this means, don't you?
Did you read me?
Hamilton?
Okay, it's on. A duel of honor.

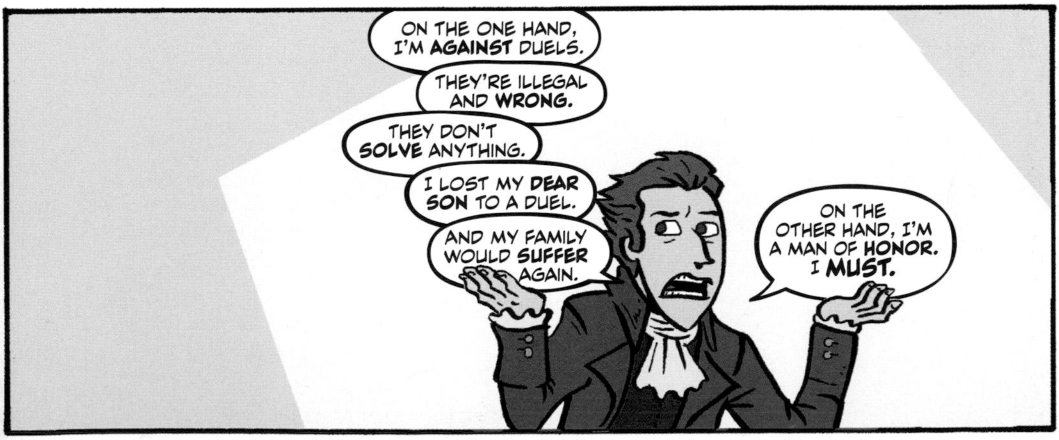
ON THE ONE HAND, I'M **AGAINST** DUELS.
THEY'RE ILLEGAL AND **WRONG.**
THEY DON'T **SOLVE** ANYTHING.
I LOST MY **DEAR SON** TO A DUEL.
AND MY FAMILY WOULD **SUFFER** AGAIN.
ON THE OTHER HAND, I'M A MAN OF **HONOR.** I **MUST.**

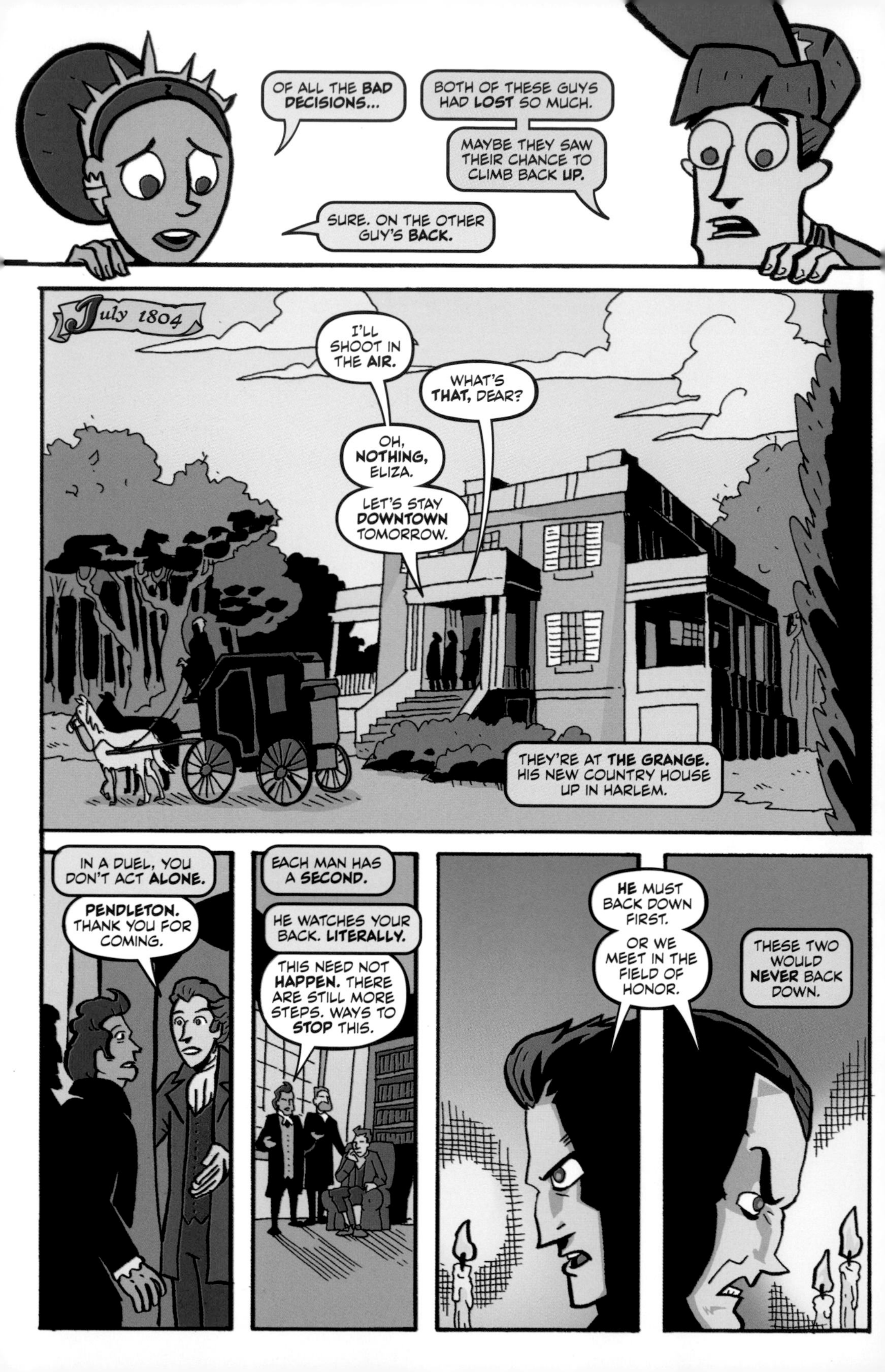
OF ALL THE BAD DECISIONS...
BOTH OF THESE GUYS HAD LOST SO MUCH.
MAYBE THEY SAW THEIR CHANCE TO CLIMB BACK UP.
SURE. ON THE OTHER GUY'S BACK.
July 1804
I'LL SHOOT IN THE AIR.
WHAT'S THAT, DEAR?
OH, NOTHING, ELIZA.
LET'S STAY DOWNTOWN TOMORROW.
THEY'RE AT THE GRANGE. HIS NEW COUNTRY HOUSE UP IN HARLEM.
IN A DUEL, YOU DON'T ACT ALONE.
PENDLETON. THANK YOU FOR COMING.
EACH MAN HAS A SECOND.
HE WATCHES YOUR BACK. LITERALLY.
THIS NEED NOT HAPPEN. THERE ARE STILL MORE STEPS. WAYS TO STOP THIS.
HE MUST BACK DOWN FIRST.
OR WE MEET IN THE FIELD OF HONOR.
THESE TWO WOULD NEVER BACK DOWN.

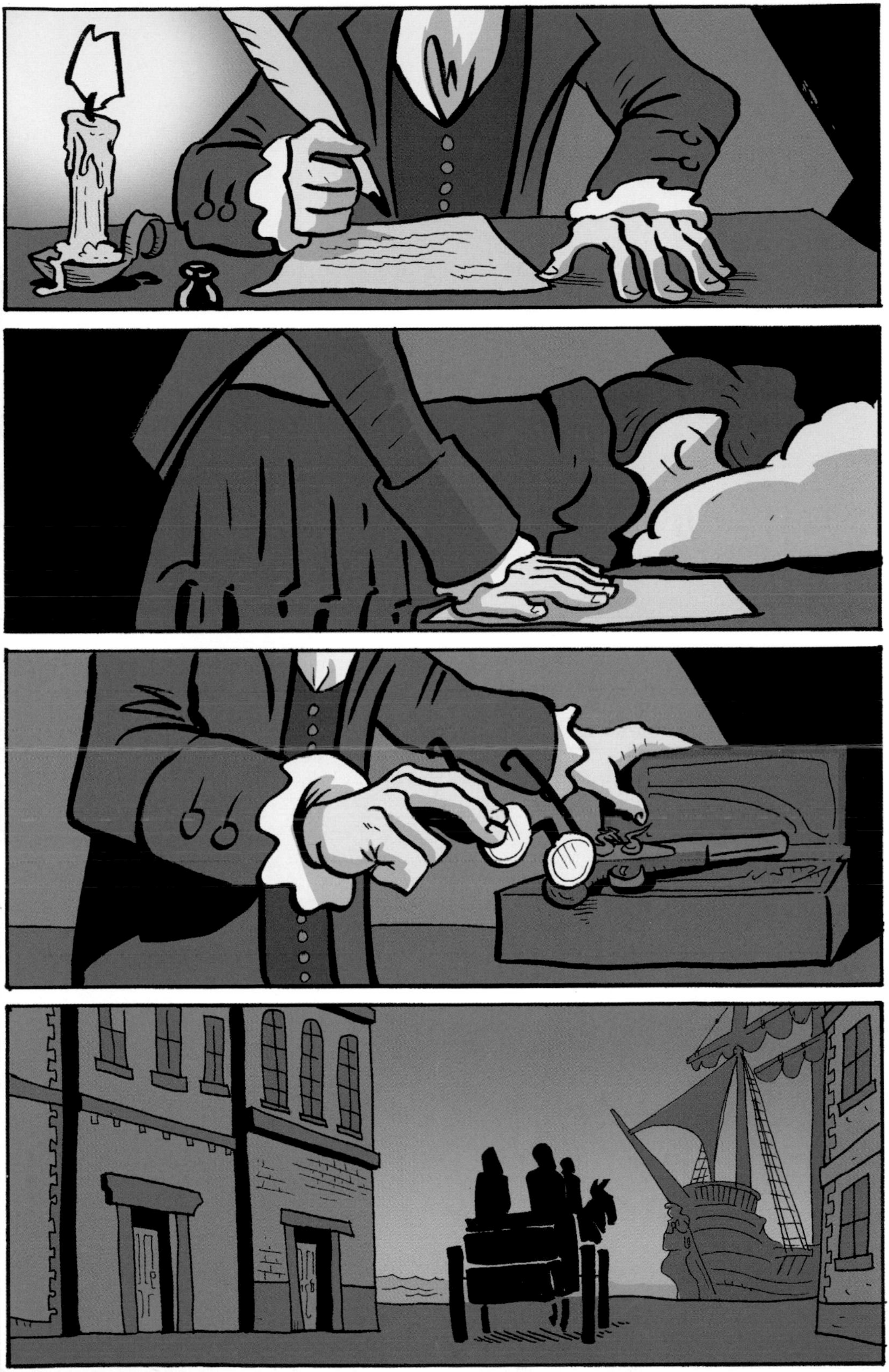

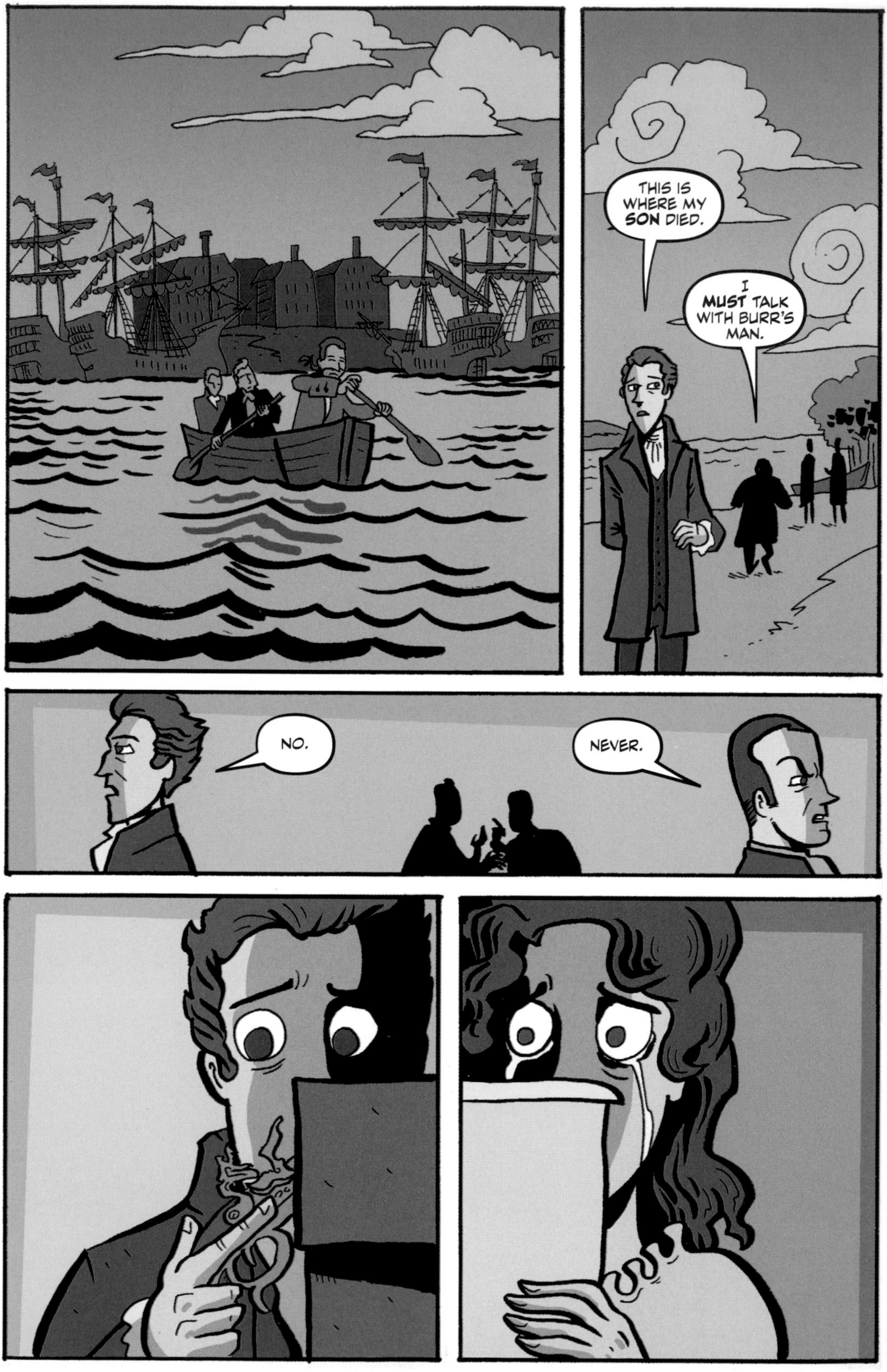

THIS IS WHERE MY **SON** DIED.
I **MUST** TALK WITH BURR'S MAN.
NO.
NEVER.

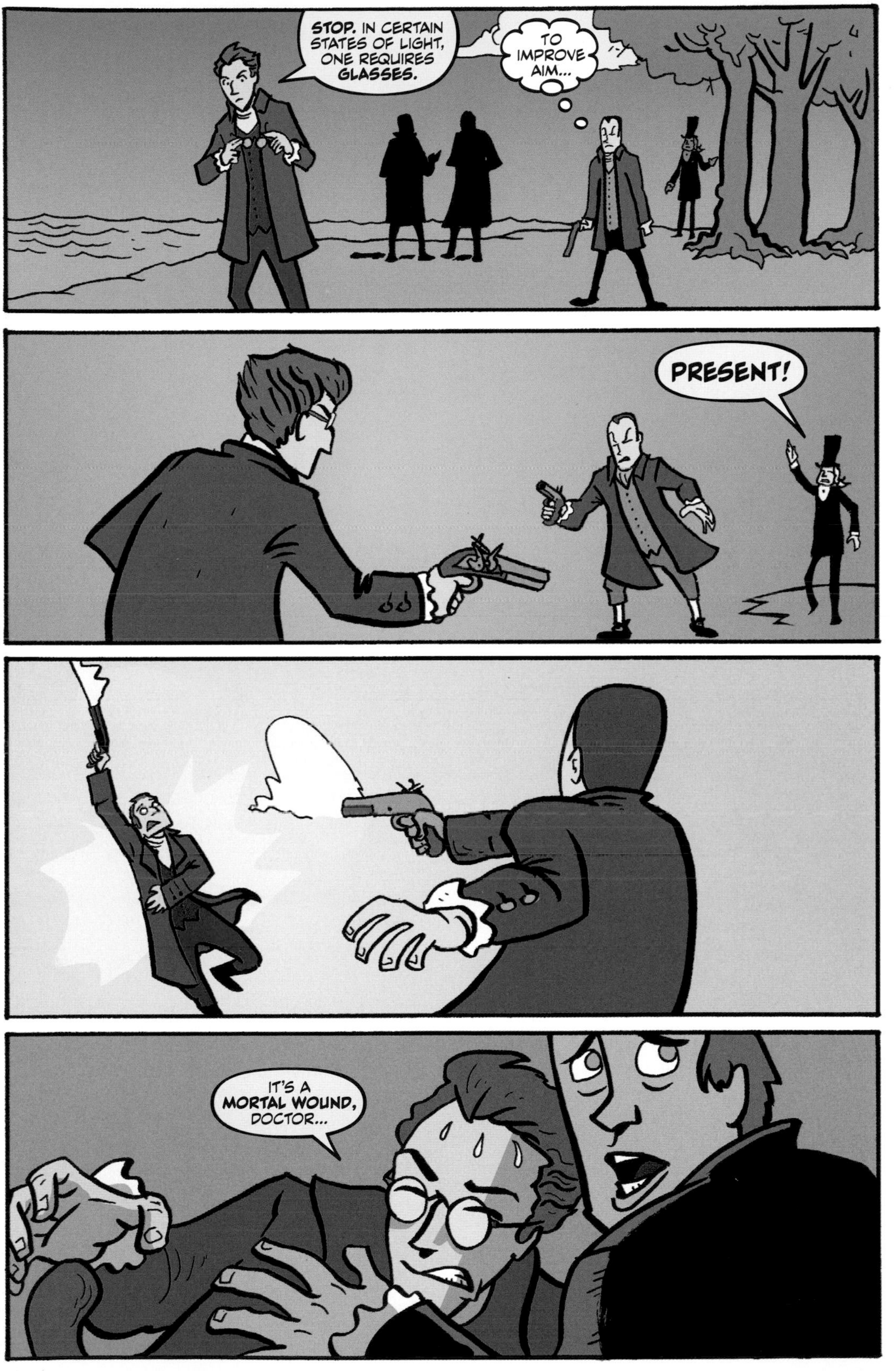
STOP. IN CERTAIN STATES OF LIGHT, ONE REQUIRES GLASSES.
TO IMPROVE AIM...
PRESENT!
IT'S A MORTAL WOUND, DOCTOR...

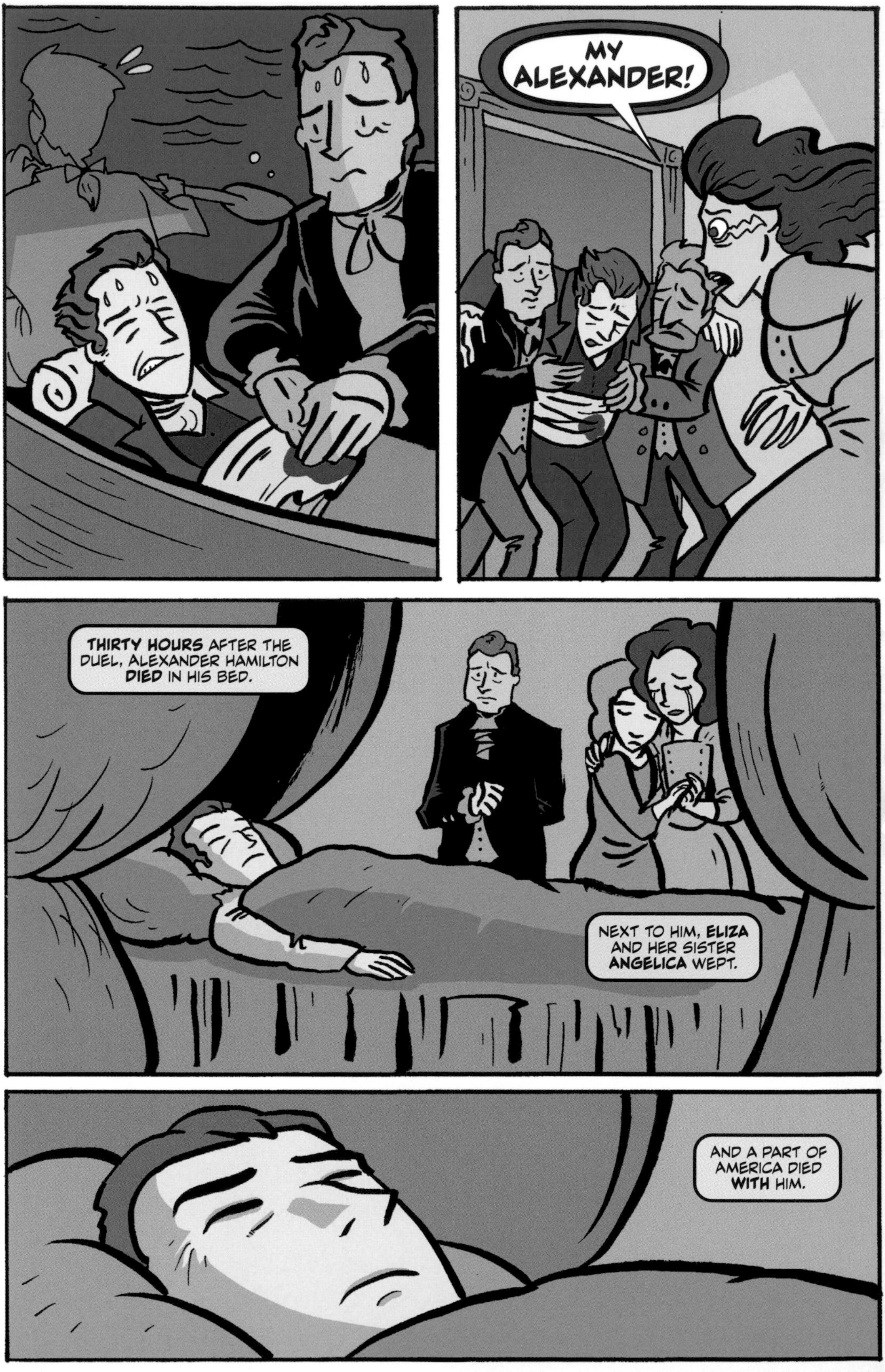
MY ALEXANDER!
THIRTY HOURS AFTER THE DUEL, ALEXANDER HAMILTON DIED IN HIS BED.
NEXT TO HIM, ELIZA AND HER SISTER ANGELICA WEPT.
AND A PART OF AMERICA DIED WITH HIM.

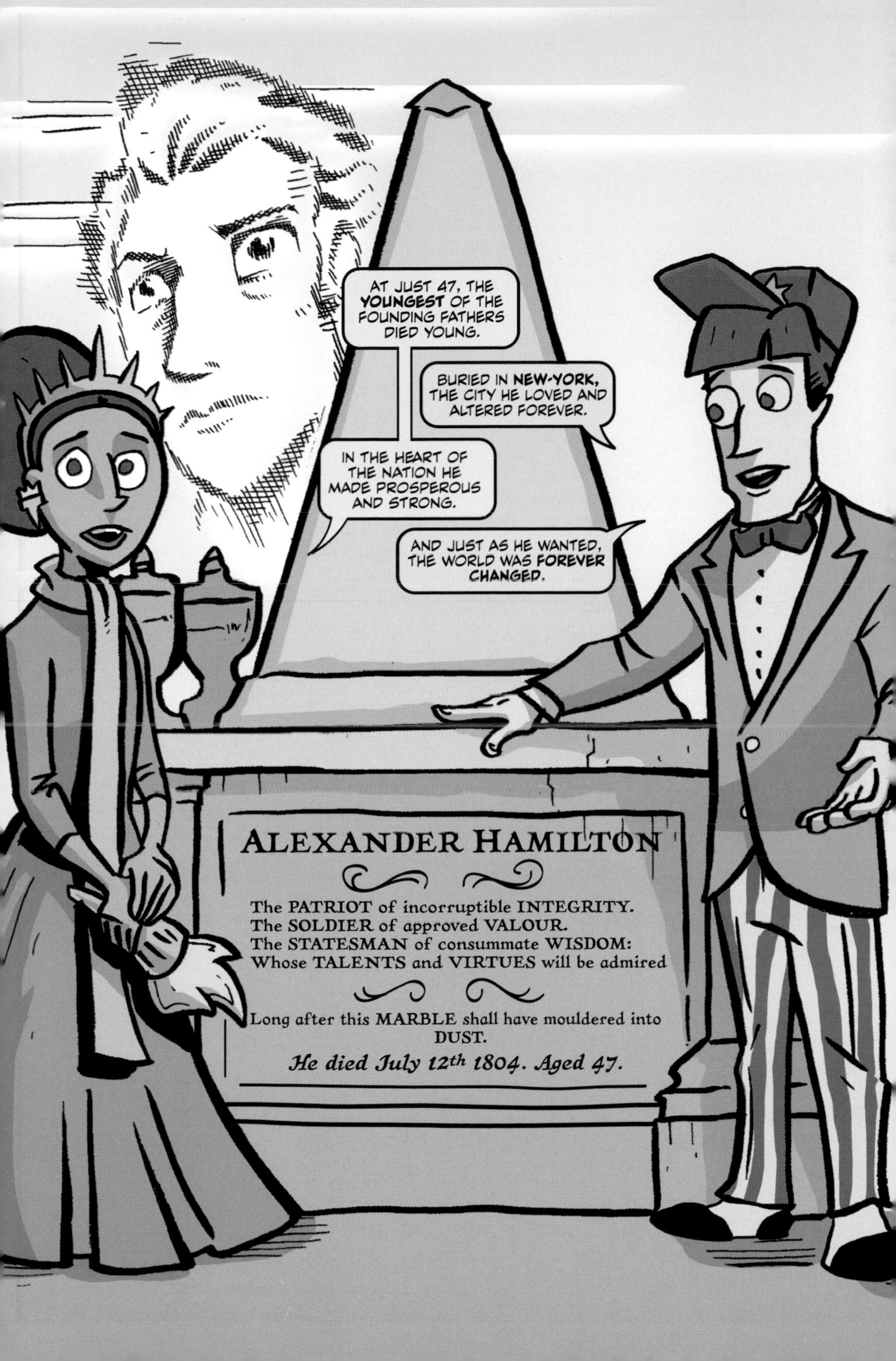
AT JUST 47, THE **YOUNGEST** OF THE FOUNDING FATHERS DIED YOUNG.
BURIED IN **NEW-YORK,** THE CITY HE LOVED AND ALTERED FOREVER.
IN THE HEART OF THE NATION HE MADE PROSPEROUS AND STRONG.
AND JUST AS HE WANTED, THE WORLD WAS **FOREVER CHANGED.**
ALEXANDER HAMILTON
The PATRIOT of incorruptible INTEGRITY.
The SOLDIER of approved VALOUR.
The STATESMAN of consummate WISDOM:
Whose TALENTS and VIRTUES will be admired
Long after this MARBLE shall have mouldered into DUST.
He died July 12th 1804. Aged 47.

DID YOU KNOW? DECLARATIONS (THAT LED TO) INDEPENDENCE!

VIRGINIA DECLARATION OF RIGHTS (1776): As the most populated state, and the home of four of the first five presidents, Virginia had lots of sway. With this document, their legislature was the first to call for independence from Britain.

LEE RESOLUTION (1776): On June 7, congressman Richard Henry Lee brought Virginia's resolution for independence to the second Continental Congress. With that action, Congress voted to draft a similar **Declaration of Independence** for all thirteen colonies.

DECLARATION OF INDEPENDENCE (1776): Written in June and adopted on July 4, it announced that the 13 British colonies were now independent, at war with their mother country, and included a long list of grievances against King George.

ARTICLES OF CONFEDERATION (1777): As the first **U.S. Constitution**, this was a cooperation agreement that made the states stronger and the central government weaker. By 1786, Hamilton, Madison, and others called for a new constitution.

CONSTITUTION OF THE UNITED STATES (1787): This document, creating a strong central power, is the world's oldest working national constitution. The government it created was a controversial idea, filled with compromises. Each state had to vote to accept it, and as with New-York, the votes were often close.

FEDERALIST PAPERS (1787-1788): Once the **U.S. Constitution** was drafted, a lot of people (and states) needed to be convinced. These 81 essays, published anonymously by Alexander Hamilton, James Madison, and John Jay, explained each of the ideas that went into the making of the government. They remain very persuasive today.

BILL OF RIGHTS (1791): Many of the framers of the **U.S. Constitution** wanted to guarantee important rights and freedoms, including freedom of the press, religion, and protections from the government. They were soon amended (added) by Congress, and they represent the first ten amendments to the **Constitution.**

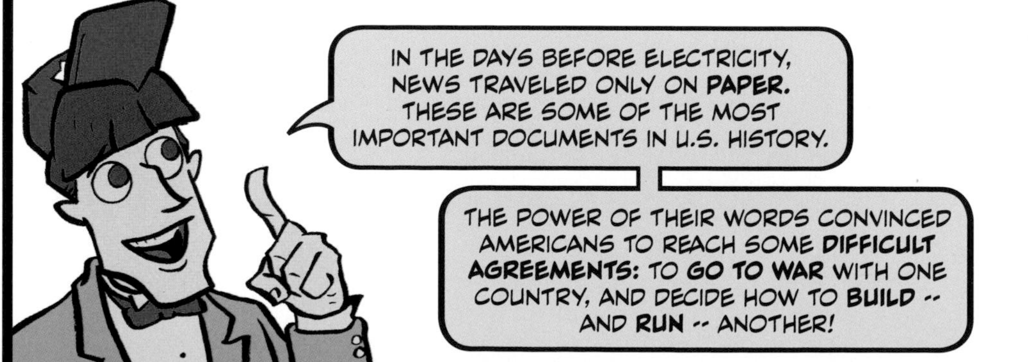
IN THE DAYS BEFORE ELECTRICITY, NEWS TRAVELED ONLY ON PAPER. THESE ARE SOME OF THE MOST IMPORTANT DOCUMENTS IN U.S. HISTORY.
THE POWER OF THEIR WORDS CONVINCED AMERICANS TO REACH SOME DIFFICULT AGREEMENTS: TO GO TO WAR WITH ONE COUNTRY, AND DECIDE HOW TO BUILD -- AND RUN -- ANOTHER!

ALEXANDER HAMILTON TIMELINE

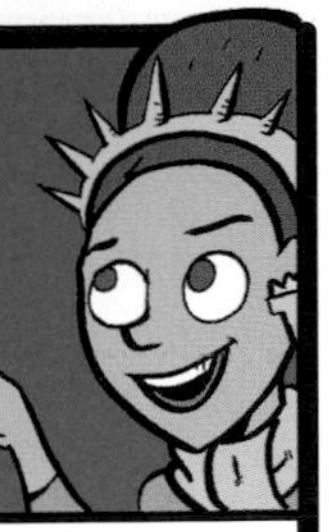

1755	Born on the tiny Caribbean island of Nevis. It may have been 1757, but most historians (and this book) use the earlier year.
1765-1775	A tragic childhood: his father leaves, his mother dies, and by age 14 he's managing a trading company. At 17, his description of a devastating hurricane inspires local leaders to send him abroad for an education.
1773-1776	Arrives in New-York City, attends King's College (Columbia University); becomes an activist against Britain and a captain in a New-York militia.
1777	Hamilton joins Washington as the general's chief of staff and proceeds to run the war's business.
1780	Marries Elizabeth Schuyler, who is from a wealthy, powerful family. They eventually have eight children.
1781	Leads his troops to victory at the Battle of Yorktown, at which the British surrender.
1782-1786	Rises in stature as a lawyer, joins the Continental Congress, the New-York Assembly, and the Constitutional Convention.
1787	Helps create the **U.S. Constitution**, writes the *Federalist Papers* essays to explain it. Persuades a wary New-York assembly to adopt it.
1789-1795	Serves as the first U.S. Treasury Secretary. Against strong opposition from many in Congress, Hamilton creates a strong financial system for the U.S.
1795	Resigns from government and returns to his law practice in New-York City.
1797	Accused of mishandling government money, he publishes the *Reynolds Pamphlet.* Hamilton admits to his having been blackmailed, but clears his name of political wrongdoing.
1799	Upon Washington's death, Hamilton becomes head of the U.S. Army.
1800	In a tied presidential election, Hamilton supports Thomas Jefferson rather than Aaron Burr, setting the stage for increased conflicts.
1801	Philip, his son, is killed in a duel. Founds the ***New-York Evening Post*** newspaper.
1804	Killed in a duel with Vice President Aaron Burr.

GLOSSARY

AIDE-DE-CAMP: The chief of staff, or top assistant, for a military officer.

ASSUMPTION: To take power or responsibility over something, such as the Federal government taking responsibility (assuming) the debts of each state.

CONFEDERATION: A group of allies that are united and organized for a shared purpose.

CONSTITUTION: A written set of principles, guidelines, and agreements that set the rules for a government or organization.

FEDERALIST: A person who supports a strong central government.

MILITIA: A military organization created by civilians to help support the regular army during an emergency.

NATIONAL DEBT: The money borrowed by a nation's government that is owed back to the lenders.

NEUTRAL: Not getting involved, or supporting, either side of a conflict or disagreement.

PAMPHLET: A booklet or miniature magazine that supports (or disses) a particular opinion or subject.

RATIFY: To make a contract or treaty valid by voting for it or signing it.

FIND OUT MORE

BOOKS

Chernow, Ron. *Alexander Hamilton*. New York: The Penguin Press, 2004.

Editors of Time, The. *Alexander Hamilton: Life Stories of Extraordinary Americans (TIME Heroes of History)*. New York: Liberty Street Books, 2018.

Miranda, Lin-Manuel. *Hamilton: The Revolution*. New York: Grand Central Publishing, 2016.

Fritz, Jean. *Alexander Hamilton: The Outsider*. New York: G.P. Putnam's Sons, 2011.

St. George, Judith. *The Duel: The Parallel Lives of Alexander Hamilton and Aaron Burr*. New York: Speak, Penguin Random House, 2016.

WEBSITES

Gloede, Jennifer. "Hamilton: How money tells his story," The Smithsonian National Museum of American History (blog), January 11, 2018, http://americanhistory.si.edu/blog/hamilton-how-money-tells-his-story
This article examines Hamilton's role in the history of American money.

National Park Service: Hamilton Grange
https://www.nps.gov/hagr/index.htm
The Grange was Alexander Hamilton's home in New York City. This website includes a photo tour if you can't make it there in person!

VIDEOS

Alexander Hamilton (American Experience Series). PBS, 2007.

I CANNOT TELL A LIE. THIS LIST OF BOOKS IS WELL WORTH THE TREES THEY CHOPPED DOWN.

FISH AND VISITORS STINK AFTER THREE DAYS.

I DON'T THINK FRANKLIN FULLY GRASPS WHAT WE'RE MEANT TO BE SAYING DOWN HERE ABOUT THOSE HORRID HAMILTON BOOKS AND WEBSITES.

CARP ALL YOU WANT, MADISON. IT'LL BE A LONG TIME BEFORE KIDS ARE SINGING SONGS ABOUT **YOUR** ACHIEVEMENTS.

GET IT, BEN? CARP!!

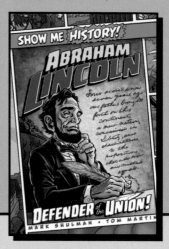

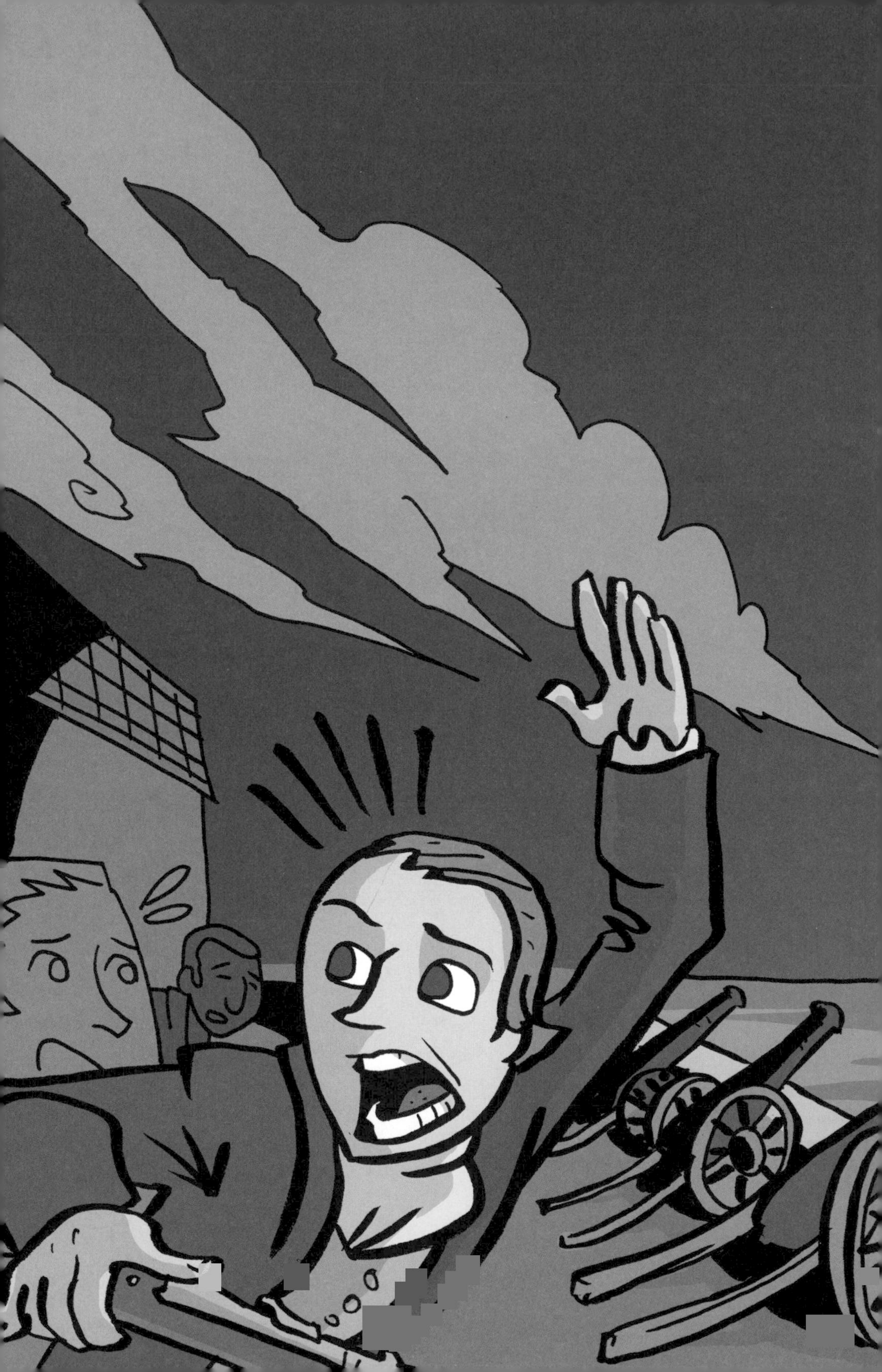